Robert Bloomfield, Romanticism and the Poetry of Community

For Rosie and Molly

Robert Bloomfield, Romanticism and the Poetry of Community

SIMON J. WHITE
Oxford Brookes University, UK

LONDON AND NEW YORK

First published 2007 by Ashgate Publishing

2 Park Square, Milton Park, Abingdon, Oxfordshire OX14 4RN
52 Vanderbilt Avenue, New York, NY 10017

Routledge is an imprint of the Taylor & Francis Group, an informa business

First issued in paperback 2019

British Library Cataloguing in Publication Data
White, Simon J.
Robert Bloomfield, romanticism and the poetry of community.
– (The nineteenth century series)
1. Bloomfield, Robert, 1766–1823 – Criticism and interpretation
2. Romanticism – Great Britain
I. Title
821.7

Library of Congress Cataloging-in-Publication Data
White, Simon J., 1962–
Robert Bloomfield, romanticism and the poetry of community / Simon J. White.
p. cm. – (The nineteenth century series)
Includes index.
ISBN 978–0–7546–5753–8 (alk. paper)
1. Bloomfield, Robert, 1766–1823 – Criticism and interpretation.
2. Pastoral poetry, English – History and criticism. 3. Romanticism – Great Britain.
I. Title.

PR4149.B6Z77 2007
821'.7–dc22

2006032257

ISBN 13: 978-0-7546-5753-8 (hbk)
ISBN 13: 978-0-367-88793-3 (pbk)

Contents

General Editors' Preface vii

Acknowledgements ix

Introduction 1

1 *The Farmer's Boy*, *The Prelude* and the Poetics of Rural Life 7

2 The Romantic Ballad and Labouring-Class Culture 31

3 The Romantic Lyric and the Lyric of Labour 57

4 Betwixt and Between Patrons, Publishers and Readers 81

5 'History from Below' on *The Banks of* [the] *Wye* 105

6 Community Labour and Poetry in *May Day with the Muses* 121

Appendices

1 Reflections on Otaheite: Cooks second Voyage (endnote to *The Farmer's Boy*, 1800, 101–102) 147

2 A Chronology of Bloomfield's Publications and their Contents 149

Bibliography 151

Index 165

The Nineteenth Century Series General Editors' Preface

The aim of the series is to reflect, develop and extend the great burgeoning of interest in the nineteenth century that has been an inevitable feature of recent years, as that former epoch has come more sharply into focus as a locus for our understanding not only of the past but of the contours of our modernity. It centres primarily upon major authors and subjects within Romantic and Victorian literature. It also includes studies of other British writers and issues, where these are matters of current debate: for example, biography and autobiography, journalism, periodical literature, travel writing, book production, gender, non-canonical writing. We are dedicated principally to publishing original monographs and symposia; our policy is to embrace a broad scope in chronology, approach and range of concern, and both to recognize and cut innovatively across such parameters as those suggested by the designations 'Romantic' and 'Victorian'. We welcome new ideas and theories, while valuing traditional scholarship. It is hoped that the world which predates yet so forcibly predicts and engages our own will emerge in parts, in the wider sweep, and in the lively streams of disputation and change that are so manifest an aspect of its intellectual, artistic and social landscape.

Vincent Newey
Joanne Shattock

University of Leicester, UK

Acknowledgements

This book began life as a doctoral thesis, and I would like to thank my supervisor Jack Donovan for his support and stimulating advice. In addition I would like to thank my external examiner John Goodridge and my internal examiner John Barrell for their ideas about the kind of revisions I would need to make to turn my thesis into a monograph. The readers appointed by Ashgate to review my initial manuscript also asked me challenging but invaluable questions, and I have followed their advice in revising my book for publication. I would also like to thank the series editors, the Ashgate staff in the UK, and particularly my commissioning editor Ann Donahue who provided me with invaluable support and guidance during the commissioning process.

Many others helped me at different stages by reading drafts of individual chapters, including David Higgins, Ve-Yin Tee, Eleni Alexandraki and Peter Denney. Bridget Keegan set aside the time to read through the final daft of the revised manuscript before I resubmitted it to Ashgate. I revised my book during the period between completing my PhD and securing my first academic post. This was not always an easy time for me, and I would also like to thank Bridget for her moral support. Last but by no means least I would like to thank my partner Rosie, who is also an academic, for her support and for putting up with me when work began to overlap with leisure.

The material from MS Eng 776 and MS Eng 776.1 is cited by permission of the Houghton Library, Harvard University. Material from Bloomfield manuscripts held by the British Library is cited by permission of the British Library. An early version of the final section of Chapter 3 appeared under the heading 'A Lyric for the Artisan Poet: "To My Old Oak Table"' in *Robert Bloomfield: Lyric, Class and the Romantic Canon* (Lewisburg PA: Bucknell University Press, 2006). An early version of part of Chapter 5 appeared under the heading 'Re-thinking the History of the Wye: Robert Bloofield's *The Banks of Wye*' in *Literature and History*, 16:1 (2007), 46–58.

Introduction

At some point between November 1801 and January 1802 Robert Bloomfield 'first got sight of' *Lyrical Ballads* (1798). He later recalled his concern on noting some similarities between a passage in Wordsworth's 'The Idiot Boy' (1798) and one in his own 'Market Night' (1802). Bloomfield was worried that he might be accused of plagiarism: 'I would say ... "Mr W. wrote and published his book first, and I had not seen it." I would beg the learned searchers after imitations and curious coincidences ... to admit, in all cases, the kindred ideas which must exist in tracing the same subject' (*Remains* II: 111). Ironically during the period when Bloomfield was completing the poems for *Rural Tales, Ballads and Songs* (March–October 1800), it was much more likely that Wordsworth would have read *The Farmer's Boy* (1800) than Bloomfield *Lyrical Ballads*. At the time, Wordsworth was still relatively unknown, but following the sensation caused by the publication of *The Farmer's Boy* in March 1800 Bloomfield had become a sought-after celebrity. Remarks made in a letter from Coleridge to James Webbe Tobin indicate that Wordsworth had seen reviews of the poem by September 1800: 'What W & I have seen of the Farmer's Boy (only a few short extracts) pleased us very much' (*Letters* I: 412). In view of its continuing popularity, and the broadly positive critical reception, it is almost certain that he would have gone on to read the rest of the poem.

It is also arguable that Wordsworth had more reason to be concerned about parallels being drawn between his poetry and that produced by labouring-class poets like Bloomfield. Francis Jeffrey's diatribe against the Lake School of Poets in the *Edinburgh Review*, and at least one review of the collection, linked *Lyrical Ballads* to the kind of poetry written by 'uneducated wonders' (*Edinburgh Review* (1802), 63–83; *New London Review* (1799), 34). Indeed it is possible that in the preface to *Lyrical Ballads* (1800) Wordsworth was 'simply giving rhetorical flight to desiderata that had been oft-rehearsed (if ne'er so well expressed) by a number of plebeian poets and their advocates in the literary establishment' (McEathron 1999, 4). It does not require a great leap of imagination to suppose that in the preface, which was written between April and September 1800 (Gill 184–5), and in several passages within *The Prelude* (1805), he was attempting to define himself against Bloomfield, at the time, with the possible exception of Robert Burns, the most well-known labouring-class poet. Indeed it may be the case that in terms of Harold Bloom's famous account of influence, Wordsworth was writing in the 'shadow' of Bloomfield rather than vice versa (Bloom 5–16).

If the question of influence is put to one side, however, Bloomfield's concern is understandable. He and Wordsworth do treat the same kind of subject matter in their poetry; both are poets of the countryside. But the resemblance is not as close as Bloomfield's sensitivity would suggest because the way the two poets respond to rural people and the countryside they inhabit is very different. In fact, in the context of the way they see rural communities, it is the differences rather than the similarities that are important. In *Lyrical Ballads* Wordsworth attempts to find meaning in the lives of 'low' people for a polite reading audience (McEathron 1999, 12–26). The ideology behind Wordsworth's response to rural life has to some extent been revealed over the last couple of decades. But the idea that community life is somehow structural to Wordsworth's poetics has survived. Timothy Clark, for example, argues that 'it is one of the ironies of *The Prelude* ... that it should eulogize the values of small rural communities at the same time as promulgating an individualistic ethos of continuous self-development far more obviously appropriate to the urban capitalism it seems to attack' (1997, 94). A comparison with Bloomfield's poetry reveals that Wordsworth neither valued nor really understood the social dynamics of labouring-class community life. Bloomfield's poetry was also read primarily in polite society, but in it he explores the meaning of rural community life and the working landscape for the labouring poor themselves. Nor is the communitarian strain in Bloomfield's poetry simply nostalgia because his poetry reveals that he understood the way in which the dynamics of social relations in the countryside were changing.

The fact that Bloomfield's contribution to the discourse of Romanticism has neither been properly acknowledged nor explored represents a gap in our understanding of late eighteenth- and early nineteenth-century literature. John Lucas rightly argues, in his introduction to *Selected Poems* (1998), that because Bloomfield provides 'a poetic testimony of the *real* language of men and of the incidents of common life ... we cannot hope to understand that historical period which is habitually called Romanticism if we do not pay attention to his works' (xxii). Jonathan Lawson's *Robert Bloomfield* (1980), the only extant book-length study of Bloomfield, includes a relatively comprehensive biography, and an extended reading of *The Farmer's Boy*, but provides only cursory accounts of his later poetry. Lawson does not attempt to situate Bloomfield within Romanticism, and argues that he is successful because the subject matter of *The Farmer's Boy* is restricted to his experience of farm service in Suffolk. He thereby intimates that like other poets from a similar background Bloomfield was only able to write about his day-to-day experience as a labouring-class subject (Lawson, 57). In focusing more or less exclusively on *The Farmer's Boy* Lawson also implies that the narrative of decline, so often applied to labouring-class poets, can be applied to Bloomfield too (Goodridge 2001, 1–2). *Robert Bloomfield: Lyric, Class and the Romantic Canon* (2006), edited by John Goodridge, Bridget Keegan and myself, includes essays that focus on particular themes in his work, and that examine his significance in a broader context. But none of the essays consider in any depth the representation of community in Bloomfield's poetry. Nor does the collection add a great deal to our understanding of the way in which his poetry evolved or his role in the development of poetics during the Romantic period.

This study aims to show why Bloomfield should be considered in any re-evaluation of Romanticism by considering his poetry alongside texts by Wordsworth and Coleridge. Despite Wordsworth's often repeated desire to write about 'low' people, in Book I of *The Prelude* he is disdainful of the ability of 'the mean and vulgar works of man' to 'build up our human soul' (434–5). His vision of rural life is also structured by his bourgeois elevation of mobility and economic/social independence. Bloomfield's poetry suggests that he believed the day-to-day life experience of the rural labouring poor to be both poetic and in a sense heroic. He foregrounds the importance of local tradition and community values in the lives of labouring people. It is only because figures like Bloomfield have been ignored for so long that Romanticism has become equated with Wordsworth's way of seeing the countryside. Chapter One considers the way that these very different poetics of the countryside and rural life take shape in *The Farmer's Boy* and *The Prelude* (1805). At the same time it shows that *The Farmer's Boy* is not the naively idealistic account of rural life that so many contemporary reviewers and later critics have taken it to be.

Despite the success that he achieved with *The Farmer's Boy* Bloomfield did not use it as a model for his subsequent 'attempts at verse'. *Rural Tales, Ballads and Songs* and *Wild Flowers; or, Pastoral and Local Poetry*, the titles of the varied collections that he published in 1802 and 1806, signal his desire to convert polite readers to a more demotic kind of poetry. Collections of poetry by labouring-class poets had in the past invariably been given the kind of neutral title with which polite readers would have been familiar; a variation upon 'Poems on Various/Several Occasions'. In Chapter Two, Bloomfield's ballads and tales are considered in the context of Wordsworth's idea of a 'new' kind of vernacular poetry as set out in the preface to *Lyrical Ballads* (1800). Like the poems produced by his contemporaries, Bloomfield's are self-consciously literary, but he uniquely attempts to foreground the importance of the ballad and tale as poetic forms within labouring-class communities. Wordsworth appropriates 'rustic' imagery in ballads and tales that reveal his property-orientated bourgeois morality. Bloomfield's poems demonstrate that for the rural labouring poor properly regulated social relations were more important than relationships between individuals and property. The connection with labouring-class poetic forms becomes weaker in later ballads and tales as Bloomfield's poetry becomes increasingly composite and sophisticated. But the less rigid formal structure of poems like 'The Broken Crutch' (1806) enables him to speak more directly of issues that were of concern to him.

Bloomfield's 1802 and 1806 collections also contain a number of extended lyrics, which demand attention if we wish to fully understand the diverse ways in which the lyric functioned as a clarificatory mode during the Romantic period. Despite the fact that he began to develop his own version of the 'greater Romantic lyric' before he had any knowledge of Wordsworth and Coleridge, there are resemblances between his lyrics and the 'conversation' poem. This suggests that in some respects at least, all three poets were endeavouring to respond to similar kinds of emotional, social and intellectual dislocation.

Chapter Three explores the differences between Bloomfield's lyrics and those produced by Wordsworth and Coleridge which again are more significant than the similarities. It also shows that Bloomfield's poems engage with some of the ways in which the status of poet of polite society was problematic for a labouring-class subject. Bloomfield's composite (lyric/topographical) poem *The Banks of Wye* (1811) is considered in detail alongside Wordsworth's best-known lyric 'Lines Written a Few Miles Above Tintern Abbey, On Revisiting the Banks of the Wye During a Tour, July 13, 1798' (1798). The cultural significance of the geography of the region, and its social, political and literary history are implicated in Bloomfield's emotional and intellectual response to the Wye. The specific associations of place were not so important for Wordsworth, and Chapter Five explores some of the reasons for this distinction.

Bloomfield's first three published works appeared through the agency of his patron or editor Capel Lofft. The story of Bloomfield's relationship with Lofft demands attention because it sheds considerable light upon changes that were taking place in the literary marketplace at the turn of the eighteenth century. Before going on to consider his later verse, this study pauses to consider his writing career in the context of that relationship. Bloomfield seems to have believed that artistic independence and integrity were crucially important, but that poets should also maintain relationships with patrons. Chapter Four explores the ways in which these apparently mutually exclusive commitments caused problems for Bloomfield, particularly in relation to the publication and presentation of *The Farmer's Boy* and *Rural Tales*. The case of Bloomfield is important because it shows that patrons had declining cultural authority, and that both they and their clients had become less certain how to conduct themselves. The way that Vernor and Hood assumed an increasing degree of authority in respect of the presentation of Bloomfield's poetry also demonstrates the growing power of large publishing houses at the turn of the eighteenth century.

Bloomfield's later work did not enjoy the same kind of unprecedented success as his first published poem, and despite his continuing popularity, he was associated with the decline that Southey regarded as 'almost inevitable' in the case of labouring-class poets (*Lives*, 118). Reviewers also argued that in his later works he did not demonstrate 'an increased intimacy with the machinery of poetry' (*Critical Review* s.4, 1 (1812), 375). The tendency to dismiss labouring-class poets once their celebrity had faded even had an impact upon the positive critical reception previously enjoyed by *The Farmer's Boy*. An obituary published shortly after the poet's death in 1823 argued that 'The world would have lost nothing by the non-appearance of the Farmer's Boy, as it then existed in Bloomfield's *original* manuscript, and the poet would have enjoyed the comforts of an industrious life, enhanced by his love of the Muses' (*Monthly Magazine* 56 (1823), 182). The editor of the *Monthly Magazine*, Sir Richard Phillips, was one of the 'literary gentlemen' who rejected *The Farmer's Boy* when the poet originally tried to get the poem published in 1798. But Bloomfield was not forgotten and remained popular throughout the nineteenth century. According to the sales figures for one major London bookseller, he was the fifth most popular poet during the period 1835–95. Only Burns, Byron, Milton and Pope eclipsed him in terms of sales (B.C. Bloomfield, 92).

This study traces Bloomfield's development as a writer during a period of over twenty-five years, and a close reading of his five major published volumes refutes the narrative of decline habitually applied to labouring-class poets. In fact, his poetry is increasingly complex and self-referential. One of the many received ideas about Bloomfield is that *The Farmer's Boy* is both his most accomplished and his most important poem. As John Lucas has pointed out, *May-Day with the Muses* (1822) contains some of Bloomfield's best poetry, and the collection is perhaps his most imaginative in overall conception (1998, 306). It has been neglected because, unlike *The Farmer's Boy*, it was not a best-seller and received no attention from contemporary reviewers. *May-Day* reiterates many of the grand themes of Bloomfield's *oeuvre* in a way that once again provides a powerful counter to Wordsworth's poetics of rural life. Chapter Six demonstrates that in the frame narrative and several sophisticated individual pieces, Bloomfield also engages with issues that were of concern to 'second-generation' Romantic poets. But *May Day* is primarily concerned with the intellectual lives of the labouring-poor, and their right of access to the literary marketplace. It is a manifesto for the talent that inequality and prejudice allow to remain dormant within the ranks of the labouring poor.

CHAPTER ONE

The Farmer's Boy, *The Prelude* and the Poetics of Rural Life

The Farmer's Boy is often seen as a derivative poem, and in some respects it is a work that marks the end of a period in literary history rather than the beginning of the new 'Romantic' age. Stylistically it does draw upon eighteenth-century georgic poems like James Thomson's *The Seasons* (1730) and John Dyer's *The Fleece* (1757), particularly in terms of its episodic structure and the fact that it encompasses a range of different poetic modes (Goodridge 1995, 5). But there are also ways in which it is driven by the same kind of preoccupations as other 'new' poetry produced at the turn of the eighteenth century. Because we are so conditioned by Wordsworthian poetics we fail to see subtly different kinds of 'Romanticism' in less well-known poetry. *The Farmer's Boy* invites comparison with *The Prelude*, a poem to which posterity has accorded great importance, because it investigates the relationship between the human subject and the countryside. *The Prelude* appropriates 'rustic' imagery in an account of Wordsworth's development into a bourgeois prophet of nature for polite readers. Bloomfield's poem focuses upon the poet's early working relationships with farm labourers in a way that gradually reveals the poetic and heroic essence of labouring-class community life. In view of the fact that *The Farmer's Boy* is a response to Bloomfield's early life, it can be argued that like *The Prelude* it is also an enquiry into the origin and development of poetic sensibility. In Book I of *The Prelude* Wordsworth pronounces that 'poetic numbers came / Spontaneously, and clothed in priestly robe / My spirit, thus singled out, as it might seem, / For holy services' (60–63). Bloomfield was not confident of his vocation as a poet when he began work on *The Farmer's Boy* and did not set out to examine the influences that had made him a poet. But the multifarious and sometimes difficult milieu in which he spent his formative years shaped the sensibility that enabled him to produce a complex poem.

Most of those who have written about *The Farmer's Boy* have focused upon the ways in which it is a limited achievement. Jonathan Lawson argues that the poem succeeds because Bloomfield chose to limit his subject matter to 'a particularized, local setting that he knew intimately and loved well' (57). John Lucas reads it as an idealized representation of rural England: 'a kind of discreetly utopian account of the "natural" world very far removed from the contentious actualities of the moment' (1994, 59). Like most labouring-class writers Bloomfield did not have many alternatives in terms of subject matter to choose from, and he would later argue in his preface to *Wild Flowers* that he wrote about the rural labouring poor 'from necessity, as well as choice' (viii). This chapter will show that the period that he spent as a farmer's boy in rural

Suffolk provided him with important things to say about human psychology and community relations. But the poem has a range of reference that extends beyond and in many ways problematizes rural life. In reading it only as the product of a severely restricted range of experience or as a representation of a kind of rural utopia, Lawson and Lucas fail to take account of this complexity and range of reference. They do not consider the impact of the poet's London life upon *The Farmer's Boy*, and perpetuate the representation of Bloomfield as a limited and unsophisticated rural poet.

Bloomfield began work on *The Farmer's Boy* in May 1796, fifteen years after leaving Suffolk, and completed it in April 1798. At the time he and his family lived in one room in a house at 14 Bell Alley, Coleman Street, and he worked as a shoemaker in an upper-floor garret with five other men (Lawson, 20). This experience had a considerable impact upon the practical production of *The Farmer's Boy*. As he remarks in the preface to the 1809 edition of his poems, much of it was composed in his head because he did not have the time or space to write: 'Nine tenths of it was put together as I sat at work, where there are usually six of us; no one in the house has any knowledge of what I have employed my thoughts about when I did not talk.' (I: xxi) In *Lives of Illustrious Shoemakers* (1883), W.E. Winks suggests that the proliferation of shoemaker poets during the eighteenth and nineteenth centuries was due to the fact that the shoemaker 'sits to his work, and, as a rule, sits *alone*; that his occupation stimulates his mind without wholly occupying and absorbing its powers; [and] that it leaves him free to break off, if he will, at intervals, and glance at the book or make notes on the paper which lies beside him' (232). It is likely that during the eighteenth century the majority of shoemakers would have worked with others in small groups. They would have been either apprentices or journeymen working for a master, or masters taking on apprentices and employing journeymen. By the time that Winks was writing, the decline of apprenticeship having been accelerated by the abolition of 5 Elizabeth in 1814 (which removed the legal requirement for artisans to undertake a seven-year apprenticeship), it is probable that many more shoemakers would have worked on their own (Keegan, 195–217). But Bloomfield did not work alone, and had to compose *The Farmer's Boy* amidst the noise made by his fellow workers.

The manner in which he was obliged to produce the poem apparently restricted Bloomfield's choice of verse form as he remarks in a letter to his brother George (he included part of this letter in his 1809 preface):

> I chose to do it in rhime for this reason; because I found always that when I put two or three lines together in blank verse, or something that sounded like it, it was a great chance if it stood right when it came to be wrote down, for blank verse has ten-syllables in a line, and this particular I could not adjust, nor bear in memory as I could rhimes. [I: xxi]

It is not entirely clear what Bloomfield means when he says that he could not 'adjust' to the ten syllables of the blank verse iambic line, because the heroic couplet also has ten syllables in a line. The most likely explanation is that he found it easier to accommodate the iambic meter in couplets because in blank verse pairs of lines are not distinctly isolated from each other by rhyme. Any difficulty in coping with this feature of blank verse would have been magnified by the fact that Bloomfield's material circumstances forced him to compose the poem in his head, and the rhyme made it easier to remember what would otherwise have been hard to recall. It could be argued that Wordsworth was able to use a more 'free' and flexible verse form for *The Prelude* because his manner of composition was not so constrained.

Roger Sales is not entirely correct when he suggests that Bloomfield 'split his personality between the farmer's boy [in poetry] and the artisan [in some of his letters]' (19). In fact, there are several ways in which *The Farmer's Boy* engages with the poet's experience of life as an artisan. It is about rural Suffolk, but begins with an invocation that links Bloomfield and his poem to his situation as a city-based shoemaker. It is not the conventional entreaty to a higher authority such as the classical Muses or God, nor is it a supplication to Spring itself as in *The Seasons*, or to the 'ministry' of nature as in *The Prelude* (I: 370). Bloomfield appeals to a power within the self: 'Oh Come, blest Spirit! whatsoe'er thou art, / Thou kindling warmth that hover'st round my heart, / Sweet inmate, hail! thou source of sterling joy, / That poverty itself cannot destroy / Be thou my Muse' (I: 1–5). As an impoverished shoemaker working amongst other artisans within a confined garret, Bloomfield had no alternative but to look to a silent inner spirit which, like himself, was an 'inmate' of a restricted space and subject to the oppressive force of poverty.

Bloomfield did not enjoy the education, leisure and relative independence of Wordsworth, who in Book III of *The Prelude* claims that he could allow 'better fruits, / Whether of truth or virtue', to mature 'naturally' (561–3). At least until he settled at Racedown with Dorothy in 1795, Wordsworth led a wandering life, visiting France twice and spending some time in London. He continued to enjoy freedom even after his marriage to Mary Hutchinson in 1802, although he might have been experienced the feeling more intermittently. In Book I of *The Prelude* he celebrates his state of freedom in 1804, when he began the poem: 'Now I am free, enfranchised and at large, / May fix my habitation where I will / ... / May dedicate myself to chosen tasks' (9–34). For middle-class poets like Wordsworth, this freedom or liberty to wander was inextricably bound up with their social status. Wordsworth even connected it with his ability to produce poetry, implicitly proscribing the creative potential of the labouring poor. He suggests that to be tied to a particular place and trade, as Bloomfield was, would hinder his development as a man and a poet. The wandering transitory life that he led as a young man: 'Did better suit ... [his] visionary mind— / Far better, than to have been bolted forth, / Thrust out abruptly into fortune's way / Among the conflicts of substantial life—' (III: 556–9).

Bloomfield's invocation distances *The Farmer's Boy* from the heroic Miltonic tradition within which Wordsworth wrote: 'Retrace the paths of wild obscurity. / No deeds of arms my humble lines rehearse; / No Alpine wonders thunder through my verse' (I: 7–8). It asserts the power of 'substantial life' to engender poets, and challenges eighteenth-century preconceptions about appropriate subject matter for poetry: 'From meaner objects far my raptures flow: / ... / Live, trifling incidents, and grace my song, / That to the humblest menial belong' (I: 13–20). For much of the eighteenth century the 'occupations of peasants' were not regarded as fit subject matter for poetry (*Monthly Review* n.s.33 (1800), 52). Thomson and Dyer both follow Addison's instruction that the georgic should single out 'the most pleasing circumstance ... and so convey ... the whole in a more diverting manner to the understanding' (Elledge I: 3). Wordsworth had contradictory views on the subject. In Book I of *The Prelude* he is disdainful of the ability of 'the mean and vulgar works of man' to 'build up our human soul' (434–5), then in Book XII he states his intention to make his 'verse / Deal boldly with substantial things'(233–4), but only when 'high service' (226), presumably to 'Nature'(225), is performed by them. In the preface to *Lyrical Ballads* (1800), he had expressed a desire to write about 'low and rustic life' because in this situation 'our essential' or 'elementary' feelings are 'more forcibly communicated' (245). The implication seems to be that the labouring poor reveal 'our elementary' feelings when their experiences are filtered through the superior sensibility of an educated and gifted poet, and that of his polite readers. Wordsworth's poetics generally gravitate towards an elevated treatment of subject matter, and this is why he struggles to find a way of justifying his poetry to his polite readers. In view of the fact that it is likely Wordsworth had read *The Farmer's Boy* before writing the preface to *Lyrical Ballads* and the thirteen-book *Prelude*, his espousal of 'low and rustic life' as subject matter for poetry might also represent a response to Bloomfield's poem (McEathron 1999, 2–4). Bloomfield wanted to demonstrate in *The Farmer's Boy* that 'meaner objects' and 'trifling incidents' in the lives of the poor could in themselves be of interest as subject matter for poetry. Implicitly his poem also adds weight to the idea that the labouring poor themselves were best placed to represent their lives in poetry (or prose), a view that was increasingly held by labouring-class intellectuals during the 1790s (Keen, 153).

Bloomfield's exposure to London artisan culture might have helped him to develop the confidence with which he introduces his subject matter. In the London of the 1790s skilled artisans like Bloomfield increasingly saw themselves as part of a public sphere or republic of letters that overlapped with and challenged the 'polite' public sphere (Keen, 142–70). Indeed members of the London Corresponding Society regarded literature as 'the greatest engine of social transformation' (Keen, 169). As his brother George reveals in the letter that Capel Lofft included within his preface to the first edition of *The Farmer's Boy*, Bloomfield attended a debating society, he saw that other artisans read widely, and he witnessed how his fellow shoemakers could be very assertive when demanding what they perceived to be their rights (1800, vii–xii). In the opening passages of the poem, Bloomfield displays a similar self-assurance in attempting to situate his poem within literary culture. No other labouring-class poet before Bloomfield had been confident enough to assert the value and originality of their poetry in this way, particularly early in their career. But because of his status even an independent-minded poet like Bloomfield was not completely free to position his own work.

Whilst the poet was attempting to signal ways in which the poem might depart from his reader's preconceptions, his self-appointed patron Capel Lofft was more concerned about fulfilling those expectations. This is apparent from one of the changes made by Lofft when he edited the poem. The original manuscript reads: 'No deeds of arms my lowly tale rehearse' (MS Eng. 776, fol. 1). His patron changed this line to read 'No deeds of arms my humble lines rehearse' (MS Eng. 776.1, fol. 1). Lofft clearly had grammatical and euphonic reasons for making the emendation because Bloomfield says the opposite of what he means, and once the grammar had been corrected the phrase 'lowly tale' could not remain. Lofft may have saved Bloomfield from possible criticism regarding his lack of education, but the new wording does subtly alter the meaning of the line. The phrase 'lowly tale' links *The Farmer's Boy* to the folktale tradition, and accords well with the poet's conception of it as a poem about the day-to-day lives of the rural poor. The word 'humble' also suggests that the poem treats 'low' subject matter, but it says more about Bloomfield's origins and pretensions than it does about the poem itself. Labouring-class poets were expected to have a deferential attitude towards more fortunate members of society, and to be satisfied with their social status (Christmas 2001, 157–234). The revision reinforces Lofft's conclusion to the preface which, despite the fact that the poet had endeavoured to find a publisher for his poem before enlisting Lofft's help, typically reminds the reader that Bloomfield is reassuringly humble:

> ... the Author, with a spirit amiable at all times, and which would have been rever'd by Antiquity, seems far less interested concerning any Fame or Advantage he may derive from it [*The Farmer's Boy*] to himself, than in the pleasure of giving a printed Copy of it, as a tribute of duty and affection to his MOTHER. [1800, xv–xvi]

Bloomfield's original suggests that *The Farmer's Boy* is rooted in popular culture, Lofft's revision that it is somehow a product of paternalism.

Lofft's preface and editorial interventions construct Bloomfield as an innocent and contented peasant who knows his place. But the way the poet attempts to position his poem in the opening passages suggests that he is not in fact poorly educated and subservient. As a consequence it is not easy for the reader to place Bloomfield. For different reasons it is also difficult to read the poet's young alter-ego. Bloomfield may not have wanted his readers to be made aware of the link between Giles and his personal experience. Because he was not consulted regarding the presentation of the poem, and did not see the prefatory material until after it had been published, the poet could not have known that Lofft would make this connection explicitly in his preface. Nevertheless, the figure of Giles is clearly based upon Bloomfield's own experience of life as a farmer's boy. Despite the fact that he returned to Suffolk a number of times after leaving as a fourteen-year-old, his memory of Breckland always took him back to those early years. As he remarks in a letter to his mother written during 1788, he could always see 'in imagination ... [his] old neighbours and things just as they were' (MS 317/3, fol. 1).

Notwithstanding Bloomfield's claim to be able to remember his past clearly, as an urban artisan he was a considerable distance away from his former self both temporally and in terms of his way of life. The process of memory clearly played an important part in the composition of *The Farmer's Boy*. This is apparent from one of the first descriptive passages in the poem, in which Giles is depicted following the ploughman with the harrow. These lines focus on Giles's status as a labourer carrying out allotted tasks: '... Giles with wearying strides / From ridge to ridge the ponderous harrow guides; / His heels deep sinking every step he goes, / Till dirt adhesive loads his clouted shoes. / Welcome green headland! firm beneath his feet; / Welcome the friendly bank's refreshing seat' (I: 79–84). The image of Giles struggling over the field with the harrow, as layer upon layer of earth builds up upon his shoes, brings into relief the gross physicality of the landscape. It is an image drawn from memory that directly connects Bloomfield the poet with his boyhood on Mr Austin's farm. The respite that the headland provided for the exhausted farm worker would have been most apparent to someone like Bloomfield who had actually performed this kind of task. But the image is also symbolic in that Giles toils within the old and fast-disappearing open field landscape in which the grassy headland between the furlongs still existed. This pre-Enclosure landscape signifies a social system rooted in commonality and tradition, indeed for labouring people 'open fields and commons' represented 'the collective memory of the community' (Bushaway 1982, 82–4). Most headlands disappeared during Enclosure when the ridge-and-furrow field system was ploughed over in order to create the new enclosed fields (Taylor 1975, 84–6). Ironically, Bloomfield was writing his poem during the years immediately preceding the enclosure of west Suffolk. Between 1800 and 1817 there were twenty-six Enclosure Acts affecting Breckland (Postgate, 87).

Following the ploughing scene there is one of the most didactic georgic passages in the poem, as Giles is given the task of scaring birds away from young seedlings. It is one of the keys to reading what is, in the georgic tradition, an episodic poem, because he is given the task on two subsequent occasions in circumstances that emphasize the protean nature of both Giles himself and rural life. The passage is almost Hesiodic in mode: 'Let then your birds lie prostrate on the earth, / In dying posture, and with wings stretcht forth; / Shift them at eve or morn from place to place, / And Death shall terrify the pilfering race' (I: 117–20). Rosenmeyer makes a distinction between the georgic and the instructive Hesiodic tradition (20–29). It is possible that Bloomfield had read Hesiod because numerous translations of his works appeared in periodicals and journals towards the end of the eighteenth century. In the context of the fact that the poem is semi-autobiographical, these variations on the georgic mode bring into relief an interesting feature of the way in which Bloomfield remembers life on Mr Austin's farm. In respect of both the bird-scaring and the ploughing scenes he focuses on everyday practical detail, and represents working life as perfunctory and task orientated. When discussing Marcel Proust's theory of the relationship between memory and art, Mary Warnock describes such recollections as 'voluntary memories' (92).

Bloomfield appears to be suffering from a lack of poetic inspiration, but this apparent crisis is resolved when he recalls the beauty of a tree-lined lane after a spring shower: 'His sandy way, deep-worn by hasty showers, / O'er arch'd with Oaks that form'd fantastic bow'rs, / Waving aloft their tow'ring branches proud, / In borrow'd tinges from the eastern cloud, / Gave inspiration, pure as ever flow'd, / And genuine transport in his bosom glow'd.' (I: 131–6). Jonathan Lawson notes the way in which this passage represents 'the poet finding inspiration' (69). There is a definite intensification of tone, but there is something else very noticeable about the passage too. The 'rapture' which the reader is told fills the mind of the young Giles appears to become merged with the poetic capacity of the mature poet. A boy walking through the early morning countryside might experience a kind of undefined joy, but 'inspiration' does not seem to be the right word to describe such a feeling. On the other hand, it is the correct word to describe the effect that the remembrance of this scene has upon the poet. The passage also articulates the manner in which he is drawn or transported back through time by making an emotional, rather than an intellectual connection with Giles's youthful sensibility. 'Transport' is a word with multiple meanings, it can mean a kind of indefinable rapture or it can mean the movement of an object, or even a sensation, through space or time. Bloomfield demonstrates the striking effect that memory can have upon the consciousness as he brings together the two senses of the word.

In the next passage Bloomfield suggests that nature's ability to 'transport' the individual will provide relief from the monotony of the walk to work. Giles's 'inspiration' continues when a profusion of images crowd into his mind:

> His own shrill matin join'd the various notes
> Of Nature's music, from a thousand throats:
> The Blackbird strove with emulation sweet,
> And Echo answer'd from her close retreat;
> The sporting White-throat on some twig's end borne,
> Pour'd hymns to freedom and the rising morn;
> Stopt in her song perchance the starting Thrush
> Shook a white shower from the black-thorn bush,
> Where dew-drops thick as early blossoms hung,
> And trembled as the minstrel sweetly sung.
> Across his path, in either grove to hide,
> The timid Rabbit scouted by his side;
> Or Pheasant boldly stalk'd along the road,
> Whose gold and purple tints alternate glow'd. [I: 137–50]

This passage celebrating the variety of nature is marked by the kind of urgency that Warnock associates with 'involuntary memory' (92–3). In that it incorporates a number of diverse images into fourteen lines it resembles numerous sonnets written by John Clare during the 1820s. Some of the images are linked syntactically in such a way that they represent 'a complex manifold of simultaneous impressions' and thereby convey a 'sense of place' (Barrell 1972, 157). But the different impressions are not always temporally and spatially related to each other. The images could easily stand in isolation and as such are like raw remembrances before they are shaped by poetry. In that his 'transport' reveals his sensitivity to the beauty of nature and causes him to sing along with the birds, it could be argued that here Giles is a kind of proto-poet.

Whether the physical hardship and drudgery of labour itself could be relieved by the variety of nature is a moot point. But these lines do evoke certain features of the agricultural landscape that must have had great personal resonances for the mature poet. Bloomfield was one of those 'poring thousands' hidden in the 'breathless rooms' of London (I: 239). Shoemakers did have ways of relieving the drudgery of their work, for example by appointing an apprentice like the young Bloomfield to read the newspaper to them. But for Bloomfield the poet, a properly functioning memory was his only regular link with the landscape of his youth, which was such an important part of his moral and intellectual being. His recollection of the way nature apparently rejuvenates the young Giles frees his poetic sensibility from a kind of enthrallment to the practical detail of rural working life. A variation in tone is brought about by the combined effect of a change in the way that he remembers the past and a new kind of poetic impulse. The celebration of natural diversity in these lines also owes something to both the Romantic belief in the nourishing power of nature, and the neoclassical conception of pastoral as a mode which should provide relief from day-to-day affairs. The ability to indulge in this kind of 'inspiration' would have provided a relief of sorts for a struggling shoemaker-poet working in a poorly lit garret.

In 'Summer' when, for the second time, Giles is given the task of scaring birds away from the growing crop, he experiences a significantly different kind of inspiration. He anticipates that the monotony of his task will again be relieved by the plenitude of nature, but his desire to find 'objects to his mind' (II: 50) indicates that he is not, as in the earlier passage, being represented as simply an enthusiastic observer. His wish is satisfied when, as he lies down on the headland to rest, he gets the opportunity to try his skill as an entomologist:

> Stretch'd on the turf he lies, a peopled bed,
> Where swarming insects creep around his head.
> The small dust-colour'd beetle climbs with pain
> O'er the smooth plantain-leaf, a spacious plain!
> Thence higher still, by countless steps convey'd,
> He gains the summit of a shiv'ring blade,
> And flirts his filmy wings, and looks around,
> Exalting in his distance from the ground.
> The tender speckled moth here dancing seen,
> The vaulting grasshopper of glossy green,
> And all prolific Summer's sporting train,
> Their little lives by various pow'rs sustain. [II: 73–84]

Here it is Giles's intellectual rather than his emotional faculties that are stimulated. This is clear from the way in which he observes minute details such as the texture of the different insects' wings. Later he even moulds his hat into a 'friendly telescope' in order to view a lark in flight, an image which speaks of intellectual aspiration restricted by poverty and lack of opportunity. The mature poet had a particular interest in the precise observation of natural objects as is clear from his 'Observations' upon spiders and their webs (*Remains* II: 54–66). Such an interest and the associated aptitude for patient observation would be more likely in a man than in a young boy. It seems that this is another example of Bloomfield's mature preoccupations being attributed to the consciousness of Giles. At the same time, the passage provides a foil to the conception of agricultural labourers as ignorant brutes. This was a view that became increasingly common amongst the more fortunate classes during the late eighteenth and early nineteenth centuries. As William Cobbett later remarked, the labouring poor were 'spoken of by everyone possessing the power to oppress them ... in just the same manner as we speak of the animals which compose the stock upon a farm' (*Political Register* 78 (1832), 710).

Bloomfield's representation of Giles brings into relief some of the problems inherent in the autobiographical project. The inflection of Giles's consciousness with that of the mature poet makes it difficult for the reader to see Giles as an innocent and contented farmer's boy. It is arguable that in *The Prelude* Wordsworth fails to deal adequately with other problems and temptations that must be negotiated by the autobiographer. Whereas Bloomfield endows Giles with an ability to appreciate the beauty of nature, and some intellectual aspiration, Wordsworth suggests that even at the age of ten he knew that he was special: 'even then I felt / Gleams like the flashing of a shield. The earth / And common face of Nature spake to me / Rememberable things' (I: 613–16). Nature not only spoke to him, it communicated things that he knew were of value. Wordsworth also traces the development of his 'poetic' capacity to this period; he is able to see 'affinities / In objects where no brotherhood exists / To common minds' (II: 403–405). The way he sees his younger self is influenced by his mature desire to present himself as the possessor of a poetic vocation that is one 'in ten thousand' (XII: 91). Had Bloomfield been confident of his vocation, the representation of his former self might have been more egoistically controlled, but then *The Farmer's Boy* would not have revealed the workings, and frailties of the memory process.

The emergence of more than one Giles from the text is probably an unintentional effect of the instability of the poet's memory. But on occasions he did remember the past vividly, particularly when *The Farmer's Boy* reflects critically upon the treatment of labour in poetry and painting by those who had not experienced agricultural work. Bloomfield acknowledged his debt to Thomson, but in *The Seasons* (1730) the description of ploughing is brief and all of the labour appears to be undertaken by the team, 'cheered by the simple song [of the ploughman] and the soaring lark' (I: 40). Late eighteenth-century poetry and painting generally naturalized the labourer within the landscape (Barrell 1980, 35–164; 1992, 105–32). Labour would not generally be marked upon the countenance of the agricultural worker. In George Stubbs's *Reapers* and *Haymakers* (1785), to cite the most obvious examples, the figures 'do their work with the same kind of gravity with which, in Italian Renaissance paintings, serious-minded archers shoot arrows at St Sebastian' (Barrell 1992, 105). Notwithstanding Wordsworth's express desire to 'speak of tillers of the soil ... / The ploughman with his team; or men and boys / ... busy with the rake' (VIII: 498–500), work itself is rarely represented in his poetry. Instead he employs suggestive rustic imagery in his quasi-philosophical response to the working countryside. In so doing he satisfies the expectations of a polite reading audience conditioned by the absence of close-up images of work from eighteenth-century georgic poetry.

William Christmas fails to take account of Bloomfield's complex imagery when he remarks that: 'the discourse on work discernable throughout the poem is repeatedly folded into pleasing images ... and the eternal optimism of a fecund natural world of labouring-class content' (2001, 270). In fact Bloomfield explicitly stresses the great physical effort involved in farm-work, in a way that echoes the representation of farm-workers in many seventeenth- and eighteenth-century popular songs (Palmer, 17–46). The ploughman in 'Spring' labours alone and 'unassisted through each toilsome day' (I: 71), and the 'Sturdy Mower' in 'Summer', 'Whose writhing form meridian heat defies, / Bends o'er his work, and every sinew tries' (II: 143–4). The mower's effort is clearly recorded on his frame, and the effect of labour upon the ploughman's countenance is ironically highlighted when Bloomfield draws attention to his furrowed brow: 'With smiling brow the plowman cleaves his way' (I: 72). The contrast between 'smiling' and 'cleaves' establishes a play upon the different senses of furrow; the ploughman's 'smiling' brow is furrowed with effort and the land is furrowed as it is cleaved apart by the plough. The words reflect backwards and forwards as they illuminate and comment upon each other. The newly ploughed fields, marked with the effort of the ploughman's labour, are not the 'smiling fields' of James Thomson's 'An Elegy on Parting' (17) or Thomas Gray's *Journal* (45). And the 'sober brown' fields are reflected on the furrowed brow of the ploughman, which is not that of the serene labourer which appears in so many poems and paintings of the period. Nor is the harsh physical effort involved in rural labour always relieved by 'Nature's music' as it is for Giles when he walks to the fields in 'Spring'. In 'Summer' Giles is given the task of threshing the newly harvested wheat in a passage that recalls Stephen Duck's *The Thresher's Labour* (1730) which had also represented unpleasant aspects of agricultural labour: 'The sweat, and dust, and suffocating smoke / Make us so much like *Ethiopians* look' (64–5). Giles is enclosed amidst 'The cobweb'd barn's impure and dusty air', and feels great relief when his work is completed: 'Laborious task! with what delight, when done / Both horse and rider greet th'unclouded sun' (II: 198, 203–204).

In the same way as the labourer has to work and does not spend his life at rest, the working landscape is constantly in a state of transition. It is neither as 'natural' nor as static as it is sometimes represented in the poetry of the period. Wordsworth sanctifies both the rural worker who resisted change like the hero of 'Michael' (1800), and, in *The Prelude*, his own response to a landscape that is often construed as in some way eternal. The countryside was generally shaped by innovation rooted in tradition in earlier eighteenth-century georgic.

In *The Farmer's Boy* the appearance of the landscape is the result of managed change. Even the apparently uncontrolled manner in which sheep graze is not what it seems, as is apparent from the description of Giles guarding the flock at the end of 'Spring':

> Small was his charge: no wilds had they to roam;
> But bright inclosures circling round their home. / … /
> Yet ever roving, ever seeking thee,
> Enchanting spirit, dear Variety!
> O happy tenants, prisoners of a day!
> Releas'd to ease, to pleasure, and to play;
> Indulg'd through every field by turns to range, / … /
> Sheep long confin'd but loathe the present good;
> Bleating around the homeward gate they meet,
> And starve, and pine, with plenty at their feet. [I: 285–98]

Christmas suggests that this passage idealizes a potentially troubling scene because it ignores the destructive aspects of enclosure, and represents it in a way that 'can only be described as positive' (2001, 282). But the adjective 'bright' was a common qualifier in eighteenth-century poetry. It was used repeatedly by Thomson in the first two books of *The Seasons*: 'Moist, bright, and green, the landscape laughs around'; 'yon bright arch, / Contracted, bends into a dusky vault' (I: 197, 1011–12). It is certain that the word was originally employed to denote features in the landscape made distinctive by the light conditions, but it eventually became a stock epithet used habitually by poets in the manner deplored by Wordsworth in the preface to *Lyrical Ballads* (1800). The phrase 'bright enclosures' might represent an attempt to suggest the way in which a particular kind of light picks out features in the landscape, or it might be an instance of the poet unconsciously employing the kind of poetic diction that he had absorbed from his reading. It is unlikely that Bloomfield would have set out to represent enclosure in a positive way because elsewhere in his early poetry and in his prose he condemns the practice. In 'The Broken Crutch' (1806) he condemns this 'scythe of desolation call'e "Reform"' (68), and in one of his 'Anecdotes and Observations' remarks: 'Inclosing Acts! I do not much like the rage for them. They cut down the solemn, the venerable tree, and *sometimes* plant another,—*not always*; like the mercenary soldier, who kills more than he begets' (*Remains* II: 53).

There is a way in which *The Farmer's Boy* complicates what had traditionally been an unequivocally idealistic pastoral scene. The idea of sheep 'seeking' variety is odd because they do not crave diversity in their food (Lynch, Hinch and Adams, 24). As long as they have lush green grass, clover pasture, or something similar to graze upon they are generally contented, although Clare would later represent the effects of enclosure in a similar manner in 'The Mores' (1821–24): 'Fence now meets fence in owners little bounds / Of field and meadow large as garden bounds / In little parcels little minds to please / With men and flocks imprisoned ill at ease' (46–50). In the context of Bloomfield's response to the way the sheep are managed, it does not matter whether they are in reality programmed to wander because he is using them as figures for the love of freedom. Unlike Clare's discontented sheep, Bloomfield's are happy because they are provided with variety, but ultimately they are still 'prisoners'. They are 'happy tenants' because they are deluded into a sense that they possess the freedom to wander, but like people sheep are easily deceived and easily led. The way in which the sheep's apparent desire for freedom is controlled suggests a way in which Bloomfield's London experience might have influenced the construction of this passage. The cycle of restraint and release mirrors the kind of effect that mental reverie might have upon the human prisoner or the discontented shoemaker confined within a city garret. As being allowed into a new enclosure does for the sheep, the memory of past freedom and happiness brings momentary relief from current pain. But as soon as the reverie ends, the walls around them make them aware that they are still restrained, just like the enclosing fences do for 'long confin'd' sheep.

Bloomfield may have disliked the lack of freedom associated with his labouring-class status. But if he had enjoyed the leisure of a poet like Wordsworth, *The Farmer's Boy* would not have revealed the way in which the working landscape and the response of the participatory observer are shaped by change. Wordsworth's poetics elevate his status as casual middle-class wanderer in the landscape, and during the period treated in *The Prelude* he did not stay in one place for very long. This meant that he did not have a sustained opportunity to observe a particular place in the working landscape through time. Bloomfield's poem describes the whole farming year, and is based upon his experience of working alongside other labourers on a single farm in Suffolk for a period of four years. In the first book of *The Farmer's Boy* there are accounts of the way in which the advent of spring cheers the labouring poor. For example, the description of Giles walking to the fields, or that of the farmyard (I: 165–230), or the account of spring's impact upon the countryside and country people: 'Where'er she [spring] treads, Love gladdens every plain, / Delight on tiptoe bears her lucid train; / Sweet Hope with conscious brow before her flies / Anticipating wealth from Summer skies' (I: 273–6). But the working landscape is marked by different kinds of seasonal change too in some much darker passages. In the closing lines of 'Spring', the narrator is again inspired by a 'transport' of memory. He imagines 'young Lambs at play', apparently one of the most pastoral of scenes. But the fact that the shadow of the metropolis also hovers over this passage is suggested by the reappearance of prison imagery. The enthusiasm of the new-born lambs for play is compared with the impatience of 'the fond dove, from fearful prison freed' (I: 227). And the innocent joy of the gambolling lambs is indeed soon cut short: 'For lo, the murd'ring Butcher, with his cart, / Demands the firstlings of his flock to die, / And makes a sport of life and liberty' (I: 346–8). The leisured visitor can avoid scenes like this, but the shepherd is a participatory observer; the sheep are his 'gay companions' (I: 349), and the scene makes a profound impression upon him: 'Care loads his brow, and pity wrings his heart' (I: 345).

In terms of the influences that acted upon Bloomfield when writing *The Farmer's Boy*, the kind of language used in his account of the death of the 'firstlings' of the flock is important. It is not quite the 'safe, symbolic language for registering social criticism' that Christmas finds in Bloomfield's animal imagery (2001, 277). Although agricultural labourers would not necessarily have been callous towards stock and working animals, nor would they have displayed this kind of sentimentality. As a London artisan, Bloomfield might have encountered a different, more politicized manner of thinking about animals, either at the debating societies that he attended or in print. In texts like John Oswald's *The Cry of Nature* (1791), the vegetable diet was associated with social progress, and with the endeavour to establish a more egalitarian order marked by a universal benevolence which also encompassed the world of 'brutes' (Morton, 25). Bloomfield's exposure to such ideas probably does not explain the point of view expressed in this passage, however, because the labouring poor; whether country or town dwellers, with whom Bloomfield generally sympathized, did not theorize or moralize diet. By the turn of the eighteenth century, the poor could hardly afford meat, and when they were able to buy it they might have eaten pork or bacon, but almost certainly never lamb (Burnett, 13). Lamb, even mutton, would have been the preserve of the better off, and were in most cases luxury items for all but the rich. Because of Suffolk's proximity to London, a significant proportion of the lamb produced in the county must have found its way into the metropolis where there was a great demand for meat (Drummond and Wilbraham, 227). Just as the 'London market' (I: 244) for butter is responsible for a decline in the quality of Suffolk cheese, the appetites of wealthy Londoners are ultimately responsible for the 'murder' of the young lambs. The anger in Bloomfield's language might therefore represent a critique of the rich in general and the metropolitan rich in particular.

At the end of 'Spring', the narrator suggests that the 'shocking image' of slaughter is inconsistent with the feelings of hope and 'universal joy' that should accompany the approach of summer. This is an expression of desire for the kind of stable rural idyll, the reality of which the poem seriously interrogates. There are many accounts of happy workers in 'Summer', for example the description of Giles lying down to rest whilst bird-scaring or the account of the ploughman admiring the ripening crop (II: 113–20). But the moment in the agricultural year which perhaps most represented a celebration of 'universal joy' in rural life at its most idyllic was the harvest festival. It was the major turning-point in the calendar for both labourers and the working landscape. The successful completion of the harvest principally benefited the farmer, but all were made to feel involved by the harvest-home feast. In *The Farmer's Boy* the 'Harvest-home' scene represents a kind of equality within inequality: 'Here once a year Distinction low'rs its crest, / The master, servant, and the merry guest, / Are equal all' (II: 323–5). The easy way in which 'Pride gave place to mirth' (II: 334) in the conduct of the farmer or landowner, also suggests that relations between all members of the community are marked by an inclusive cordiality. Freedom itself is not so much a matter of the absence of restraints. For Bloomfield the 'unaffected Freedom' (I: 377) of rural communities is dependent upon the presence and acceptance by all of certain constraints and responsibilities.

The nature of freedom is also a question that preoccupied Wordsworth, but on the evidence of *The Prelude*, the word had a very different meaning for him. It has been suggested that 'it is one of the ironies of *The Prelude* ... that it should eulogize the values of small rural communities at the same time as promulgating an individualistic ethos of continuous self development' (Clark 1997, 94). But Wordsworth does not 'eulogize' rural communities because of the commonality and mutuality that he finds in them. In Book VIII of *The Prelude* he admires the communities that he found in Cumberland, and which had such an impact on all of his verse, because there he found 'Man free, man working for himself, with choice / Of time, and place, and object; by his wants, / His comforts, native occupations, cares, / Conducted on to individual ends / Or social' (152–6). There were more small semi-independent cottagers in Cumberland than in Suffolk at the end of the eighteenth century, but they were probably not quite as independent as Wordsworth suggests, and the majority of the population had to sell all of their labour to others in order to survive (Snell, 95–6). In other words, Wordsworth only sees the better-off minority. Notwithstanding the view of a number of critics that Wordsworth's poetry represents a critique of bourgeois capitalism (Clark 1997, 94; Turner 1986, 218), the ethos that regulates conduct within his Cumberland communities has much in common with the modern *laissez-faire* version of freedom which depends upon the absence of restraints and responsibilities towards others. In Wordsworth's ideal community, each person is 'free' to labour 'for himself' towards 'individual ends', and, but only if he chooses to do so, engage in 'social' labour. He individualizes rural 'custom' in order to show that moral and market economics are not in conflict. A natural corollary of the way Wordsworth conceives of rural communities in Cumberland is that labourers have no grounds upon which to resist the advance of agrarian capitalism. In Bloomfield's ideal community everyone has a 'duty' rooted in custom to labour for everyone else towards common ends. For Bloomfield, custom binds the community together in a way that allows everyone, rather than just possessors of independent property and wealth, to enjoy the benefits of 'unaffected freedom'.

The closing passages of 'Summer' demonstrate the importance of the 'Harvest-home' to the rural labouring poor, but also reveal the fragility of the customary practices which sustained it through time. Customs are dependent upon the attitudes which underpin them, and Bloomfield suggests that new 'tyrant customs', underpinned by different attitudes, such as a trend towards greater 'refinement' amongst farmers, have started to replace the older customs (II: 338). Critiques of London wealth, fashion and refinement began to appear in rural popular songs over a century before Bloomfield started work on *The Farmer's Boy* (Dyck, 91–3). In his *Rural Rides* (1830) a quarter of a century later, William Cobbett remarked upon the way this trend had changed the face of rural England: farm-houses which were formerly the 'scene of *plain* manners and *plentiful* living' had become cluttered with 'decanters ... glasses, the "dinner set" of crockery ware, and all just in the true stock jobber style' (226–7). The attitudes which resulted in this change evolved as the inward-looking approach to life of the new capitalist middle class spread from the towns and cities to the countryside (Hay and Rogers, 85). It is an approach to life that is mirrored, to some extent at least, in Wordsworth's Cumberland communities. The fact that in *The Farmer's Boy* the luxury of the farmer is described as a 'tyrant' custom, an emotionally and politically charged phrase, suggests that their middle-class liberty to choose their way of living is actually repressive and works against freedom.

This new bourgeois 'refinement' has a detrimental effect upon everyone within the rural community, it 'Destroys life's intercourse; the social plan / That rank to rank cements, as man to man' (II: 241–2). In destroying the wider community, the farmer's empty posturing also destroys the individuals within it; the labourer is impoverished materially, but the farmer's social impoverishment is greater. His social 'display' is psychologically damaging: 'Wealth flows around him, Fashion lordly reigns; / Yet poverty is his, and mental pains' (II: 343–4). The labourer is left with the vestiges of an admittedly declining popular culture, but the farmer is left isolated in his new '*parlour*' (*Rural Rides*, 227). It could be argued that in this passage Bloomfield echoes the way London radicals deployed rural topoi in order to legitimize their criticism of 'providence'. In *The Peripatetic* (1793), John Thelwall argues that the indifference of those who 'loll ... on the couch of luxurious affluence' might impel individuals, like unemployed hay-makers forced into beggary, to improve their situation by violent means (87).

This part of *The Farmer's Boy* is 'rather out of key with the rest of the poem', and further illustrates the manner in which Bloomfield's encounters with the fringes of the London radical movement influenced him (Sambrook, 169). It is easy to see why for the *British Critic* it constitutes evidence 'that the author received some impressions, probably at the debating society, of a questionable kind' (15 (1800), 602). The reviewer had in mind Bloomfield's brother's account of the poet's visit to 'a dissenting *Meeting-house* in the *Old Jewry*, where a Gentleman was lecturing' which Capel Lofft included within his preface. The gentleman was the radical Unitarian minister Joseph Fawcett: 'one of the great voices of radical dissent of his time' (Lucas 1994, 58). This man 'fill'd *Robert* with astonishment' and as a consequence he also 'went sometimes ... to a *Debating Society* at *Coachmaker's-hall*, but not often' (1800, vi–vii). At the turn of the eighteenth century, debating houses would have been associated with radical politics, particularly by a journal with impeccable Tory credentials like the *British Critic* (Roper, 180). As Lofft's footnote to the preface reminds the reader, the activities of debating houses were feared by the government and were severely curtailed by the Two Acts of 1795. The radical connotations of these revelations about Bloomfield's interests are undercut in the preface by the fact that it focuses upon the way the encounters improved the poet's command English. But according to his brother, the young Bloomfield did gain 'the most enlarg'd notions of PROVIDENCE' from his interest in radical lectures and debating houses (1800, vii). George seems to be suggesting that Bloomfield's notion of providence became larger than the 'whatever is, is right' idea of the world, promoted with increasing fervour and frequency during the 1790s by the religiously orthodox. In other words he developed a wider sense of the governance of the world than that it is directed by God and so must be just as it is, and came to understand that a religious view of life was compatible with a commitment to social and political change for the better.

Bloomfield might have flirted with radical politics during the 1780s and 1790s, but his poetry has generally been read as politically conservative. Roger Sales concludes that he 'was successful because he knew that the reading public expected farmer's boys to show that they were blissfully contented with their place in society' (20). In a more recent essay William Christmas, whilst conceding that 'Bloomfield's poem does reproduce at one level a degree of rural idealization that both reinforces the status quo and harks back to traditional eighteenth-century pastoral', goes on to demonstrate that it 'is far more complex in its modes, and in its implied politics, than Sales allows' (2006, 32). Christmas focuses on three political 'interludes' within the poem: the response to tail-docking in 'Summer'; the 'Harvest-home' scene; and the post-horse/plough horse comparison in 'Winter'. With regard to the 'Harvest-home' scene, he argues that Bloomfield, whilst adopting a rationalist standpoint in order to expose the 'destructive effects of "refinement," "Wealth," and "Fashion" on the old, organic social order ... stops short of articulating the natural and civil right of individuals to challenge that power and forge a new government based on Paine's republican principles' (2006, 42). Christmas is right to question the view that *The Farmer's Boy* unquestioningly upholds the status quo, and the poem does adopt a rationalist position in its critique of the new order in the countryside. But if Bloomfield was concerned to defend the 'old, organic social order' he could not have done so by invoking 'Paine's republican principles'. The 'Harvest-home' festivities in *The Farmer's Boy* are underpinned 'by right' (II: 303) of a quite specific network of customs, that is related to, but independent of the Burkean conception of custom as the foundation of the constitution. It is a quite different nexus from that which produced the Painite rationalist liberal view that it is the right of each generation to form its own system of governance. Bloomfield's 'Harvest-home' is legitimized by 'manorial custom' or a complex of custom, law and common rights operating at a local level (Hay and Rogers, 97–184).

The closing passages of 'Summer' are clearly full of oppositions and contradictions, and perhaps more than any other part of *The Farmer's Boy* reveal that critics like Lawson and Sales are wrong to endorse Lofft's presentation of Bloomfield as a simple rural poet. But the composite nature of Bloomfield's response to rural England becomes particularly evident if his appendix is considered alongside the poem (Appendix 1 reproduces the full text of Bloomfield's appendix). In fact the appendix problematizes Christmas's conclusion that Bloomfield's only answer to the 'destruction' caused by bourgeois 'refinement' is 'the old organic order that 'linked landowner to tenant farmer to labourer' (2001, 275). A note appended to his 1807 fair copy MS of the poem suggests that Bloomfield had wanted readers to take a particular message away from *The Farmer's Boy*:

> In reference to this passage, and as I thought, by way of illustration, I subjoined an extract from Cook's voyage [the appendix] not knowing but it was written by Cook himself, which I now find was not the case ... I was pleading for kindness between the ranks of society, and it seem'd to suit my purpose. And if I could believe that what I have said of letting "Labour have its due" would in only one instance persuade a Farmer to give his men more wages, instead of giving, or suffering him to buy cheap corn in the time of trouble, I should feel a pleasure of the most lasting sort, having no doubt but that an extra half crown carried is worth, morally, and substantially, a five shilling Gift, to those who in the House of their fathers work for bread. [MS Eng. 776.1, fol. 27]

The extract from 'Cook's voyage' appeared at the end of the poem in all early editions of *The Farmer's Boy*, up to and including the tenth edition which was published in 1808 (it was omitted from *The Poems of Robert Bloomfield* published in 1809). As Bloomfield appears to have realized some time after publication, it did not come from Cook's own account of his second voyage. In fact it originally appeared in George Forster's 1777 account entitled *A Voyage Around the World* (198–200). Bloomfield could have quoted from any one of the many works and periodicals in which sections of Forster's text appeared. As the introduction to Thomas and Bergof's edition notes, it was 'abridged, pirated, printed in excerpt – in short, every thing but sold' (xxxvi).

The passage fulfils Bloomfield's stated purpose because in many ways Otaheite society does mirror the kind of community that is represented in the harvest-home feast described in *The Farmer's Boy*. Very definite hierarchies exist amongst the Otaheite, but distinctions between social groupings are veiled by the simple lifestyle of all: 'The simplicity of their whole life contributes to soften the appearance of distinctions, and to reduce them to a level.' There is free and easy intercourse between everyone:

> The lowest man in the Nation speaks as freely with his King as with his equal, and has the pleasure of seeing him as often as he likes. The King, at times, amuses himself with the occupations of his subjects; and not yet deprav'd by false notions of empty state, he often paddles his own canoe, without considering such an employment derogatory to his dignity.

The implication is that the King and his subjects eat together on occasion, unlike the new kind of farmer who dines apart from his workers with 'selected guests' even on the occasion of the harvest-home feast (II: 378–85). Empty posturing and display play no part in Otaheite society; the King does not require the Otaheite equivalent of 'decanters' or canteens of cutlery to maintain his position and set him apart from his subjects. That he is 'not yet deprav'd by false notions of empty state' represents an implied criticism of the farmer's luxury.

Bloomfield may have included the Otaheite passage to reinforce his defence of the old social order, but far from clarifying the situation, the Cook passage and the 1807 MS note actually draw Bloomfield's poem further into a London-oriented political milieu. When he says 'I was pleading for kindness between the ranks of society' he is being a little disingenuous because he was not providing a neutral commentary upon the theme of his text by citing, as he thought at the time, from Cook's journal. From the time of their first encounter with the South Pacific, Europeans viewed it and its inhabitants in a variety of ways (Smith 1985, 133–54). Some accounts of Cook's voyages were received with horror by conservative commentators, fearful that idealistic visions of the South Sea Islands might foster attempts to overturn both gender relations and the political order in Britain (Maxwell, 247). In this context it is clear that Bloomfield was entering into a pre-existing and highly charged political debate. Especially in view of the fact that the passage cited in his appendix contrasts the Otaheite with the English social order in a way that reflects negatively upon the latter:

> Absolute want occasions the miseries of the lower class in some civiliz'd states, and is the result of the unbounded voluptuousness of their superiors. At Otaheite there is not, in general, that disparity between the highest and the meanest man, that subsists in England between a reputable tradesman and a labourer.

Notwithstanding the fact that social ills were widely blamed upon luxury during the eighteenth century, texts which criticized the status quo and advocated the levelling of society in this manner were often regarded as seditious by those in positions of authority.

Bloomfield's plea for labour to be given 'its due' appears to be an almost pitiful cry for the return of organic rural communities (II: 399). The kind of 'Harvest-home' that Bloomfield's 'mourner' (II: 345) appears to lament is located in the primitive, uncorrupted and innocent Golden Age that some observers saw in Otaheite society. The 1807 MS note, on the other hand, suggests that Bloomfield believed wages in the hand might be of greater value than some of the rewards that workers received under the old system of custom and right. For a figure so often seen as firmly rooted in the past this is significant. Bloomfield does not consider the sort of action that might be necessary to achieve better wages and conditions for workers, such as political reform or the development of strong trade unions. But his revelation is surprisingly progressive, and does indicate that Bloomfield was aware of the advantages of an alternative, if traditionally rooted, social order. It does not necessarily represent an abandonment of the poet's commitment to customary practices. It links him to the intellectual milieu that existed in late eighteenth-century London, when

> ... the opposition between historicist and rationalist logics was not secure on street level, where rationalists borrowed from and contributed to the languages of both custom and millenarianism, and, significantly, the meaning of custom itself was far more dialectical and internally various than the elite version purveyed by Burke. [Janowitz 1998, 63]

The Farmer's Boy, when read in the context of the Otaheite passage and the 1807 MS note, indicates that Bloomfield believed both the maintenance of traditional customary practices (at a local level) and political change were required to improve the lives of the labouring poor.

Both 'Spring' and 'Summer' conclude with passages that show rural life to be both potentially shocking and unpredictable: the description of the slaughter of the lambs and the account of the changing harvest-home. *The Farmer's Boy* also explores the way in which the shadow of the metropolis impacted upon life in the countryside, and presents a rural community that is complex, multi-faceted, and not always easy to understand. The complexity of Bloomfield's representation would perhaps have been missed by his polite reading audience, used to an idealized and simplified portrayal of rural life and labour. The incomprehensibility of aspects of life in the countryside would, however, have been felt by the labouring poor. The way in which life in the countryside could injure the mental health of some is explored through the story of 'Lovely Ann' in 'Autumn' ('Lovely Poll' in early editions). An obvious source is crazy Kate in Book I of *The Task* (1785), a less obvious one the figure of 'the fair Maniac' Louisa in Ann Yearsley's 'Clifton Hill. Written in January 1785' (534–6; 206–96). On another level the story is a sentimental exemplum, the kind of character digression that occurred in much of the poetry and fiction written at the turn of the eighteenth century, for example 'The Female Vagrant', 'The Thorn' and 'The Mad Mother' in *Lyrical Ballads* (1798). Like 'the gaily-passing stranger' in *The Farmer's Boy*, in Wordsworth's poems the reader is drawn into a transport of sentimental pity by empathizing with the suffering of the characters. In *The Farmer's Boy* the stranger also feeds his sentimentality through Ann's pain, but Bloomfield reveals the disturbing nature of such voyeurism as Ann becomes imprisoned by a ring of 'gazers': 'And oft the gaily-passing stranger stays / His well-tim'd step, and takes a silent gaze, / Till sympathetic drops unbidden start, / And pangs quick springing muster round his heart; / And soft he treads with other gazers round' (III: 151–5). Bloomfield stresses that the observers are strangers, and the fact that they pass 'gaily' indicates a lack of occupation and a degree of removal, in social terms, from the suffering village girl. In fact the conduct of the observers becomes de-humanized and vaguely threatening as they mechanically tread round the frightened and reclusive girl.

Although Ann does not understand what is wrong with her, and 'fancied wrongs bewails' (III: 140), there is an indication within the text as to what has unsettled her mind. According to the world-view of *The Farmer's Boy* 'unaffected freedom' rather paradoxically depends upon a sense of belonging (II: 377). Ann is affected by the feeling that she belongs nowhere, and the fact that she is a slave to 'inverted customs' (III: 130). She sleeps in the 'sty' with the swine, and, like the new kind of farmer in the account of the harvest-home, eats her meals alone and in secret. It is legitimate to consider the broader connotations of the phrase 'inverted customs' especially in view of the fact that the word 'custom' had such significance for Bloomfield. There may be contributory causes of her mental ill-health, but the phrase connects her situation with the 'tyrant' customs that psychologically damage the farmer and destabilize the entire community at the end of 'Summer'. It suggests that

Ann's plight might at least partially be a consequence of broader social change in the countryside.

It is not only social change that unsettles the mind, the changing seasons can also have an impact upon rural workers, perhaps more so than upon town and city dwellers. In 'Spring' and 'Summer' the task of guarding the new crop from thieving birds is relieved by the variety of nature which presents 'objects' to the 'mind'. In 'Autumn' Giles is given the same task, but, although his time in 'the lonely fields' is relieved by 'A frost-nipt feast' of 'clust'ring sloes' (III: 212–13) and the expectation of a visit from 'playmates young and gay' (III: 217), his state of mind mirrors the melancholy of the season 'Bereft of song, and ever-cheering green' (III: 253). Giles has lost the balance that had earlier sustained him through his 'Gibeonite' (I: 223) labours, and his spirits wane until the 'field becomes his prison' (III: 223). The way in which the previously happy and tranquil Giles is disturbed causes the narrator to question the freedom and liberty that he had previously located in the countryside: 'If fields are prisons, where is Liberty? / Here still she dwells, and here her votaries stroll; / But disappointed hope untunes the soul: / Restraints unfelt whilst hours of rapture flow, / When troubles press, to chains and barriers grow' (III: 226–30). Even isolation within nature can lead to an inability properly to value present good, and on one level this is a warning against the narrowing in perspective that can result from the solitude that Wordsworth celebrates in *The Prelude*. The lines realize their moralizing in the imagery of restraint that runs through the poem.

The question 'where is Liberty?' seems to receive some kind of answer, and the whole problem of the nature of freedom some kind of resolution in 'Winter'. A shift of focus is signalled by the opening passage: 'Who lives the daily partner of our hours, / ... / In mutual labour and fatigue and thirst; / The kindly intercourse will ever prove / A bond of amity and social love' (IV: 3–8). Whether due to solitude or alienation, isolation is destructive. Bonds rooted in commonality are restraining, but they are also liberating in that they promote the 'social love' which fosters good relations between members of a community. The prisoner in 'Autumn' is isolated by physical restraints, but as *The Farmer's Boy* demonstrates, a feeling of confinement or restraint can result from numerous other causes. The ability of an individual to enjoy 'unaffected freedom' depends upon the nature of their relationships with others. The 'Harvest-home' passage in 'Summer' focused upon a particular event which had the effect of cementing 'rank to rank'. This passage is suggestive of a social system which brought farmers and labourers together daily during their work and their leisure; 'living in hiring' or farm service. This system involved the hiring of farm workers on a long-term basis – usually for a year or more – after which they would be entitled to settlement in the parish. Those working in such conditions lived on the farm, and both ate and socialized with the farmer and his family. Farm workers valued service because it provided them with security, but also because of the communal living that it involved. During his tour of Suffolk in 1784, just three years after Bloomfield left, the Frenchman François de La Rochefoucauld noted the prevalence of the service system in the county (55). But towards the end of the eighteenth century and during the early decades of the nineteenth century, it was felt by many to be in decline, with harmful consequences for rural communities. In *Rural Rides* William Cobbett noted that the disappearance of service resulted in a deterioration of social relations and led to 'the *pauperism* and the *crimes* that now disgrace this once happy and moral England' (227). There has been some debate over how widespread farm service was, and over when and for what reasons it began to decline, but in a recent and detailed study K.D.M. Snell finds that it did decline during the late eighteenth century and that this decline did have an impact upon social relations (Snell 67–103; see also Kussmaul 49–93, 120–34).

The care that Bloomfield's 'social love' inspires extends beyond the matter of relations between human beings to incorporate farm animals in a way that promotes good husbandry and increased productivity: 'To more than man this generous warmth extends, / And oft the team and shiv'ring herd befriends; / Tender solicitude the bosom fills, / And Pity executes what Reason wills' (IV: 9–11). In the original MS 'Around their home the storm-pinch'd cattle lows' (IV: 17) reads 'Around their home dependent cattle low' (MS Eng. 776, fol. 58), emphasizing the manner in which the livestock are involved in this complex of dependencies. Those living and working in such conditions are motivated by the knowledge that they are implicated in this network and as such are responsible for the performance of certain actions. Giles goes out in the bitter cold of a winter morning to dig the frozen ground for turnips to feed the hungry cattle: 'On Giles, and such as Giles, the labour falls, / To strew the frequent load where hunger calls. / On driving gales sharp hail indignant flies, / And sleet, more irksome still, assails his eyes; / Snow clogs his feet' (IV: 26–31). They are also motivated by other feelings promoted by the conditions in which they live and work such as 'pity' for domesticated animals. Such animals rarely appear in Wordsworth's poetry, and when they do they are treated as an item of property or 'a practical feature of a hard life' (Kenyon-Jones, 157). But in *The Farmer's Boy* the last thought of the ploughman before he sleeps is for his team. 'Short-sighted Dobbin', the plough-horse, is protected by the 'care' that permeates the rural community, unlike the 'poor post horse' who labours within a fragmented world for strangers in whose 'business' he is not implicated (IV: 159–65). The reference to 'business' locates the source of the horse's pain in the new capital-driven and largely city-based industry and commerce that alienates 'rank' from 'rank', and humankind from other species. The most telling example of the way this extension of compassion works for both the farmer and his stock occurs when the bereaved ewes and the orphaned lambs are brought together. The orphan wears the skin of the dead lamb: 'Till, cheated into tenderness and cares, / The unsuspecting dam, contented grown, / Cherish and guard the fondling as her own' (IV: 358–60).

Animal welfare was implicated in progressive political theory at the end of the eighteenth century. Bloomfield may have been aware of this proto-animal rights movement, but in these passages his point of departure was elsewhere. Whilst his opposition to practices such as tail-docking might align him with such a movement, his concern was always with the practicalities of farming and the quality of life of those that live off the land. For example he had little sympathy for the rooks and crows that were 'To level crops most formidable foes' (I: 106). At the same time he clearly felt that as far as was practically possible 'social love' and a feeling of compassion should be extended to incorporate humankind's animal companions in the countryside. The same kind of feeling would be expressed in later poems such as 'Abner and the Widow Jones' (1806), when Abner feels compassion for an old horse at the end of its useful working life. On each of these occasions, however, it seems that Bloomfield was looking backwards to his own experience of farm service in Suffolk between 1778 and 1781, rather than to a more utopian world located in the future.

The cottage evening scene demonstrates the way in which all farm-workers are enveloped within a micro-network of egalitarian regard. As the fire 'Throws round its welcome heat: – the ploughman smiles, / And oft the joke runs hard on sheepish Giles, / Who sits joint tenant of the corner–stool, / The converse sharing, though in duty's school' (IV: 83–6). Giles is an equal beneficiary of the joint labour effort, and, as a result of the fact that he spends his leisure time with the other workers, including the farmer, he benefits from their experience:

> Left ye your bleating charge, when day-light fled,
> Near where the hay-stack lifts its snowy head? / … /
> The Fox in silent darkness seems to glide / … /
> If chance the Cock or stamm'ring Capon crows / … /
> Destruction waits them, Giles, if e'er you fail
> To bolt their doors against the driving gale.
> Strew'd you (still mindful of th' unshelter'd head)
> Burdens of straw, the cattle's welcome bed? [IV: 89–104]

More importantly Giles also learns '*That duty's basis is humanity*' (IV: 106). This phrase reiterates one of the grand themes of the poem; that humankind are above all social beings, and that our 'social bonds' are reflected in the duty that psychologically healthy human beings feel towards each other.

As the poem completes its circuit of the seasons and spring re-emerges, it focuses on the shepherd 'in his small contracted round of cares' (IV: 369). The shepherd 'cares' for his sheep, but he also labours under a burden of 'cares' or rather tasks. He has a duty to the sheep in that it is his responsibility to protect them, and a duty to his fellow workers to perform his tasks well. In *The Prelude*, the shepherd is cut off from 'crowded life', but in *The Farmer's Boy* he performs his tasks within a community sustained and bound together by 'social love'. Like Giles, the shepherd learns from his fellow workers and 'Adjusts the practice of each hint he hears' (IV: 370). This is apparently a scene of order and pastoral quietude. But the reader knows that the shepherd's joy, as he observes the 'healthful show / Of well-grown Lambs, the glory of the Spring' (IV: 72–3), will soon be succeeded by 'care' and 'pity' as the butcher's knife 'plunges thro' their throats' (I: 352). The fact that the lambs are 'well-grown' also suggests that their demise is imminent, and that the annual cycle of potentially unsettling transformations is about to begin again.

Notwithstanding the fact that rural life is subject to change, social bonds and human interaction help both individuals, including poets, and communities to survive and develop. *The Prelude* focuses on the way healthy human development, particularly in respect of 'great minds', occurs in isolation from 'the deformities of crowded life' (VIII: 465). It is for this reason that of all rural workers, Wordsworth learns most from the shepherd, albeit a different kind of shepherd from the individual that appears in *The Farmer's Boy*. Wordsworth admires the shepherd for his 'solitary' and 'sublime' characteristics (VIII: 407), and does not see him as a 'husband' and 'father' who 'suffered with the rest / From vice and folly, wretchedness and fear' (VIII: 424–6). *The Prelude* represents Wordsworth as 'a chosen son' (III: 83) of nature, nurtured by the 'self-sufficing power of solitude' (III: 78), so it is unsurprising that the kind of communal learning that is encountered in *The Farmer's Boy* should not be valued by him. *The Farmer's Boy* explores both the functioning and the vulnerability of a particular kind of self-sustaining and nurturing community life that Bloomfield felt represented humankind at their best.

In the last verse paragraph Giles wills the continuation of his community and way of life: '"Another Spring!" his heart exulting cries; / "Another year!" with promis'd blessings rise!' (IV: 385–6) In terms of what the poem has revealed about the working landscape, it is clear that life is not always comprised of 'blessings' and that social relations are subject to change. Moreover, having read the preface, the reader of *The Farmer's Boy* knows that the young Bloomfield was soon to leave Suffolk. The reader knows that the mature Bloomfield is one of those 'poring thousands' in London's 'breathless rooms'. In this context the plaintive closing lines can be read as ambiguous: 'Seed-time and Harvest let me see again; / Wander the leaf-strewn wood, the frozen plain: / Let the first flower, corn-waving field, plain, tree, / Here round my home, still lift my soul to Thee; / And let me ever, midst thy bounties, raise / An humble note of thankfulness and praise!' (IV: 389–95) Is this the voice of Giles, Bloomfield's young alter-ego, or is it that of the poet wishing to be delivered back to his youth in rural Suffolk? Is it the young shepherd's prayer of thanksgiving, or is it the urban poet's lamentation for the loss of a beloved home?

In the original MS the second line of the passage read 'Pierce the dark wood, the frozen plain', but at the suggestion of Capel Lofft, Bloomfield altered the wording and in a note appended to the 1807 MS remarked:

> This alteration in one circumstance differs from all the foregoing. With all the preceding Mr Lofft dealt according to his own good judgment without consulting me. But in this case he proposed the above lines [line] in one of his earliest letters to me, as forming a kind of "Recapitulation of the subject and Seasons" and thereby forming a more appropriate close than mine, I agreed to it. [MS Eng. 776.1, fol. 57]

The alteration is more appropriate in the way that it completes the compression of the varied weather conditions of the four seasons into three lines. In a way, however, the slightly unsettling and strange nature of the original wording does say something of the kind of mental processes involved in the composition of the poem. Sitting in his cramped and ill-lit garret Bloomfield did have to 'pierce' the darkness of the present, and penetrate the 'dark wood' of his distant past, in order to produce *The Farmer's Boy*.

The poem that resulted from this act of recall is not the straightforward idealization of life in rural Suffolk that it is often said to be. This is because Bloomfield was not an uncomplicated labouring-class writer. On the evidence of *The Farmer's Boy*, his boyhood experience of life in Suffolk was fundamental to his world-view, but his attitude to rural life was also shaped by his contact with London artisan culture. He was an educated and self-conscious poet, as is apparent from the manner in which he introduces his subject matter in the opening passages of the poem. Partly because the mature Bloomfield was so far away from his young alter-ego, *The Farmer's Boy* does not reveal one Giles, but several, including the contented swain, the sensitive admirer of nature, and the 'untaught' but aspirant intellectual. For Bloomfield, the composition of the poem was a reflective process that also enabled him to see there is no point in the farming year when the world is static and comprehensible. Just as there is no single 'pure' text of *The Farmer's Boy*, distorted as it is by Lofft's preface and editorial emendations, rural communities are not timeless pastoral idylls.

The Farmer's Boy is certainly not an anti-pastoral, however, and represents many positive aspects of rural life. It investigates the potential for rural communities, if properly organized, to engender healthy well-balanced human beings, better able to cope with change. If the account of 'lovely Ann' and the bird-scaring passage in 'Autumn' demonstrate that isolation unsettles the mind, the accounts of the harvest-home feast and the cottage evening argue the value of supportive interaction between individuals. The poem also reveals and investigates the way in which his experience of commonality was instrumental in the development of Bloomfield's poetic voice, and made it distinctive from 'mainstream' Romantic poets like Wordsworth. According to *The Prelude*, Wordsworth's development as a poet principally resulted from his interaction with nature. Like Giles and the shepherd, who learn their trades from others, Bloomfield learnt the sensibility that shaped his poetry from interaction with others in close and supportive communities; first as a farmer's boy and later as a London artisan. Although Wordsworth apparently valued 'creative communities' such as that consisting of Coleridge, Tom Poole, Dorothy Wordsworth and himself, he believed that his calling set him apart from the rest of humankind. A revealing passage in *The Prelude* suggests that he felt it was his vocation to speak to and educate those not so privileged: 'hither had I come with holy powers / And faculties' to 'work / Like changes ... ['upon the visible universe'] by the force of my own mind' (III: 83–8). Bloomfield set out not to 'work ... changes' on the labouring poor, but to speak 'of' the value and beauty of traditionally orientated labouring-class culture.

CHAPTER TWO

The Romantic Ballad and Labouring-Class Culture

At the turn of the eighteenth century many poets turned to labouring-class poetic forms in order to make a connection with the vernacular origins of English poetry. This is particularly so of Wordsworth and Coleridge whose *Lyrical Ballads* engage with 'low' subject-matter in order to explore the ability of polite narrators (and readers) to derive meaning from the lives of the labouring poor (McEathron 1999, 5–26). But the fact that twentieth-century criticism has focused upon a limited number of poets has skewed our understanding of the response to the traditional ballad and the folktale during the Romantic period. The poems contained within *Lyrical Ballads* have received exhaustive attention from critics. The ballads and tales written by the other 'major' Romantic poets such as Keats and Shelley have been considered too, but those written by less well-known poets have been largely ignored. Robert Bloomfield's deserve to be considered as part of his attempt to forge a distinctive labouring-class poetics. He produced numerous ballads and tales between 1798 and 1804; they were published in *Rural Tales, Ballads and Songs* and *Wild Flowers; or, Pastoral and Local Poetry*. Like those written by his contemporaries, most of his poems are self-consciously literary, but Bloomfield uniquely attempts to foreground their relationship with traditional labouring-class culture. This chapter assesses the way in which, as a consequence, his tales and ballads differ from those within *Lyrical Ballads*, and asks whether the increased sophistication of his later poetry obscured its origin in the lived experience of the rural labouring poor.

Bloomfield would have known that a poetics rooted in labouring-class culture would attract criticism, and that the occupations of peasants would not necessarily be considered fit subject-matter for poetry. Reviews of *The Farmer's Boy* tended to focus upon the author's humble origins and the way in which he had been influenced by Thomson's *The Seasons*. When reviewers commented upon the subject-matter of the poem they viewed it as a hindrance, and argued that it was only Bloomfield's skill as a poet that had enabled him to produce a work of quality from such inauspicious material. The remarks made in the *Monthly Review* for September 1800 are typical:

> To describe the various occupations of a farmer's boy, in the four seasons of the year, is the main design of the poem; and however humble these employments may appear as objects for poetical attention, the very ingenious writer has contrived to embellish their rusticity and meanness with a harmony of numbers, which could not be expected from an uncultivated mind; to soften the harshness of minute detail, by blending

> apt and picturesque descriptions; and to enliven the whole by strokes of poetic imagery, and unaffected sentiment. [n.s.33 (1800), 52]

Although it is not possible to say whether he was responding either directly or indirectly to reviews of *The Farmer's Boy*, in his preface to *Rural Tales* Bloomfield attempts to vindicate his choice of subject-matter. Gerard Genette suggests that the most common means by which writers attribute value to their work through prefaces is to give prominence to the subject-matter 'by demonstrating its importance and – inseparable from that – the usefulness of examining it' (199). This approach enables writers to confer a high value upon the work without praising themselves overtly. Bloomfield initially appears to assert the value of his subject-matter in a statement that directly contradicts the kind of sentiment expressed in the *Monthly Review*: 'As they [the poems in the collection] treat of village manners, and rural scenes, it appears to me not ill-tim'd to avow, that I have hopes of meeting in some degree the approbation of my Country' (iii). The passage that follows this declaration suggests that he was not quite so confident of approval. In what can only be described as a somewhat reticent 'marketing ploy', Bloomfield immediately goes on to refer to the reception of *The Farmer's Boy*: 'I was not prepar'd for the decided, and I may surely say extraordinary attention which The Public has shown towards the Farmer's Boy'(iv). He is implicitly asking readers to approve his new work because it treats the same subject-matter as this hugely successful poem.

Bloomfield's most bold and didactic statement of the critical assumptions behind his ballads and tales occurs in the preface to *Wild Flowers*. This is an important text for two reasons. First, unlike the hesitant preface to *Rural Tales*, it attempts to argue the value of a poetics based upon 'local' Suffolk labouring-class culture. Secondly it distinguishes Bloomfield's poetics from Wordsworth's as expressed in the preface to *Lyrical Ballads* (1800). It engages with the criticism of Samuel Johnson, and in some respects Wordsworth's preface represents a restatement of Johnson's views. Bloomfield's increasing confidence and independence is clear from the first sentence. He describes Samuel Johnson as 'A MAN of the first eminence', and expresses relief that he was spared the 'the Herculean crab-tree of his criticism' (vii). He then quotes Johnson's well-known remarks from the preface to his edition of Shakespeare: 'Nothing can please many, and please long, but just representations of general nature' (vii). Shortly after the passage referred to by Bloomfield, Johnson goes on to elaborate exactly what he means: in 'just representations of general nature ... characters are not modified by the customs of particular places, unpractised by the rest of the world' or 'by the peculiarities of studies or professions, which can operate but upon small numbers' (*Works* VII: 62). It is not unreasonable to see Johnson's 'just representations of general nature' as a precedent for Wordsworth's programme for a poetry rooted in the 'essential passions of the heart' (245) in the preface to *Lyrical Ballads* (1800). Johnson also had quite explicit views regarding fit subject matter for poetry. He had considerable disdain for the pastoral mode, and did not believe that poetry about the lives of ordinary people could sustain interest, or be of lasting value: 'We have all been born; we have most of us been married; and so many have died before us that our deaths can supply but few materials for a poet' (*Lives of the Poets* I: 424).

That Bloomfield did not agree becomes clear as his discussion of Johnson's statement continues. In a somewhat perfunctory manner that veils the serious import of his remarks, he proceeds to discuss the question of whether his own representations of nature are general. At first he suggests that they are 'not *general*', but finally concludes that they are because 'nature in a village is very much like nature everywhere else' (vii). Bloomfield then confidently asserts his decision to concentrate upon the ordinary lives of a particular group within society: 'all my pictures are from humble life, and most of my heroines [are] servant maids. Such would I have them: being fully persuaded that in no other way would my endeavours, either to please or to instruct, have an equal chance of success' (vii). The local nature of his poetics is evident from a number of the poems that appear in *Rural Tales* and *Wild Flowers; or, Pastoral and Local Poetry*, and is emphasized by the title of the latter volume. Even in verse that is more autobiographical in mode, or more concerned with the process of writing itself, Bloomfield's poetry is usually driven by what is identifiably local and personal. He is endeavouring to say that events in the day-to-day lives of the labouring poor in rural Suffolk can be of poetic value and illuminate the general nature of humankind. It appears that, like Johnson's Imlac, he did see it as the poet's role to 'write as the interpreter of nature, and the legislator of mankind' (*Rasselas*, 62), but believed that he could perform this function by deriving his subject-matter from a particular locality. Bloomfield did not see it as the business of a poet to 'number the streaks of the tulip', or to 'describe the different shades in the verdure of the forest' (*Rasselas*, 61), but he did see it as his business to develop a specifically local descriptive idiom in his work.

As a critic of literature Johnson had a second major preoccupation that reappeared again and again both in his major works and in periodical essays. This was the question of what constituted the proper language of poetry. Johnson believed that Dryden had developed an appropriate diction that was 'at once refined from the grossness of domestic use and free from the harshness of terms appropriated to particular arts' (*Lives of the Poets* I: 420). The use of the word 'domestic' is significant here because one of Bloomfield's favourite themes was private or 'domestic' affairs, and the language of his poetry was appropriately 'domestic' as 'Richard and Kate' makes amply clear. It contains language that is at once local, 'domestic' and 'appropriated to particular arts'. The eighth stanza is marked by all three qualities, and Bloomfield was sufficiently aware of this to gloss its language in footnotes to the first edition of *Rural Tales*: the word 'Hutch' is used locally in Suffolk to describe a chest (Ellis, 180); the phrase she 'gave him out his Sunday Breeches' is clearly 'domestic' in tone; and 'Lucks and Twitches' are 'Terms used in spinning' (1802, 3).

Notwithstanding the fact that his verse was compared with that of Dryden, Bloomfield is implicitly asserting the poetic authenticity and value of a language quite different from that which Johnson had approved. His position is as innovative as that of Wordsworth even though it is established in a much less direct manner than in the preface to *Lyrical Ballads*. A reading of Bloomfield's poetry alongside this, his first confident and critical preface, reveals that his range of acceptable language taken from 'low and rustic life' is broader than that of Wordsworth. Bloomfield did not necessarily agree with Wordsworth's view that the language of poetry should be 'purified ... from what appear to be its real defects, [and] from all lasting and rational causes of dislike and disgust' (245). In the preface to *Wild Flowers*, he anticipates that something akin to 'disgust' might be felt by some readers regarding certain poems within the collection, and he attempts to forestall possible criticism:

> Perhaps, in some of them, more of mirth is intermingled than many who know me would expect, or than the severe will be inclined to approve. But surely what I can say, or can be expected to say, on subjects of country life, would gain little by the seriousness of a preacher, or by exhibiting fallacious representations of what has long been termed *Rural Innocence*. [viii]

And in 'The Horkey. A Provincial Ballad' Bloomfield was specifically concerned to recreate the local idiomatic speech patterns of rural Suffolk. In order to avoid any possible uncertainty regarding the origin of the custom that represents the major theme of the poem, he informs the reader in an advertisement that it originates in 'Suffolk husbandry' (31). Despite his belief that the linguistic idiom in which he chose to write was the right one, he was correct to be nervous about whether it would be universally accepted. The *Annual Review* considered Bloomfield's native dialect to be 'the corrupt and clownish dialect of an obscure county' and was particularly critical of 'The Horkey' (1806, 526).

Bloomfield's discussion of Johnson's criticism and the outline of a programme for poetry about 'rural scenes and village manners' that arises out of it performs several functions at the same time. It is an attempt to assert the value of the subject-matter treated in *Wild Flowers* and *Rural Tales* without simply alluding to the success of his previous work, and without any submissive reference to the approval of 'Friends'. It also performs a second primary function of the original preface in that it constitutes Bloomfield's 'interpretation of ... [his] text' or 'his statement of intent' (Genette, 221). Like Wordsworth in the preface to *Lyrical Ballads*, but in a less convoluted manner, he argues that his poetry has the power to improve his readers. He also challenges the better educated amongst his readers to accept his poetic agenda: 'The path I have thus taken, from necessity, as well as from choice, is well understood and approved by hundreds, who are capable of ranging in the higher walks of literature' (viii). Bloomfield is in effect reminding such readers that the simplicity and naturalness to be found in his verse is not the result of ineptitude, and so should not be unthinkingly equated with insipidity or triteness. Finally, the discussion of Johnson addresses two secondary purposes of an original preface; it stresses the thematic unity of the collection, an important motif of value enhancement in collections of poetry, and it accounts for the title (Genette, 210, 213). The contrast between this and the opening passages of the preface to *Rural Tales* could not be greater. No other eighteenth-century labouring-class poet had endeavoured to articulate his or her critical perspective in an authorial preface. Later John Clare could be quite self-assured in letters regarding his poetics, but remarks made in letters are not public statements, and the short preface that he wrote for *The Rural Muse* (1835), the last volume of poetry published in his lifetime, is still that of the 'peasant' poet with obligations to patrons: 'it will be ... gratifying ... to find that my old friends are as warm as usual, and waiting to cheer me with the welcome praises that encouraged me in the beginning' (22).

The first poem in *Rural Tales* exemplifies Bloomfield's 'statement of intent', as expressed later in the preface to *Wild Flowers*, in a number of ways. The title of 'Richard and Kate; or Fair-Day. A Suffolk Ballad', a poem which Clare considered to be 'inimitable, and above praise' (*Letters*, 302), clearly indicates that the style and theme are to be local. By choosing to tell a tale of village life in Suffolk through the medium of an imitation 'Suffolk Ballad', Bloomfield connects his poetry, and the inspiration for that poetry directly with rural Suffolk. The imitation of dialect speech patterns together with the repeated use of dialect words reinforces this localness. Bloomfield may also have had in mind the sentimental ballads that filled the pages of magazines during the 1790s, because his title explicitly distances 'Richard and Kate' from such poems. Nor would such a low-key theme be chosen for sentimental ballads which, although they professed to be tales of country people, focused on ageing beggars, repentant convicts, bereaved parents, village idiots, orphans and village maids or swains driven mad by the death or betrayal of their lovers. In *May Day* Sir Ambrose criticizes such poems within his 'Invitation': 'harkye, bring / No stupid ghost, no vulgar thing; / ... surely fancy need not brood / O'er midnight darkness, crimes, and blood, / In magic cave or monks retreat' (93–103). Sir Ambrose could easily have in mind Robert Southey's 'Mary [the Maid of the Inn]' (1797) or 'The Cross Roads' (1799), because these poems have all of the ingredients to which he refers. The former is a tale about the fear of ghosts, a midnight murder in a ruined abbey, and the decline of 'Poor Mary the Maniac' (12), the latter a tale of the seduction and subsequent suicide of a female farm-worker. Traditional ballads did engage with violent transformational subject-matter, but they did not, like the sentimental ballad, sensationalize village life and make moral judgements about the labouring poor. Furthermore, the style and language of the sentimental ballad was marked by a decorum that is absent from the traditional ballad, and they were new compositions, rather than collected ballads and songs. In *Lyrical Ballads* Wordsworth was also responding to the sentimental ballad, but did not feel the need explicitly to distance his poems from such poems in the same way. This is perhaps because he was not interested in labouring-class culture as such; he chose 'low and rustic life' as subject matter 'because in that situation the essential passions of the heart find a better soil in which they can attain their maturity ... [and] because in that situation the essential feelings exist in a state of greater simplicity' (245). This is not to say that Wordsworth does not do something peculiarly his own with the ballad, because he clearly does. The poetics of Wordsworth and Bloomfield appear to differ in the degree of specificity with which each treats the rural labouring poor, that specificity being the index of the value accorded by each to the particular and local.

As was often the case in sentimental ballads, 'Richard and Kate' begins with a journey away from the safety of the cottage. Many of the sentimental magazine ballads begin in the same way, for example 'A Ballad: The busy crowd had hush'd their woes' which appeared in the *New London Magazine* in March 1788. In this poem Colinet, the hero, who has been betrayed by his beloved Ellen, forsakes 'his little cot' and 'Unknowing where to find relief, / The Derwent's banks he sought' (6–8). Colinet's journey does not end in relief as these lines at the end of the second stanza would have indicated to the reader. After complaints about the unfaithfulness of women, and curses directed at Ellen, 'he plunged into the tide, / And sought untimely doom' (85–6). In 'Richard and Kate' the journey does not lead to tragedy. The two old people in Bloomfield's poem reach their destination and meet 'Their lusty *Sons*, and *Daughters* dear' (70). Their sons and daughters have clearly been forced to migrate some distance from the cottage of their parents, but migration, albeit mainly local, was a normal part of rural life in the eighteenth century (Laslett, 75).

To some extent, Bloomfield is attempting to manipulate reader response through his modification of sentimental ballad conventions, just as Wordsworth does in 'Simon Lee, the old Huntsman, with an incident in which he was concerned' (1798). In this poem the event to which the title refers is merely the assistance which the narrator gives to Simon Lee in severing the root of an old tree. Before relating the circumstances of the incident the narrator makes his design on reader expectations explicit:

> O reader! Had you in your mind
> Such stores as silent thought can bring,
> O gentle reader! You would find
> A tale in every thing.
> What more I have to say is short,
> I hope you'll kindly take it;
> It is no tale; but should you think,
> Perhaps a tale you'll make it. [73–80]

Simon Lee's previous employment as a huntsman and the social implications of his impoverished situation are significant. But in terms of Wordsworth's poetics, it could be argued that the details of Simon's life and of the incident described in the poem are secondary. The kind of 'tale' that the reader makes of the materials provided by the narrator is perhaps less important than that they should be affected and improved by vicariously sharing the gratitude felt by Simon. It is the power of Simon's emotion that is important rather than the circumstances which led to its expression. 'Simon Lee' thus exemplifies Wordsworth's 'statement of intent', as expressed in his preface to the 1800 edition of *Lyrical Ballads*. It shows that the right kind of poetry can make an impression upon the reader through the empathetic experience of beneficial emotional states, or place the reader 'in the way of receiving from ordinary moral sensations another and more salutary impression than we are accustomed to receive from them' (248).

As in Wordsworth's poem, not much happens in 'Richard and Kate', but behind this apparently limited account of country life there is a more complex story. In 'Simon Lee' the 'incident' is given meaning because it is filtered through the consciousness of the gentleman narrator and his polite reader (McEathron 1999, 14). The fact that Bloomfield's poem is an imitation Suffolk ballad means that the social status of the narrator is roughly equivalent to that of Richard and Kate. Moreover, the local and domestic details of the two old people's lives, and what they signify, are important in themselves in a way that they would not have been for Wordsworth. Both Richard and Kate have to cease their work in order to journey to the fair; Kate has to stop her 'humdrum wheel, and Richard 'His Mattock he behind the door / And Hedging-gloves again replac'd' (33–4). It is implied that they have to work in order to support themselves, and Bloomfield is concerned to show that they are still, even at their advanced age, performing useful functions. The relaxed and contented tone of their conversation in the opening stanzas of the poem does nevertheless suggest that they are able to work at a leisurely pace. Bloomfield's picture of old age is a long way from Crabbe's dour images of the 'rural tribe' in *The Village* (1783). Crabbe's 'weary sires' and 'pale matrons' fade quickly in old age: 'Nor yet can time itself obtain for these / Life's latest comforts, due respect, and ease; / For yonder see that hoary swain, whose age / Can with no cares except its own engage' (177–84). The use of the impersonal pronoun emphasizes the dehumanization and isolation inherent in the condition of the old man. Bloomfield does not refer to Crabbe in his correspondence, and an edition of Crabbe's poetry does not appear on the list of books sold at the auction that took place after his death. But in view of the fact that *The Village* was a very widely read poem, and because Crabbe was, like Bloomfield, a Suffolk poet, it is probable that he was familiar with it. *The Village* might be based upon Crabbe's observations of Suffolk because, at the time of writing the poem, he had more experience of rural life there than in any other county, and a number of the descriptive passages point to the area around Aldborough.

To some extent Crabbe wished to correct 'the deliberate idealization of the English labourer in almost all eighteenth-century discussion of him, which allowed the pastoral to flourish and the poor to starve' (Barrell and Bull, 379). In particular Crabbe's poem was a response to the representation of the rural labourer in later eighteenth-century writing, for example the pre-Enclosure Auburn of Oliver Goldsmith's *The Deserted Village* (1770) 'Where health and plenty cheered the labouring swain' (2). In endeavouring to correct these images of rural life Crabbe emphasizes the negative, but Bloomfield chooses to celebrate the positive aspects of this life. His ageing swains are not ground down by the demands of subsistence, and they do have time for other 'cares'. On the way to the fair and throughout the day described in the poem Richard recounts pleasant memories of village life: 'Once, passing by this very Tree, / A Gotch of Milk I'd been to fill, / You shoulder'd me; then laugh'd to see / Me and my Gotch spin down the Hill' (49–52). For Crabbe's 'hoary swain' on the other hand: 'The bare arms broken from the withering tree; / On which, a boy, he climbed the loftiest bough, / [were] Then his first joy, but [are] his sad emblem now' (187–9).

The ageing Richard and Kate are able to attend the fair, which along with the weekly market day was one of the main ways that country people came together. When they reach their destination it becomes clear that they are still part of a 'known community': 'Now friendly nods and smiles had they, / From many a kind *Fair-going* face' (61–2). Bloomfield does not indulge in excessive idealization, but there are numerous reminders of the reasons why their community is knowable. For example there are the sports and games for both children and adults, such as 'the DICKY [donkey] RACES', which were a regular part of village life and did not only take place at fairs. Such popular recreations 'served to foster social cohesiveness and group unity' (Malcolmson, 84). Then there is the custom of giving '*fairings*' or gifts brought back from the fair. The existence of this particular custom reveals that people in eighteenth-century rural communities were not as selfishly isolated as a poem like *The Village* implies. Such communities were, however, dying as a result of the drive for agricultural improvement, and Bloomfield's poem powerfully evokes what was being lost as a consequence.

The fact that 'Richard and Kate' is principally orientated towards events that occur away from the cottage suggests another way in which Bloomfield's poems are different from Wordsworth's ballads and tales which generally focus upon the internal dynamics of the independent cottage unit. This feature of Wordsworth's poetry is perhaps a consequence of his understanding of freedom. In *The Prelude* he praises Cumberland 'communities' because they consist of men who, although they can choose to work towards 'social' ends, are essentially independent and 'free' from any obligation or duty towards one another (VIII: 153–7). Crabbe sees isolation as a corollary of the moral and spiritual bankruptcy of the labouring poor, for Wordsworth it is a reason for approbation. It has also been argued that Wordsworth was interested in the landscape rather than the people who inhabit it (Wesling, 14). This is overstating the case, but it is true to say that he was interested in interaction between individuals and the land or property, rather than relationships between people. Wordsworth remarked of 'Michael': 'I have attempted to give a picture of a man ... agitated by two of the most powerful affections of the human heart; the parental affection, and the love of property, *landed* property, including the feelings of inheritance, home and personal and family independence' (*Letters*: 322). When the relationship between an individual and his property fails, as in poems like 'The Female Vagrant' (1798), 'The Last of the Flock' (1798) or 'Michael', the protagonists do not have recourse to any sources of assistance because they are 'free' and 'working' for themselves, and their family units are isolated from others within their communities. Bloomfield believed in the social and cultural value of the semi-independent cottager. But he was more interested in exploring through his poetry the social structures that supported the cottager within a properly functioning community.

Notwithstanding the fact that it alludes to cultural practises which bring people together, 'Richard and Kate' does not explicitly engage with the community structures that support the two old people. It could be argued that like the folktale, it 'presents us with a world that is blissfully self-sufficient' (Luthi, 84). Individuals and family units within the village communities that Bloomfield admires were not, however, self-sufficient, and they often had to help each other to survive. Communities were not held together only through being 'knowable', the 'kindness' and 'mutuality that still ... [managed] to flow' within them was also important (Williams, 106). 'Walter and Jane' and 'The Miller's Maid. A Tale', the next two poems in *Rural Tales*, explore some of the ways in which social and communal structures operate when things go wrong, and how they help village communities to evolve and move forward. In these poems, Bloomfield further manipulates the folktale tradition that formed an important part of the lives of the labouring people who inspired him, by drawing upon a common element of the folktale: characters who function as helpers and thereby advance the plot.

In both poems the hero derives his power to act from assistance offered by other members of the community. With regard to the hero of 'Walter and Jane', it is the 'First on the list of active Country Squires' who enables him to take up his position within the community and establish control over his environment (268). This 'active' squire brings Walter news of his inheritance, and, more significantly, provides him with 'a spare Shed' (289) adjacent to the public road where he can trade as a blacksmith. The squire clearly resides on his estate and takes an interest in those that dwell on his land. He is part of that wider paternalist structure of mutual dependencies and obligations that supports the retirement of the old couple in 'Richard and Kate', the loss of which is mourned in the closing passages of 'Summer' in *The Farmer's Boy*. He justifies his position in society by being active within the community of which he is clearly an important part. E.P. Thompson claims that the paternalist system was held together by a tension between the self-interested hegemony of the gentry and the group identity of the labouring class, rather than by feelings of 'kindness' and 'mutuality': 'There is a sense in which rulers and crowd needed each other, watched each other, performed theatre and counter-theatre in each other's auditorium, moderated each other's political behaviour' (Thompson 1993, 71). Whether he is motivated by feelings of kindness or by self-interest, as in the folktale this helper arrives at just the right time and is able to bestow gifts that precisely meet the requirements of Walter. Like many folktale helpers, once his much-needed assistance has been provided he disappears from the plot just as suddenly as he had appeared.

Helpers do not often feature in Wordsworth's ballads and tales, and when they do they tend to be outsiders like the gypsies who assist the protagonist in 'The Female Vagrant'. The narrator praises this 'wild brood' because of their kindness and because 'all belonged to all, and each was chief' (221). This could be read as a critique of failing mutuality within the protagonist's native village which fails to offer assistance when an interloper; presumably the possessor of new capitalist wealth, forces her father out of his 'hereditary nook' (44).

But there is nothing in this poem, or any of the others within *Lyrical Ballads* that treat the collapse of the independent cottage unit, to suggest that a decline in mutuality contributes to the fate of the central character. Wordsworth, it seems, dislikes the predatory ethic that is fundamental to capitalism, but he admires the kind of independence and self-reliance that capitalism fosters. Indeed, the very survival of Wordsworth's protagonists indicates that they are self-reliant and resilient, and his poems foreground the importance of these qualities rather than the ability to cooperate with, and assist others.

The plot-line of 'Walter and Jane' resembles the folktale in another respect that also sets it apart from Wordsworth's tales. It employs a variation of the lost-child-found motif, a common transformation narrative in folktales. This motif dramatizes a process that, according to Freud, all children must pass through if they are to develop into healthy adults. According to Freud, when children approach puberty they start to see faults in their parents, and begin, imaginatively, 'the task of getting free from the parents of whom ... [they] now ... [have] a low opinion and of replacing them by others, who, as a rule, are of a higher social standing' (222). In folktales it is often the case that events which have occurred before the time that the story depicted actually begins turn out to be the cause of a crucial transformation. This is the case within Bloomfield's poem in which the establishment of a trust in Walter's name and the subsequent death of his kinsman are crucial events that occur before the poem takes up his story. Much of the dramatic tension generated by the poem is due to the fact that the reader only learns of these important events towards the conclusion of the narrative. The unexpected, but perfectly feasible transformation that occurs is, however, to a large extent dependent upon them. It is significant that the fictional quality of the narrative is exposed by the way the tale is structured, but at the same time events are narrated in such a manner that they appear natural and everyday. This is another characteristic of the typical folktale.

As in 'Walter and Jane' the events that result in the transformation of the hero and heroine in 'The Miller's Maid' are narrated in a naturalistic manner. The fact that it is a wealthy miller who performs quite remarkable acts of beneficence and generosity is significant. The miller occupies a major place in English popular culture not only as a lecher, but also as someone who cheats the honest labourer. During the eighteenth century, millers were often the target of food rioters as a result of grievances about price rises, or unscrupulous activities such as the adulteration of flour (Thompson 1993, 219–21). When Bloomfield reminds the reader in the second line of the poem that his miller is 'An honest Miller' (2) he is making an indirect criticism of the many dishonest contemporary millers who did not perform their duty within their respective communities. The fact that his wife is 'the Doctress of the neighb'ring Poor' (5) reinforces the impression that the miller's household is part of the affective cement that binds the rural community together.

The miller's treatment of Phoebe is inspired partly by feelings of 'kindness', and partly by a feeling that it is his duty to assist her. The inherent benevolence of the miller is clear both from his response to the child's plea that she should not be sent back to her tormentors: 'I send you back! (The Miller cried) "no, no"', and from the narrator's commentary: 'Th' appeals of Wretchedness had weight with him, / And Sympathy would warm him every limb' (76–8). The Miller goes on to inform Phoebe that she shall have all the assistance that he can offer: 'My house has childless been this many a year; / While you deserve it you shall tarry here.' (83–4) The commentary makes explicit the fact that the provision of this assistance is the duty of the miller. After Phoebe has thanked him 'with a sigh' the narrator remarks: 'Thus was the sacred compact doubly seal'd' (87). The earlier dialogue between the Miller and Phoebe had revealed that her arrival on his doorstep in the midst of a storm was in some way the result of a breakdown of another earlier 'sacred compact'. In response to the miller's enquiries about her past Phoebe informs him that she has 'no Parents; and no friends beside' (53). The death of her mother was perhaps unavoidable, but as the reader learns later, like Margaret's husband in Wordsworth's 'The Ruined Cottage' (1798), her father had been forced to enlist when 'Employment fail'd, and poverty was come' (304). Unlike the hero of 'Walter and Jane', Phoebe's father had not been saved from this fate by an 'active' country squire. This is a sign of failing mutuality within Phoebe's home village, as is the fact that following her mother's death Phoebe and her brother only have recourse to the '*Workhouse*' (58).

The assistance provided by the helpers in both of these tales could be seen as unique single acts that are unlikely to be repeated. The fact that the Miller saves Phoebe from the workhouse will not prevent others being forced to live out their lives within such institutions. At least one reviewer did point this out. The *Critical Review* considered the story of 'The Miller's Maid' to be 'improbable' (s.2, 35 (1802), 72). But the establishment of men in respectable trades, marriages and family reunions represent the kind of subject matter that Johnson believed to be too dull and therefore unfit for poetry. They are everyday events, but are represented in Bloomfield's poetry in a manner that captures the attention. The poems are meant to be representative of the real world in that they are rooted in Bloomfield's own experience of rural life in Suffolk during the last quarter of the eighteenth century. But at the same time they depict that world as he believed it should be, and are meant to be read as exemplary. These tales do not present the reader with a possible world order so that the real world can be contrasted with it. Like the folktale both show us '*the* world that is in order' rather than '*a* world that is in order' (Luthi, 89). At one and the same time they represent the world as it is and as it should be.

The behaviour of the miller and that of the active country squire in 'Walter and Jane' can also be read as motifs of patronage. This was another feature of the 'affective community' which Bloomfield clearly considered to be of great importance, and which was of considerable personal significance to him. Figures like Bloomfield's miller and squire are the principal foundation of a socially integrated community, but they can also be seen as patrons of deserving individuals within those communities. If their exemplary acts are seen as the bestowal of patronage, the poems also express the point of view that patronage is, or rather should be, a structural attribute of a properly functioning rural community. It was a traditional belief that patronage was a duty and a responsibility, rather than an optional indulgence which the country squirearchy and aristocracy could choose to ignore; in a sense Wordsworth's Simon Lee is suffering from the consequences of a breakdown of patronage. Nor did Bloomfield believe that acts of patronage should call forth an excessive display of gratitude from the recipient in a world where all are bound to each other by mutual responsibility. The patronage offered by the squire and the miller is for example very different from that of the bad patron Mrs Howard in Charlotte Lennox's novel *The Life of Harriot Stuart* (1751), who 'took care to be fully repaid for any act of benevolence' (652). Bloomfield does not dwell upon Walter's response to the squire's act of patronage in 'Walter and Jane'. Walter is not even heard to proffer thanks for the considerable assistance that he receives in addition to what is his as of right. Likewise in 'The Miller's Maid' George is not required to elevate the miller through subservient gratitude, even though the miller has conferred virtually his whole estate upon his former assistant. George came into the miller's household as a wage-labourer, but was drawn into the community as he proved himself a responsible member of that household. The act of patronage that allows George to take over from the miller represents the last step in his assimilation into the community. The adoption plot of 'The Miller's Maid', a variation of the lost-child-found plot, emphasizes worth and benevolence; social virtues that bind the community together, rather than ties of blood, as the criteria of succession. Moreover in neither tale is the giving and receiving of assistance undertaken according to a deferential code that increases the social division between rich and poor. In fact the support given to Walter and George occurs within a community in which familiar social interaction serves to reduce social distinctions.

The full significance of the point of view expressed in the tales only becomes apparent when it is considered alongside Bloomfield's own conduct. The manner in which the patronal gifts are received by the heroes of the two tales is quite different from the tone of humble gratitude which characterizes various references to his own patrons in the preface to *Rural Tales*. Bloomfield's repeated subservient gestures to the friends who have supported him and approved his achievements are the words of a client of patronage with a debt to discharge. His particular expression of gratitude to his 'first great friend' in the preface to *Rural Tales* is couched in terms which could only have magnified the character of Capel Lofft, Bloomfield's most important patron, in the minds of his readers: 'his private life is a lesson of morality; his manners gentle, his heart sincere' (v). During the eighteenth century, patrons were generally motivated by the expectation of some form of recompense, and in making these remarks Bloomfield was rewarding his patron with acclamation (Griffin 1996, 16–17). As has been remarked by a number of critics, labouring-class poets 'were often used by ... patrons for their own purposes' (Rizzo, 244). For example Betty Rizzo suggests that Bridget Freemantle, Mary Leapor's first patron, used her to 'promote proto-feminist ideas about, particularly, the superiority of a single life for a woman' (Rizzo, 250). Interestingly, Leapor was used for different purposes by a later posthumous 'patron'. Samuel Richardson wished to show, through the achievement of Leapor, that writers who, like himself, lacked a formal education could produce works of the highest quality. Chapter Four of this study examines the ways in which Lofft endeavoured to take advantage of Bloomfield's success, for example by using *The Farmer's Boy* as a vehicle to promote his political views.

Bloomfield's declaration of praise for his patron focuses upon Lofft's apparently 'exemplary' character. It could therefore also be argued that it aligns him with the patrons within the tales who are not primarily motivated by desire for personal benefit. This construal is apparently undermined by Lofft's response, contained within a footnote that he appended when preparing the manuscript of *Rural Tales* for publication. It appears to add considerably to the degree of personal aggrandizement that the poet's remarks confer upon him: 'I dare not take to myself praise like this; and yet I was, perhaps, hardly at liberty to disclaim what should be mine and the endeavour of every one to deserve.' (v) The note is not, however, as straightforward as might appear to be the case at first glance, particularly when it is considered in the context of Bloomfield's exemplary tales. Lofft acknowledges the flattery inherent in Bloomfield's remarks and does with a show of reluctance accept the praise, but, as his final comment makes clear, only in so far as it can serve as an example to others. He subtly alters the import of the poet's remarks, and they develop an exemplary function when read in the light of the note. Lofft's comment suggests that he understood Bloomfield's poetry, but also indicates that he was not entirely comfortable with his position as patron.

All of the poems examined so far are primarily concerned with the conduct of human relationships. 'Walter and Jane' and 'The Miller's Maid' demonstrate that patronage can be conducted in a manner that promotes the development of both relationships between individuals and communities. Because the poems are derived structurally from the traditional ballad and the folktale they are also rooted in labouring-class culture. In 'The French Mariner. A Ballad' and 'Dolly', Bloomfield looks away from the internal relational dynamics of rural communities for his subject matter in that both poems are principally concerned with the ongoing war with France. The effect of war had already been alluded to in 'Walter and Jane' and 'The Miller's Maid', but it is more centrally the concern of these poems. In 'The Miller's Maid' war had taken away the father of Phoebe and George, but the point of view of the poem is more or less neutral in relation to the overall impact of war. It is hardly surprising that the theme of conflict should recur throughout *Rural Tales*, especially in view of Bloomfield's interest in 'humble life' and his express desire that his poetry should possess the power to 'instruct'. During most of the 1790s England had been at war with France, and it was a common and reasonable belief amongst the labouring poor that their suffering was disproportionately greater during wartime. It was felt that the commercial and landed classes prospered, whilst the poor suffered because of higher taxes, higher prices and lower wages.

The rise in the level of consumption taxes in order to pay for war was a particular source of resentment amongst the labouring poor. The resentment against the tax on beer, for example, is articulated by Thomas Paine in *The Rights of Man* (1791 and 1792):

> The tax upon beer brewed for sale does not affect the aristocracy, who brew their own beer free of this duty. It falls only on those who have not the conveniency or ability to brew, and who must purchase it in small quantities. But what will mankind think of the justice of taxation, when they know that this tax alone, from which the aristocracy are from circumstances exempt, is nearly equal to the whole of the land tax, ... and with its proportion of the taxes on malt and hops, it exceeds it. [225]

The early years of the war were characterized by extreme scarcity, and this was particularly so during the years 1795–96 and 1800–01 (Wells, 1–181). This scarcity often amounted to actual famine, and on some occasions led to food riots, attacks upon the property of farmers and various other manifestations of unrest. Whatever the cause of scarcity and higher prices, both would have been attributed to the war by those already predisposed to view it as fundamentally against the interests of the poor.

During the early years of the war many poems were written which opposed it upon the grounds that it was fought primarily for the rich, but paid for with the lives of the poor, or at best resulted in the loss of their modest security. 'Effects of War', published in *The Cambridge Intelligencer* on 22 February 1794, begins 'Come proud unfeeling pomp – Come luxury, / And ye, who thoughtless frolic in the round / of mirth and joy, or revel out the night / Where dissipation mads her festive sons!', and provides an account of the way war destroys the domestic 'innocence and peace' of the cottage: 'Alas! How chang'd! each smiling joy is fled, / Fled to return no more, – while sickness, want, / Famine, and all the complicated woes, / That haunt the desolating steps of war, / With dismal gloom o'erspread the sadden'd scene' (Bennett, 22–6). Wordsworth was also concerned about the impact of war upon independent cottagers. His poetry focuses upon the experience of war widows, whose suffering was a recurrent theme of the anti-war poetry. It is the dominant theme of 'Anna's Complaint; Or the Miseries of War; Written in the Isle of Thanet, 1794' published in *The Universal Magazine* for March 1795 and 'The Widow' published in *The Morning Post* on 22 June 1795. In Wordsworth's 'The Ruined Cottage', poverty forces Margaret's husband to join the army, and the family suffers an irreversible decline. The same thing happens in 'The Female Vagrant' (1798). The former is more complex in the way it represents the psychological deterioration of the female protagonist, but then 'The Female Vagrant' is based upon an extract taken from an earlier poem; 'Salisbury Plain' (1793), reworked as 'Adventures on Salisbury Plain' (1795). Bloomfield's 'Dolly' also treats the suffering of war widows, although it is a minor poem and demands attention only in so far as it considers the impact of personality upon an individual's view of the conflict. The quiet and submissive patience of Dolly is linked to the peace and beauty of the rural scenes described in the opening stanzas. Her quiet, penetrating intelligence and common sense are contrasted with the shallow, brash and superficial character of her betrothed as he leaves to take part in the war.

Scott McEathron suggests that Bloomfield's later poems treating the subject of war 'are more agitated, more ideologically fragmented, and more desperate, revealing just how much the actual fact of war had altered Bloomfield's consciousness' (2006, 225) over the decade since he had written 'On Seeing the Launch of the Boyne' (1790). McEathron is right to argue that Bloomfield's view of war had become much more pessimistic by 1798, but 'Dolly' and 'The French Mariner' are not as incoherent as he suggests. As far as it goes, 'Dolly' offers a consistent point of view and 'The French Mariner' is coherent and approaches the question of war from a challenging and progressive perspective. The mariner complains of the increase in poverty suffered by returning soldiers and the labouring poor left at home: 'Ah! why do these old Eyes remain / To see succeeding mornings rise! / My Wife is dead, my Children slain, / And Poverty is all my prize.' (45–8) Wordsworth does not make an explicit connection between deficient government and the poverty that draws the husbands of Margaret and the female vagrant into the war, and the account of the discharged soldier in *The Prelude* focuses upon the pitiful physical degeneration of the man. Bloomfield directly attributes the suffering of the poor in wartime to the motives of the rich and powerful: 'Proud crested Fiend, the World's worst foe, / Ambition; canst thou boast one deed, / Whence no unsightly horrors flow, / Nor private peace is seen to bleed' (41–4).

Wordsworth considers the war from a French perspective in *The Prelude*, a poem that was not of course published during his lifetime. He remembers his youthful belief in 'Liberty' and consequent support for the French cause, and regrets that he 'Exalted in the triumph of ... [his] soul / When Englishmen by thousands were o'erthrown' (X: 260–61). The point of view of 'The French Mariner' is progressive in a subtly different way from that of *The Prelude* because Bloomfield makes his speaker an enemy serviceman. Even in 1802 this was a courageous thing for him to do because the threat of invasion had only recently passed, and the majority of English people believed all things French to be either wicked or depraved, as is apparent from David Garrick's 'France and England' (1793): 'With lanthern jaws and croaking gut / See how the half-starv'd Frenchmen strut, / And call us English dogs; / But soon we'll teach these bragging foes, / That beef and beer give heavier blows, / Than soup and roasted frogs' (Bennett, 1–6). Even Coleridge came to see the French as a 'light yet cruel race' (140) by the time he wrote 'Fears in Solitude' (1798). Bloomfield's mariner expresses anger and resentment, curses the 'conquering Foe', and is seemingly patriotic and nationalistic. At the same time he is aware that many of those on the side of the victorious armies would suffer the very same 'private woe'. In stanza nine the mariner explicitly acknowledges this: 'E'en all the joy that Vict'ry brings, / (Her bellowing Guns, and flaming pride) / Cold, momentary comfort flings / Around where weeping Friends reside' (33–6). Despite himself, in concentrating on the effects of war upon the poor, the speaker expresses solidarity with the labouring poor and the common soldiery of England. In an annotation to his 1807 fair copy MS of *The Farmer's*

Boy, Bloomfield had revealed a progressive attitude towards relations in the workplace (MS Eng. 776.1, fol. 27). In this poem he implicitly suggests that the labouring poor of France and England have more in common with each other than they do with their own rich and powerful countrymen.

In 'The French Mariner' Bloomfield uses a traditional poetic form in order to make a sophisticated political point. He had expressed oppositional political views in *The Farmer's Boy*. But both the title and preface to *Rural Tales, Ballads and Songs* declare that he was concerned to demonstrate the value of labouring-class culture, rather than use the collection as a vehicle for the dissemination of views that would not normally be articulated in ballads or songs by the rural labouring poor. 'The French Mariner' does retain some of the formal characteristics of the traditional ballad. It is written in ballad metre, and descriptions of conflict in the poem are in direct and simple ballad language: 'I've rode o'er many a dreadful wave, / I've seen the reeking blood descend: / I've heard the last groans of the brave;— / The shipmate dear, the steady Friend' (5–8). The images appear to be drawn directly from the personal experiences of the speaker, and the immediacy of the opening stanza is enhanced by the appearance of the personal pronoun 'I' at the beginning of the first three lines. The passages that focus on the mariner's reflections would not, however, be found in traditional ballads which generally concentrate upon narrative, and avoid either elaboration or narratorial comment. This feature of the poem is a departure from the formal norms of the traditional ballad or tale which occurs more often in his later collection *Wild Flowers*.

There are other ways in which the *Wild Flower* poems can be said to be more sophisticated than those contained within the earlier volume. This might be explained by Bloomfield's new familiarity with the poetry of Wordsworth and Coleridge. He first read *Lyrical Ballads* after he had finished writing the pieces for *Rural Tales*, and it seems that he immediately became aware of striking similarities between some of the poems in the two collections. In a critical fragment under the heading 'Coincidences' he notes a specific resemblance between a line in his own 'Market Night' and one in 'The Idiot Boy': he 'was startled to find ... [Wordsworth] saying, in the "Idiot Boy," "That Pony's worth his weight in gold." I had written, without seeing or dreaming of Mr. Wordsworth's remark, almost the same words in "Market Night:" "That Beast is worth his weight in gold"' (*Remains* II: 111). He was clearly concerned to defend the authenticity and originality of his work, but 'Market Night' and 'The Fakenham Ghost' are marked by a somewhat lighter tone than the other poems in *Rural Tales*, and in many respects they do bear a resemblance to Wordsworth's 'The Idiot Boy'. Like Wordsworth, Bloomfield was responding to those sentimental ballads, marred by the 'stupid ghost' or 'vulgar thing' that Sir Ambrose criticizes in the 'Invitation' to *May Day*.

'Market Night' describes the thoughts of the female protagonist as she and her family wait at home for her husband to return from market on a stormy night. She visualizes the various dangers that he is likely to face, as well as the events that might speed his journey home. The poem shows how the mind, when excited by fear or fed by superstition, makes strange and irrational associations: 'There shines a *Star*!—O welcome Sight!— / Through the thin vapours bright'ning still! / Yet, 'twas beneath the fairest night / The murd'rer stain'd yon lonely Hill' (41–4). This passage and others like it resemble those sections of 'The Idiot Boy' which describe the thoughts of Betty Foy as she searches impatiently for her son: '[perhaps] him that wicked pony's carried / To the dark cave, the goblin's hall, / Or in the castle he's pursuing, / Among the ghosts, his own undoing; / Or playing with the waterfall' (237–41). In both poems the humour inherent in these associations is augmented by the manner in which the short four-stress metre produces a hurrying forward movement. 'The Fakenham Ghost' employs the traditional alternate three and four-stress ballad metre for perhaps a greater sense of forward movement, but relies upon the same kind of thought associations to generate humour. In this poem the female protagonist is followed home at night by a 'trotting ghost' (31) which turns out to be 'an *Ass's Foal* [that] had lost its Dam / Within the spacious Park' (61–2).

It is not possible to say whether Bloomfield felt the need to distinguish his poetry from that of Wordsworth, who adopts a serious tone in all of the poetry within *Lyrical Ballads*, with the exception of 'The Idiot Boy'. But it is certainly the case that humour, particularly mock-heroic, is used in a more sophisticated way within *Wild Flowers* than in the two earlier poems. The humour if not the increased sophistication was acknowledged and approved by some reviewers. The *Literary Journal* is one example, although in this case approval is tinged with condescension towards the rural labouring poor: 'Some of the pieces are of a more playful and humorous cast, and in these we think he particularly excels, as they are descriptive of those scenes which place the manners of the common villagers in the most pleasing and entertaining point of view.' (2 (1806), 62) Bloomfield did have access to a tradition of mock-heroic romance literary ballads at the time that he was writing, the most well known was probably William Cowper's 'The Diverting History of John Gilpin' (1782). It is quite likely that he was familiar with this poem because it was disseminated widely as a broadside and was often included in chapbooks during the latter part of the eighteenth century. 'Abner and the Widow Jones' resembles Cowper's poem in that the narrative concerns a comic journey made by the principal character. In Bloomfield's poem, however, the humour arises from its concentration upon the inner world of Abner rather than the physical comedy of the journey.

The fact that Bloomfield's poem is about the wooing of a widow with some means is, as always, a strong indication that the poem is going to be comic or satirical. And the self-important calculating voice in which Abner's emotions are articulated is clearly intended to heighten the humorous tone. In the first stanza, Abner's principal feeling is determination 'To go and court the Widow Jones' (4). This feeling is quickly succeeded in the second stanza by sympathy for his old horse which faces the 'pole axe' at the knacker's yard (13). There was real concern about cruelty to animals at the beginning of the nineteenth century. Bloomfield himself had written about the cruelty of tail docking and the poor treatment of post-horses in *The Farmer's Boy*, and an anonymous tract published in 1827 particularly noted the pitiful treatment of horses at the end of their lives:

> They are turned into an open yard or pound, with no covering from the inclemency of cold and rain; no bed but the filth of the place; and all suffering pain from those diseases that have incapacitated them for future usefulness. Even death by starvation is very frequently added, as they have no food given them, and are slaughtered either according to the number in hand, or the demand for their flesh, it being often a matter of *indifference* whether they die in this way or are slaughtered. [4]

During his journey to the widow's cottage Abner experiences a series of different emotions; from confidence that he will win her hand and with her financial assistance save Baynard from this fate, to uncertainty about the widow's intentions, and finally to determination '.... whatever might betide, / To speak his mind ...' (42–3). He feels excitement at having gained her acquiescence to his courtship and the purchase of the old horse, subject to an unspecified delay for the sake of decency. This emotion is immediately succeeded again by uncertainty about whether she will change her mind, leading him to reconsider the purchase of the horse: 'Suppose she should refuse her hand? / Such thoughts will come, I know not why; / Shall I, without a wife or land, / Want an old horse? then wherefore buy?' (149–52). The romance mode in this poem arises from the physical journey or quest to win the widow's hand, the mock-heroic from the link that Abner establishes in his mind between the saving of the horse and his courtship of Mary.

Bloomfield's growing sophistication as a poet is evident from the manipulation of poetic voices in the poem. It is this, together with its mock-heroic vein that makes 'Abner and the Widow Jones' a greater achievement than some contemporary reviewers allowed. The *Annual Review*, for example, considered it 'vulgar and childish in the extreme' (1806, 526). The humour generated in the poem is augmented through the tension that often exists between stanzas of speech imitation and narrative stanzas. There is a series of three stanzas at the beginning of the poem which illustrate this point quite well; one stanza of speech imitation followed by two narrative stanzas. In stanza four Abner expresses his determination to save Baynard 'If .... [he] can win the Widow Jones' (16). The narrator describes Abner departing jauntily on his quest in the fifth stanza, and then remarks in the sixth: 'And every spark of love reviv'd / That had perplex'd him long ago' (21–2). The irony is heavy because the reasons given by Abner to justify his courtship of the widow had exclusively concerned his desire to save the old horse, and he is later described mulling over the financial implications of his decision to marry: 'From bush to bush, from stile to stile, / Perplex'd he trod the fallow ground, / And told his money all the while, / And weighed the matter round and round' (153–6). The motivations of the widow are also subjected to the ironic gaze of the narrator: 'But whether, freed from recent vows, / *Her* heart had back to Abner flown, / And mark'd him for a second spouse, / In truth is not exactly known' (25–8). There is a thinly veiled suggestion here, either that their relationship had not always been platonic in the past, or that she was not above viewing courtship in a calculating manner.

Bloomfield always valued affection between the members of a family, and had an evident distaste for marriages of convenience. The 'fallow ground' upon which Abner treads symbolizes the barren and spiritually unproductive nature of his materialistic attitude to marriage. It is important to note, however, that amongst the labouring poor at the turn of the eighteenth century financial considerations would have played at least as great a part in decisions to marry as would the degree of affection present (Stone, 237–8). Bloomfield, like other members of the rural labouring classes, would have had little time for excessively romantic love. In *Hazelwood-Hall: A Village Drama* (1823) Spoken censures Joel for his self indulgent conduct towards Mary: 'could you not love her as other people do, that is, reasonably?' (2). On the other hand, Bloomfield did believe that the kind of companionable affection which exists between Richard and Kate was of great value. The satirical tone of some passages within 'Abner and the Widow Jones' might be explained by the poet's fear that the narrow mercenary values which drove agricultural improvement were beginning to impinge upon other aspects of rural life.

The way in which the narrative is constructed so as to stress Walter's mercenary mindset is not explained only by the fact that Bloomfield is endeavouring to provoke a humorous response. The narrative techniques employed in all of his ballads and tales contribute to their point of view. But the earlier poems derive their impact from the clarity of their exemplary plot, and this is enhanced by essentially mono-tonal narration and the presence of only one distinctive voice. In 'Abner and the Widow Jones' the manipulation of voices and the tonal variation encourage the reader to respond critically to the practical, and perhaps more importantly the emotional impact of social change in the countryside. This feature of 'Abner and the Widow Jones' sets it apart from the narrative poems in *Lyrical Ballads* which, like those in *Rural Tales*, are characterized by what Wordsworth in the preface calls a direct, 'naked and simple' narrative style (261). The narrative style also represents a departure from the kind of direct story telling that is ordinarily found in the traditional ballad. Having said this, the poem does focus upon what is essentially a simple story, and is recognizably a ballad.

'The Broken Crutch. A Tale' is a more complex poem, and more difficult to position within Bloomfield's labouring-class poetics. When the heroine first encounters her future husband, the narrator's commentary sets up the expectation that what follows will be the kind of story regularly encountered in the literature of the period. The narrative involving an aristocratic or gentleman libertine and a defenceless girl was an established trope in eighteenth-century magazine poems and in novels, the most well-known example being Mr B's imprisonment of Pamela in Samuel Richardson's *Pamela* (1740). In the context of the poet's life in the metropolis, something which he did not write about explicitly in his verse, he may also have had in mind the libertinism that dominated artisan culture in late eighteenth-century London. He would have observed reckless and lascivious behaviour amongst apprentices and journeymen (*Autobiography of Francis Place*, 74–8; Clark, 1995, 31–4). At the beginning of 'The Broken Crutch' the narrator suggests that Peggy's beauty and purity would provoke such behaviour:

> At such a sight the libertine would glow
> With all the warmth that *he* can ever know:
> Would send his thoughts abroad without control,
> The glimmering moonshine of his little soul.
> Above the reach of justice I shall soar,
> Her friends may weep, not punish; they're too poor:
> That very thought the rapture will enhance,
> Poor, young, and friendless; what a glorious chance! [35–41]

Bloomfield's description of his hypothetical villain spans fourteen lines, but is in fact a play upon reader expectations because at the end of the passage the narrator remarks: 'Such was not Herbert' (49). The narrator abruptly disrupts the orientation of the narrative towards a sensational denouement in a way that raises the question; what kind of poem is 'The Broken Crutch', and what is it about?

The narrative not only manipulates reader expectations, it also adopts a playful attitude towards certain characters in the poem. The behaviour of Peggy's father, and that of her uncle Gilbert, is based upon an understanding of social interaction in the countryside that might have been acquired from the sentimental ballad. The scene is set for Gilbert's mock-heroic quest when the squire's messenger Nathan falls into a drunken stupor on his way to collect Peggy's relatives, and fails to bring them to the wedding. Ignorant of Herbert's honourable intentions, the suspicions of Peggy's father and uncle increase until, in a moment of frustration and anger, John Meldrum breaks his crutch on a stile. Carrying one of the broken ends, Gilbert then sets off to confront Herbert 'with enormous strides, / Rebellious mutterings and oaths besides' (185–6), but Herbert has honourably married Peggy by the time he arrives. The comic quality of the meeting between 'hero' and 'villain' is enhanced when Herbert enquires of Gilbert: 'What meant this cudgel? What was it to do?' (302). After explaining the reasons for his suspicions, Gilbert can only reply: 'An' please you, Sir, I meant to knock you down' (322). Notwithstanding the humour, the scene also dramatizes the threat of labouring-class resistance to tyranny which emerges on several occasions in 'The Broken Crutch'.

Story-telling artifice of the sort employed by Bloomfield in 'The Broken Crutch' would not be found in the traditional 'local poetry' that both the title and preface announce *Wild Flowers* to contain. In the folktale the narrator simply describes the twists and turns of the story-line, but in Bloomfield's poem sophisticated narrative techniques generate considerable tension. The integrity of the poem in terms of narrative is further interrupted by the kind of intrusive commentary that is present in 'Abner and the Widow Jones', but much more common in 'The Broken Crutch'. One example is the passage describing the hypothetical villainous squire. The thirty-four-line passage which begins immediately after it is, however, more disruptive of the 'unity of action' in the poem (57–90). It is rooted in the lyric mode and was in fact anthologized as a separate poem under the title 'Burnt Hall' in *The Suffolk Garland* (1818). There is a sense in which the narrative momentum ceases. Moreover, the predominant polemic tone of this passage is out of place in a tale, and it is not always clear who is speaking.

The first four lines of the passage are rhapsodic in tone, but the mood changes abruptly in line five when the speaking voice becomes angry at the destruction caused by the axe 'in Gain's rude service, and in Pity's smite' (62), and at 'this scythe of desolation call'd "Reform"' (68). This section of the passage is marked by its emotionally engaged language. It is conservative in that it is backward looking, but in a sense it is radical too because it represents a criticism of the enclosure and agricultural improvement that generally followed the removal of trees. The disappearance of common land had touched Bloomfield personally through the enclosure of 'his native Green', of which he remarks:

> To take such a small bit of ground and divide it into three, was hardly worth while. What man, with a sack of wheat on his back, would stoop for one grain? Inclosing Acts? I do not much like the rage for them. They cut down the solemn, the venerable tree, and sometimes plant another, – *not always*; like a mercenary soldier, who kills more than he begets. [*Remains* II: 53]

His brother Nathaniel also lamented this event in his enclosure elegy 'Honington Green: A Ballad' (1803): 'Such lucrative maxim as this / The Lords of the Land all pursue, / For who such advantage wou'd miss? / Self-int'rest we all keep in view. / By it, they still more wealth amass, / Who posses'd great abundance before; / It gives pow'r to the Great, but alas! / Still poorer it renders the Poor' (30). Notwithstanding the enclosure of Honington Green, Suffolk was left virtually unaffected by eighteenth-century Enclosure Acts. There were only ten Acts affecting Suffolk between 1727 and 1801, although these did mainly concern the western half of the county (the eastern half, the inspiration for many of Gainsborough's rustic landscapes, had been subject to small-scale enclosure during the sixteenth century). Much more of western Suffolk would be enclosed during the first decades of the nineteenth century. Nevertheless the enclosure of 'his native green' clearly affected Bloomfield, and the angry tone of his language at this point in 'The Broken Crutch' is very similar to that of John Clare fourteen years later in 'Helpstone' (1820), when he denounces 'Accursed wealth [for] o'er bounding human laws' (127). And Clare was criticized by Lord Radstock for 'conveying Radical and ungrateful sentiments' in this passage (Storey, 61). Bloomfield was aware that some of the sentiments expressed in his poem might be disapproved. He remarks near the end of the first verse paragraph: '"Warmth," they will term it, that I speak so free' (75). From the beginning of the eighteenth century the word warmth was often used to describe an 'excited or fevered state of the feelings' or a 'fervent or vehement character' (*OED*). Like labouring-class resistance to change in the countryside, such displays of enthusiasm were often linked to radical politics by those in positions of authority and were mistrusted accordingly.

The poor resisted change because it undermined a way of life that they saw as in some way inviolable, the paternalist regulation of their lives within known communities. By the turn of the eighteenth century the customs and rites upon which they depended were regarded by many as obstacles to progress. In *General View of the Agriculture of the County of Lincolnshire* (1779), Arthur Young, one of the main proponents of agricultural 'Reform', categorized common lands in the following way: 'I must consider commons, however naturally rich in soil, as wastes' (253), and concurred with the view that they were responsible for 'nursing up a mischievous race of people' (255). A note to the section on wastes in *General View of the Agriculture of the County of Suffolk* (1794) justifies the enclosure of commons on the basis that 'the men who usually reside near a common, are the depredators of the neighbourhood: smugglers, sheep-stealers, horse-jockies, and jobbers of every denomination, here find their abode' (168). Remarks such as these suggest that enclosure only affected those living at the margins of society. This was not the case, and although Young continued to support the principle of enclosure, he later observed the brutality with which it was carried out and the kind of people that were affected. By the time he came to write his *Inquiry into the Propriety of Applying Wastes to the Better Management of the Poor* (1801) he had a very different view of the subject:

> I will not dispute their meaning; but the poor look to facts, not meanings: and the fact is that by nineteen out of twenty Enclosure Acts the poor are injured, in some grossly injured ... The poor in these parishes may say, and with truth, *Parliament may be the tender of property; all I know is, I had a cow, and an Act of Parliament has taken it from me.* [42–3]

In *The Village Labourer* (1911) the Hammonds agreed that enclosure had a serious impact upon the standard of living of the rural labouring poor, and, although their work has been questioned, some recent historians have supported their view. K.D.M. Snell argues that enclosure reduced the previously varied sources of food and fuel available to the poor to just two: wages and poor relief (Snell, 149–54). As E.P. Thompson suggests, it seems that ultimately ideology became an expression of self-interest: 'It became a matter of public-spirited policy for the gentleman to remove cottagers from the commons, reduce his labourers to dependence, pare away at supplementary earnings, drive out the small holder' (Thompson 1963, 243).

Herbert Brooks, the hero of 'The Broken Crutch', is a member of the class whose conduct Thompson condemns, and it is unlikely that he would share the kind of view that is expressed in this passage of the poem. Even if he felt some sympathy for the plight of the poor, he would not use such emotionally charged language in condemning the actions of his own class. But at the beginning of the passage there is an indication that the speaking voice is his. Immediately after the reader has been informed that Herbert is innocent and uncorrupted, the passage begins: 'On thy calm joys with what delight

I dream, / Thou dear green valley of my native stream!' (57–8). It does not become clear until the end of the verse paragraph that it is the narrator who is speaking. The language is more appropriate for someone who had worked as a farm-labourer in an area of Suffolk that was being enclosed at the time that 'The Broken Crutch' was written. Bloomfield felt immense anger at the way in which agricultural improvement affected the poor, and as it progresses the passage becomes increasingly personal:

> No army past that way! yet they are fled,
> The boughs that, when a school-boy, screen'd my head:
> I hate the murderous axe; estranging more
> The winding vale from what it was of yore,
> Than e'en mortality in all its rage,
> And all the change of faces in an age. [69–74]

The narrator draws attention to the fact that this lyric digression represents a pause in the narrative momentum by signalling his return to the story: 'In Herbert's days woods cloth'd both hill and dale; / But peace, Remembrance! let us tell the tale' (78).

On the surface, the second verse paragraph of the lyric is an account of Herbert's ancestral home and its environs, but it is also an implied commentary upon the content of the previous paragraph: 'His home was in the valley, elms grew round / His moated mansion, and the pleasant sound / Of woodland birds that loud at day-break sing, / With the first cuckoos that proclaim the spring, / Flock'd round his dwelling' (79–83). The growing elms and woods full of birds are opposed to the transformed barren landscape that remains after the disappearance of the alders and poplars. It is also significant that these harmonious scenes are directly associated with the responsible community of which Herbert was an important part: 'his kitchen smoke, / That from the towering rookery upward broke, / Of joyful import to the poor hard by, / Stream'd a glad sign of hospitality' (83–6). The hypothetical libertine imposes upon the helpless poor with whom he shares no common purpose, but Herbert is a source of support and assistance to poor neighbours within a known community. This affective harmony between human beings and between humankind and nature is lost when the landscape is destroyed and agriculture "Reformed".

The last lines of the lyric explicitly locate Herbert's community in the past: 'So fancy pictures; but its day is o'er; / The moat remains; the dwelling is no more! / Its name denotes its melancholy fall, / For village children call the spot "Burnt Hall"' (87–90). The name given to the site of the hall suggests that ashes are all that remain of the old world in which Herbert was a 'crutch' for those in need. The poem does, however, end with an appeal from Peggy's father suggesting that the type of community celebrated in the poem is not completely irretrievable:

> But from my soul I wish and wish again,
> *That brave good gentlemen would not disdain*
> *The poor, because they're poor*: for, if they live

> Midst crimes that parents *never can* forgive,
> If, like the forest beast, they wander wild,
> To rob a father, or to crush a child,
> Nature *will* speak, aye, just as Nature feels,
> And wish—a Gilbert Meldrum at their heels. [369–76]

As the first set of italics emphasize, the implication of this statement is that communities are built out of the attitudes of people towards one another. The words are spoken by a character in the tale rather than by the narrator, and the reader is left to ask in what way rural life has changed since the period in which the tale is set. This passage invites reflection, the reader is being asked to stop and think about the dynamics of the community portrayed, as well as the one in which they live. The closing lines do not refer explicitly to the crimes of libertines, and could easily represent an implied warning to the proponents of "Reform" who often adopted a disdainful attitude towards the poor. Nature, or the labouring poor in possession of broken crutches or similar weapons, will punish those who offend against her; '*Nature* will speak'.

John Meldrum's closing words are politically engaged, like the lyric passage attacking enclosure. His words are not those of a semi-literate rural worker, and it is not the kind of speech that a father would make following his daughter's wedding. The speech does achieve a sense of closure, but it is out of key with the narrative resolution of the tale. It reinforces the dislocation between narrative tenor and point of view that had been present elsewhere in 'The Broken Crutch'. The narrative structure of 'Abner and the Widow Jones' is controlled; the structure of 'The Broken Crutch' is more composite, comprising lengthy passages in different poetic modes. But in both the connection with labouring-class poetic forms that had been central to the point of view in earlier poems is less important. Bloomfield's desire to speak directly of matters that affected the lives of the rural labouring poor is more apparent than in exemplary tales such as 'Walter and Jane' and 'The Miller's Maid'. He departs from the critical agenda set out in the prefaces to *Rural Tales* and *Wild Flowers*, but it is perhaps the case that a more composite structure suited his developing ideas regarding the purpose of poetry, and he turned away from the self-contained ballad or tale in his later published verse.

This development in Bloomfield's poetics can also be explained in terms of the distinction drawn earlier in this chapter between his and Wordsworth's poetics. The latter was relatively uninterested in communal interaction, and it seems that he neither saw nor understood the impact of social change upon the psychology of rural communities. Bloomfield was primarily interested in the social dynamic of rural communities, but his early ballads and tales treat the effect of social change upon human relationships in a restrained manner that he perhaps came to feel did not make a sufficiently forceful impression upon his readers. The later poems engage more directly with the motivations and thought processes of the characters. Bloomfield produces engaging poetry about everyday events partly through his humorous treatment, but also because his poetry recognizes that the day-to-day lives of the labouring poor were becoming increasingly fraught with uncertainty. The narratorial commentary draws attention to the way in which agricultural improvement driven by self-interest and the dictates of political economy was sweeping away the paternalistic certainties that had in the past regulated the lives of the poor, and reshaping the psychology of social interaction within rural communities.

CHAPTER THREE

The Romantic Lyric and the Lyric of Labour

The lyric has been central to our understanding of Romanticism, indeed 'defining the mode once meant, in effect, defining Romanticism' (Zimmerman, 9). One of the principal reasons for this tendency in criticism has been the influence of M.H. Abrams' seminal essay 'Structure and Style in the Greater Romantic Lyric', first published in 1965. Abrams identifies Coleridge as the mainspring behind the development of the Romantic lyric because, inspired by William Lisle Bowles's *Sonnets, Written Chiefly on Picturesque Spots, During a Tour* (1788), he had begun to produce poems which brought about 'the Romantic interfusion of subject and object' (550). According to Abrams, a new kind of lyric poem began to emerge in which an identified speaker in a localized outdoor setting engages in a colloquy with himself, the scene or a silent human auditor. The narrator generally begins with a description of the landscape, some aspect of which provokes a sustained 'process of memory, thought, anticipation and feeling', in the course of which an emotional problem is resolved. 'The Eolian Harp' (1796) is identified as Coleridge's first experiment; his greatest poems 'This Lime Tree Bower My Prison' (1797), 'Frost at Midnight' (1798) and 'Dejection: an Ode' (1802). All of this seems incontestable, with the exception of the suggestion made by Abrams that Coleridge, and perhaps Wordsworth in 'Tintern Abbey', were developing this new mode in isolation.

New historicism has critiqued the ideological implications of the poetics of interiority and transcendence identified by Abrams, but the terms of that critique have ironically reinforced the equation of the extended Romantic lyric with these extra-formal qualities (Zimmerman, 3). Not all the extended lyric poems written during the Romantic period can be characterized in this way, and Bloomfield's lyric poems should certainly be considered in any revaluation. They respond to the kind of problems typically addressed in the 'conversation' poem in a way that is actually rooted in the material circumstances of the speaker. This is particularly so of Bloomfield's most accomplished extended lyrics; 'Shooter's Hill' and 'To My Old Oak Table', both of which were published in *Wild Flowers*. But in order to appreciate how Bloomfield's meditative lyric poetry evolved it is necessary to consider early poems too. 'The Widow to her Hour-Glass' was published in *Rural Tales*, it is not narrated in the first person, but it is a lyric response to the relationship between the human psyche and domestic security. The widow's meditation is addressed to her hour-glass, rather than a feature of the landscape. This in itself is significant, because the use of such a device is suggestive of a particular way of life, and a particular class of people amongst the labouring poor.

The precise period in time when it first appeared is not known, but by the fourteenth and fifteenth centuries 'the sand-glass was a common object of daily life' (Turner 1984, 78). Although it was normally described as an hour-glass during the eighteenth century, the period of time which it measured was decided 'by the whim of the maker or the task for which the glass ... [was] required, and may ... [have been] for any interval from a few seconds up to 24 hours' (Turner 1984, 76). From the beginning it was also seen as a symbol of temperance, regularity and the need to make good use of each passing moment. The earliest known illustration of the sand-glass dates from the middle of the fourteenth century. It is in a series of frescoes by Ambrosio Lorenzetti in the Sala del Pace of the Palazzo Publico, Sienna, and depicts Temperantia holding aloft a sand-glass. The hour-glass reminded people of the value of each moment, and that they were ever that bit closer to their final judgement: 'in the hands of Death the hour-glass reminded ... [people] of their final hour, and urged them to make use of the moment for as long as there was still time ... [for] "Your last hour is one of these"' (Borst, 96). It is also significant that an hour was, for a long time, seen as the standard time for a formal meditation, as is suggested by the opening lines of a poem by Henry Vaughan: 'I walkt the other day (to spend my hour,) / Into a field' (1–2).

In Britain, unlike continental Europe, 'sand-glasses' were 'never ... more than utilitarian time-pieces ... for which ... the less prosperous classes supplied a ready market', and were produced by an 'unregulated, itinerant, perhaps rural out-industry' (Turner 1982, 171). By the turn of the eighteenth century some of the better off within the labouring classes might have owned clocks or watches which, apart from their obvious function, were also status symbols: 'Whenever any group of workers passed into a phase of improving living standards, the acquisition of time-pieces was one of the first things noted by observers' (Thompson 1993, 370). According to W. Radcliffe's account of Lancashire hand-loom weavers during the 1790s, when they were at their most prosperous, each man had 'a watch in his pocket', and each house was 'well furnished with a clock in elegant mahogany or fancy case' (67). But at the beginning of the nineteenth century, an artisan possessing a clock would still have been an exception. And the possession of all but the most simple mechanical time-keeping devices, such as shadow clocks and hour-glasses, would have been well beyond the means of the poorest among the labouring classes.

For the labouring poor in the countryside, the possession of a clock or watch to measure time might not have been so important anyway. Life was still largely regulated according to cyclical seasonal rhythms, and work organized according to the demands of agriculture and animal husbandry, which varied depending upon the time of year. Time measured in minutes and hours would have been more important for a factory-worker required to start and finish work at a set time. But it would often be necessary for the rural labouring poor to perform numerous tasks during the course of a day, and to ensure that too much time was not devoted to one occupation. Hour-glasses would have been used to keep track of passing time whilst people were engaged in activities such as basket-making or weaving. Within the poetry of the period there are numerous examples of the hour-glass being used to symbolize the ephemeral nature of earthly lives. But there are also poems in which the hour-glass is employed for the apparently secular purpose of measuring the time spent upon a particular task. In 'Days Departed; or, Banwell Hill, A Lay of The Severn Sea' (1828) by William Lisle Bowles, as in Bloomfield's poem, the hour-glass is used by a country maid to measure the time she devotes to spinning: 'As lovely, in her lowly path. She turned / The hour-glass, while the humming wheel went round' (150–51).

A poem about a poor widow using an hour-glass to measure the time spent upon a particular task is strongly evocative of the lifestyle and work rhythms of the semi-independent cottager. Time is, however, important within the architecture of Bloomfield's poem in more ways than one. The widow's meditation concerns the common vacillations of human existence, taking both a seasonal and a lifetime perspective. The uncertainty and variations in fortune that afflict humankind are reflected in the movement of the sand within the hour-glass:

> I've often watch'd thy streaming sand
> And seen the growing Mountain rise,
> And often found Life's hopes to stand
> On props as weak in Wisdom's eyes:
> Its conic crown
> Still sliding down,
> Again heap'd up, then down again;
> The sand above more hollow grew,
> Like days and years still filt'ring through,
> And mingling joy and pain. [11–20]

The hour-glass represents the mutability of fate that manifests itself in human joy and pain. Because it does so whilst in a sense remaining constant, it also symbolizes a kind of stability within change, or change within stability. The relative durability of the widow's domestic economy, despite disruptive events, is impressed upon the reader during the address to the hour-glass at the very beginning of the poem: 'Spring thirty times hath fed with rain / And cloth'd with leaves my humble bower, / Since thou hast stood / In frame of wood, / On Chest or Window by my side' (3–7). None of the events to which she alludes in the poem, not even the death of her husband, probably her principal source of material support, have resulted in the loss of her security.

In the third stanza it is revealed that the widow has enjoyed security despite the fact that she has been forced to resort to some precarious means of support. She informs the reader that one of her occupations is to 'glean the sultry fields' (28). The fact that in the closing stanza attention is drawn to the manner in which the hour-glass 'strik'st the Heart without a Bell' (34) might be a further allusion to the practice of gleaning. In many parishes the poor were allowed to begin gleaning after the ringing of a bell: this was sometimes a hand bell, but often the church bell would be used. The regulation of the practice implicit in the use of a bell was enforced by the gleaners themselves, and 'any woman bold enough to start work before the signal to do so was given' was set upon by other gleaners and 'had all her gleanings snatched from her and scattered on the ground by her fellow workers' (Porter, 124). Sometimes the bell would be rung again in the evening as a signal that the time allowed for the practice was over. When the gleaners within a particular parish sought to restrict gleaning to local parishioners only, the bell was often used to reinforce this direction as well (Bushaway 1982, 145). On its own, gleaning would not have supported the widow, but it might have formed an important part of her means of subsistence. In a letter to Lord Egremont, cited in Arthur Young's *General View of the Agriculture of the County of Sussex* (1808), Bloomfield's patron Capel Lofft suggested that in Suffolk in 1795 a labourer could add £4 to an average income of £27.9s through gleaning and other subsidiary activities such as pease and wheat dropping (sowing) and his children's spinning (407–409). Later, in 1832, as part of a call for stricter regulation of gleaning, Jefferys Taylor remarked that 'A family has been known, by mere gleaning, to gather up a quarter of corn, that is, eight threshed and dressed bushels, in a season – worth, we may say, three pounds or guineas' (Taylor 1832, 140). Through that of his widow, Bloomfield is representing one of the households that was most needful of the extra income provided by gleaning. It has been noted that gleaning would have 'been particularly valuable in households headed by widows; that is about 1 household in 8' (King, 466). Furthermore, when combined with the numerous other customary rights supported by the paternalist system, gleaning might have made the difference that meant survival for the labouring poor during times of scarcity, particularly because there was often as much corn to be gleaned during lean years as in times of plenty (King, 466).

The practice of gleaning was attacked by the rural improvement lobby towards the end of the eighteenth century. A common defence was that these '*unhired* harvest folks' had 'immemorial usage on their side' (Taylor 1832, 139, 140). The story of Ruth and Boaz in the Book of Leviticus was invoked by some in support of this view. But in the rhetoric of figures such as Thomas Ruggles, the fact that gleaning was allowed by Mosaic law did not necessarily have universal application. According to Ruggles, Mosiac law referred the right of gleaning

> ... to the vineyard, to the olive grounds; and, by parity of reasoning, in this country, it would go to the orchard, to the hopground; and apples should be left upon the trees, and hops on the bines; and these not for the poor, the fatherless, and the widows only, but for the stranger; not for the poor of a particular village, district, or for our poor countrymen only, but for the whole world. [639]

Some also attempted to prevent gleaning by recourse to the law of England. The case of *Steel* vs. *Houghton and Uxor* (1788) went a considerable way towards undermining the customary defence of gleaning. Like Ruggles,

Lord Loughborough appeared to dislike gleaning because he felt it to be incompatible with the requirements of agrarian capitalism and the associated need for an ordered and manageable workforce. He 'thought it inconsistent with the nature of property which imports exclusive enjoyment ... Destructive of the peace and good order in society, and amounting to a general vagrancy' (Blackstone, 52). Contrary to the provisions of a recent Enclosure Act which had implicitly allowed gleaning by incorporating regulations relating to the custom, the judgment maintained that: 'No person has, at common law, a right to *glean* the harvest field. Neither have the *poor* of a parish *legally settled* as such any such right' (Blackstone, 51) According to the commentator in W.H. Pyne's *Microcosm* (1806), even where gleaning was permitted, many farmers thinking 'only of making the most money' admitted 'the *fatherless*, *the widow*, and *the stranger* ... only after the corn ... [was] carried, and the field perhaps well raked', and 'generally ... [took] care to loose ... [the] pigs to glean along with the less fortunate *partners of* ... [their] *kind*' (30).

Bloomfield's poem does make reference to the widow's spinning, and this was perhaps her principal occupation. At the same time, especially during times of scarcity or high prices, she would have needed to rely upon other means of support. Although the reference to gleaning is the only allusion to the manner in which the widow sustains herself on these occasions, it is none the less significant for two important reasons. It was one of the customary communitarian indulgences allowed to the labouring poor by the more fortunate members of the community, and it was highly valued by them accordingly. Such indulgences can be construed as a kind of structural generosity; the labouring poor might have seen the proceeds of gleaning as both a gift and something that was theirs by right. More importantly, Bloomfield's polite readers would have been alert to the ideological connotations of the reference to gleaning within a poem which is apparently about domestic contentment. The subtext of the poem is a politically charged defence of people like Bloomfield's widow, whose modest domestic economy was being disrupted by agricultural "Reform". The poem suggests that to undermine the domestic contentment of such individuals would not promote the stability of the village, or that of the country as a whole.

In respect of his attitude to customs such as gleaning, Bloomfield had found a like-minded patron in Capel Lofft. Lofft had defended gleaning in an exchange of correspondence with Thomas Ruggles, published in the *Annals of Agriculture* (1788). In 'On the Gleaning Question', he clarifies his position regarding an earlier reference to Mosaic law, arguing that it was not intended to be taken literally, but was rather an attempt to illustrate the '*general principle*' that 'our common wants and enjoyments are the proper basis for a custom' (220). He also discusses the previously mentioned court case, and his remarks could be said to summarize the point of view of so many of Bloomfield's poems regarding mutual responsibility within the community:

> To a legal custom that it be *just* in its principle and *reasonable* in its extent, is indispensably requisite – A custom founded in benevolence, ascertained

> by immemorial usage, traceable to a moral precept of divine benevolence, and limited to the indigent, and those who are not of strength or habit to the more profitable labours of the field; nor claimed till the farmer has, in fair construction, carried his crop. – A custom recognised under all these features, by our most eminent legal writers, might, I still think, warrant me, or any man, in the supposition of its legality. [227]

Lofft argues that the opportunity to glean the harvest field is of particular importance to individuals within rural communities 'who are not of strength or habit to the more profitable labours of the field' – people like Bloomfield's widow. The real significance of the passage, however, is that the view which it expresses rests upon a singular authority. Lofft is invoking a kind of law that is different from either Mosaic or human law. He is concerned with the law that has its origin in the 'divine benevolence' of nature. This is the same natural law that Bloomfield would later invoke in the closing lines of 'The Broken Crutch'. In this sense the views of Lofft and Bloomfield coincide; both are conservative in that they detest the changes that agrarian capitalism brought to the rural communities that they believed ought to be organized according to the dictates of nature. As argued in the previous chapter of this study, such conservative resistance to change was often conflated with radicalism by those in positions of authority. As a consequence, Bloomfield's treatment of the gleaning question might easily have been seen as seditious or radical despite the fact that he did not necessarily share all of Lofft's radical sentiments.

Lofft defended practices like gleaning because he was concerned about the economic security of the labouring poor. For the poor themselves, however, the range of practices which they considered to be part of their cultural heritage had more profound significance. Gleaning was regulated according to a time-scale that was different from, and much older than that denoted by the hour-glass; time measured by the sun rather than by a device. Bloomfield's widow conducts her gleaning outside of the time-scale denoted by the hour-glass, as she suggests at the end of the third stanza: 'When Earth her yellow Harvest yields, / Thou get'st a Holliday' (29–30). The origin of the practice was believed to be beyond memory, and was perceived to have been a right of the poor since before humankind began to use abstract recording systems, such as the division of time into hours and minutes. This different kind of time was linked to the less disciplined work rhythms of the rural labouring poor, before the demands of agrarian capitalism turned them into wage-slaves.

The manner in which Bloomfield's cottagers control their own time, and the domestic self-sufficiency which is linked to their conceptualization of time, finds its archetype in the widow's life, and is given symbolic resonance through the hour-glass. The intensity of the widow's meditation and the structure of the poem further concentrate this representative power. The circumstances of her life are symbolically drawn to her home, and to the hour-glass. There is a suggestion that this is happening in the opening invocation, when she visualizes her cottage separated and hidden from the outside world. Then in the closing lines she invites the natural world to turn back on itself and shrink within the cottage: 'Curl inward here, sweet Woodbine flower' (38). The way in which she ends her address establishes a link between the structure of the poem and the hour-glass. She turns the hour-glass over, and the poem ends with a phrasal inversion of the opening lines that wills the continuance of her way of life. The poem begins 'Come, friend, I'll turn thee up again: / Companion of the lonely hour' (1–2), and ends 'Companion of the lonely hour, / I'll turn thee up again' (39–40).

'The Widow to Her Hour-Glass' is a sophisticated poem. This is surprising given Bloomfield's own self-deprecating account of its gestation in the preface to the 1809 edition of his poems: 'it has nothing remarkable belonging to it, but that it is the only piece in the book which was written quick. Had an Hour-glass before me; my wife singing softly; my girls at school. Made a shoe between dinner and tea time, and composed the 'Widow' beside' (I: ii). In that it focuses upon the emotions and thought processes of the central character, and her response to both her past, and her current situation, it is the first of Bloomfield's poems to explore human subjectivity. Bloomfield achieves the same kind of lyric intensity as Wordsworth and Coleridge, but as he had done with the ballad and the tale, he makes use of the lyric to explore the experience of the labouring poor. It is because the poem represents hidden recesses within the mind of the widow that it is so evocative of the value, and subconscious significance to the poor of custom and rite regulated locally within village communities. The widow's meditation is of course distanced from the poet's own subject position, but this was not the case in 'Lines Occasioned by a Visit to Whittlebury Forest, Northamptonshire, In August, 1800, Addressed to My Children ', the second extended lyric in *Rural Tales*. Like Wordsworth in 'Tintern Abbey' or Coleridge in 'This Lime Tree Bower My Prison' and 'Frost at Midnight', Bloomfield addresses the question of his own status as a human subject in this poem, in terms of his relationship with others.

The full title of 'Lines Occasioned by a Visit to Whittlebury Forest' would have suggested a particular type of poem to readers at the turn of the eighteenth century; the loco-descriptive poem which combines a description of a scene with an account of the thoughts that the scene suggests. The title would often name both a specific location, and a specific moment in time. As numerous critics have argued, such poems are part of a tradition that probably began with Sir John Denham's 'Cooper's Hill' (1642). Although many of the associations made in Denham's poem are political, his successors came to concentrate upon sententious moralization of the countryside. This is the case, for example, in Richard Jago's 'Edge Hill: The Rural Prospect Delineated and Moralized' (1767), the subtitle to which, as M.H. Abrams remarks, 'neatly defines the double function' (537). In his introduction to the 1989 reprint, Jonathan Wordsworth suggests that William Crowe's *Lewesdon Hill* (1788) represents a bridge between the loco-descriptive poem and the Romantic lyric (v–vii). The style is much less rooted in the Augustan tradition than that of poems like 'Edge Hill', and, as is often the case in the conversation poem, the meditation narrated in *Lewesdon Hill* is directly related to a formative period in the life of the poet. It was admired by both Wordsworth and Coleridge, and, although there is no direct evidence that Bloomfield had read the poem, it is quite likely that he was familiar with it, and there are some similarities between Crowe's poem and 'A Visit to Whitlebury Forest'.

Bloomfield's poem might be indebted to the eighteenth-century loco-descriptive poem in general and to Crowe in particular, but he was definitely not familiar with the work of either Wordsworth or Coleridge when writing 'A Visit to Whittlebury Forest'. In the absence of a direct influence, any parallels between their poetry are probably explained by that fact that all three poets were endeavouring to develop a distinctive kind of lyric mode that could respond to their particular emotional and artistic needs. 'A Visit to Whittlebury Forest' is certainly the product of a crisis in Bloomfield's life. *The Farmer's Boy* had recently been published and he was being courted by the rich and powerful, but celebrity presented Bloomfield with difficulties that an individual from a more privileged background would not have encountered.

The speaker in Coleridge's 'This Lime-Tree Bower My Prison' is physically separated from his 'friends', but his sense of loss is ameliorated by the knowledge that he and they share the same sensibility towards nature. This helps him develop an appreciation of his environment, and re-establish an easy sense of unity with his friends and with nature. Bloomfield's sense of separation, when writing 'A Visit to Whittlebury Forest', went much deeper because his status as a published poet was beginning to distance him from the kind of people with whom he would previously have had an easy understanding. It is not apparent from either the title or the poem itself, but 'A Visit to Whittlebury Forest' is the product of an act of patronage. In his 1809 preface Bloomfield informs the reader that during an audience with the Duke of Grafton on 4 March 1800 he received an invitation to spend a month at Wakefield Lodge in Whittlebury Forest on the Duke's estate in Northamptonshire (I: xxxiv). Bloomfield was clearly ambivalent about the Duke's patronage because in a revealing passage he remarks: 'When I was at Wakefield Lodge I conceited that I saw the workmen and neighbours look at me as an idle fellow. I had nothing to do but to read, look at them, and their country and concerns. They did not seem to know how to estimate me' (I: xxxv). This must have been unsettling for the poet, and the experience could have impelled him to find a way of re-establishing some emotional and psychological certainties for himself and his family.

'A Visit to Whittlebury Forrest' begins with a conventional invocation to the 'GENIUS of the Forest Shades' (1), but Bloomfield's wish to speak of the beauty of nature is quickly transformed into an expression of unity with the labouring poor. In stanza four, the silence of the birds suggests to the poet that he might replace their song with his own, and thereby achieve greater access to nature: 'From my charm'd heart the numbers sprung, / Though Birds had ceas'd the choral lay: / I pour'd wild raptures from my tongue, / And gave delicious tears their way' (25–8). The speaker is revived in the process, but the catalyst which brings about this change is not nature, as in the typical conversation poem, but a 'song' of the labouring poor. At the beginning of the nineteenth century 'The Nut-Brown Maid' was believed to be a traditional ballad dating from the fifteenth century. According to Percy it was first printed in *Arnold's Chronicle* (c.1521) and 'first revived in "The Muses" Mercury for June 1707' (22). Bloomfield re-establishes a link with the watching labourers because of the kind of song he chooses to sing, but also because of the fact that when oral utterances are addressed to an audience, and the poet's audience is both the 'hills' and the 'workmen' and 'neighbours', 'the members of the audience normally become a unity with each other and with the speaker' (Ong, 74).

Bloomfield not only wishes to re-establish links with the labouring poor, he also wants to recover the tranquillity that he has lost in his new life as a poet, and the approach of a storm suggests a way in which he might do so. The storm passes some distance away, but the speaker imagines how the trees resist its disturbing power: 'How would each sweeping pond'rous bough / Resist, when straight the Whirlwind cleaves, / Dashing in strength'ning eddies through / A roaring wilderness of leaves!' (41–4). He also visualizes the manner in which the rain would 'From the [forest's] green Canopy rebound' (46) leaving an area of relative tranquillity beneath. The storm disrupts the outer canopy, but underneath, the heart of the forest remains at peace. For Bloomfield home is always a paradigm for peace, and as a consequence his thoughts turn to his own household, particularly his children: 'But Peace was there: no lightnings blaz'd: — / No clouds obscur'd the face of heav'n: / Down each green op'ning while I gaz'd / My thoughts to home, and you, were giv'n' (49–52). His observation of nature has led him to the reflection that if, like the forest, his children can avoid the temptations of 'bootless pride and falsehood' (55), and remain satisfied by domestic peace, life's storms will be more likely to pass them by: 'And peace like this shall cheer ... [their] way' (56).

There is a sense in which the association made between the hidden calm beneath the canopy and domestic tranquillity is inward-looking, both in terms of the consolation that it offers, and the way it represents the 'genius loci' of the forest. Bloomfield believed that individual peace and prosperity was possible for the labouring poor only within a properly functioning community, and his meditation does not end with the thought that happiness can be found in a life of domestic isolation. This becomes apparent in stanza eight as his mind is prompted back to the scene around him by the sight of 'many an Oak ... stretch'd at length, / Whose trunks (with bark no longer sheath'd) / Had reach'd their full meridian strength / Before your Father's Father breath'd' (61–4). The developing chain of mental association leads him to speculate upon the role that the great trees, symbols of strength and solidarity, will play in protecting his country and its people: 'Perhaps they'll many a conflict brave, / And many a dreadful storm defy; / Then groaning o'er the adverse wave / Bring home the flag of victory' (65–8).

The meditation remains orientated towards the outside world in the next stanza, as the speaker turns to the rural communities that exist within the 'domain' of the forest: 'Sweet, from the heights of thy domain, / When the grey ev'ning shadow fades, / To view the Country's golden grain! / To view the gleaming Village Spire / 'Midst distant groves unknown to me' (74–8). In Coleridge's conversation poems the perspective usually expands from the particular to the general as the speaker resolves his emotional crises. This is the case in 'Frost at Midnight' and at the end of 'This Lime-Tree Bower My Prison' when the speaker is consoled by the general power of nature to 'keep the heart / Awake to Love and Beauty' (63–4). In 'A Visit to Whittlebury Forest' the perspective narrows from the general moral association between the heart of the forest and domestic peace, to the particular people living out their lives within local villages. They are represented by the church; one of the focal points of community life, and the ripening corn, soon to be gathered in the harvest; the most celebrated example of co-operative rural labour. The knowledge that community life still exists is some consolation, but the local village communities are 'unknown' to the poet, and he remains cut off from the labouring poor by his new status despite the symbolic union achieved with his rendition of 'The Nut-Brown Maid'.

Towards the end of the poem, the fleeting nature of this reconnection through song becomes apparent, and the tone grows plaintive as the speaker is denied access to the lives of the poor as represented by myth and fable: 'Where was the Elfin train, that play / Round *Wake's* huge Oak ... / Why were they not revealed to me!'(80–4). Bloomfield's attempt to develop a poetic rooted in labouring-class community life was dependent upon his ability to access the cultural heritage of the rural labouring poor. It was not enough to possess knowledge or physical records like the antiquary and ballad collector, it was necessary to know the meaning of legends as part of a shared living culture, and to comprehend their spiritual significance for the poor. The labouring poor understood the landscape, and found meaning in lives of great hardship, through the tales that were passed from generation to generation. The diminution in understanding implied in these lines would therefore have profound significance for Bloomfield, both in terms of his struggle to re-establish his own identity, and his apparent desire to write poetry that enabled the reader to better understand the poor.

In some respects, 'A Visit to Whittlebury Forest' corresponds with Abram's model for the Romantic lyric. During his meditation various features in the landscape provoke processes of 'memory, thought, anticipation and feeling', in the course of which the speaker is clearly endeavouring to resolve an unspecified emotional problem. As is often the case in this type of poem, for example Coleridge's 'Frost at Midnight' and Wordsworth's 'Tintern Abbey', 'A Visit to Whittlebury Forrest' ends with a private prayer: 'Genius of the Forest Shades, / Lend thy power, and lend thine ear; / Let dreams still lengthen thy long glades, / And bring thy peace and silence here' (95–8). His meditation is primarily introspective, but he addresses a public audience in those passages which articulate England's national spirit as represented and shaped by the rural spirit that dwells in Whittlebury Forest. This spirit is spread symbolically through the arteries and veins of England's rivers in the penultimate stanza of the poem. Refreshed by a sleep within the realm of the forest 'Genius', Bloomfield traces the origin of some of these rivers to its domain: 'I trac'd the births of various streams. / From beds of Clay, here creeping rills / Unseen to parent *Ouse* would steal; / Or, gushing from the northward Hills, / Would glitter through *Toves*' winding dale' (85–90). In this respect, and although Hartman's remarks are specifically directed at Wordsworth's poetry, 'A Visit to Whittlebury Forest' is 'a meditation on English landscape as alma mater – where landscape is storied England, its legends, history, and rural-reflective spirit' (Hartman, 319).

There is a tension between both of these impulses; the introspective and that which invokes the English national spirit, and Bloomfield's personal struggle to reconcile his position as a member of the labouring class with his new-found status as a poet. The speaker's meditation does not engage with the lives of the labouring poor as they are represented in the physical landscape. Even his survey of the rural communities that exist within the locality of the forest is conducted from an elevated perspective; 'from the heights of thy [the Genius's] domain' (74). But then Bloomfield did not have any links with the landscape of Whittlebury Forest which related to his experience as a farm-worker or a shoemaker. The sense of dislocation that pervades the poem is not only a consequence of the fact that Bloomfield was a leisured visitor, a guest of the Duke of Grafton. It also results from the speaker's attempt to derive both identity and consolation from interaction with a personified abstraction. Bloomfield's 'Genius of the forest shades' has something in common with Wordsworth's 'sense sublime' in 'Tintern Abbey' (96) or Coleridge's 'eternal language' in 'Frost at Midnight' (60). But Bloomfield's ability to remain both a 'brother bard *and* [a] fellow labourer' (MS Eng. 2245, fol. 186), as John Clare called him in a letter written in July 1820, depended upon his ability to maintain a relationship with the physical landscape.

The location of the speaker's meditation in 'Shooter's Hill' (first published in *Wild Flowers*) has direct associations with labouring-class culture. At the beginning of the nineteenth century, Shooter's Hill was a common destination for day trips amongst artisans and labourers in London. The landscape in the vicinity of Shooter's Hill also incorporated an area of ancient common land, which, along with the kind of customary usages that were associated with it, had deep-rooted cultural associations for Bloomfield in particular and the labouring poor in general (Everitt, 211–12). The poem represents a development in Bloomfield's response to the lyric mode too, in that it engages with some of the representational tensions in 'A Visit to Whittlebury Forest'. Nature and the landscape are confronted as physical phenomena, rather than as a key to emotional and psychological transcendence.

'Shooter's Hill' begins with the invocation 'HEALTH! I seek thee' (1) and the link between physical well-being and the physical environment is a dominant theme in the poem. This is not surprising given that during the years immediately after the publication of *Rural Tales* illness and death affected Bloomfield's family many times. His mother died in 1804 and the family correspondence is full of references to failing health. The family's major, but by no means only, concern was Charles's (Bloomfield's son) knee, which failed to respond to all of their endeavours to affect a cure. At the end of 1804 he was taken to Worthing by Bloomfield's wife Mary, whose own health was not good, in the hope that sea air might have a beneficial effect. The letters also reveal acute uncertainty over the question of whether they should continue to discharge a build-up of fluid on the knee through an open wound. In a letter to his wife, written on 28 May 1805, Bloomfield remarks: 'I almost now advise to continue the discharge though my heart aches at the thought of your trouble and the Boy's pain' (Add. MS 28 268, fol. 174). The letters written over the following two weeks illustrate the way that health matters dominated their lives. In his next letter written on 3 June the poet informs his wife that his own health 'was much worse than [he] ... thought it prudent to tell [her] ... when [he] ... wrote last' (Add. MS 28 268, fol. 176). Eleven days later he writes of his two youngest daughters: 'Mary has still a very precarious state of health, with frequent headaches ... . Charlotte's persistent cough troubles her in the night sometimes' (Add. MS 28 268, fol. 180).

Both Bloomfield's physical and his mental health were made worse by other material concerns. He was beset by financial difficulties due to the fact that he did not have a regular income, and his problems were aggravated by his desire to provide as much support as he could for his extended family. An attempt to provide the financial security which the poet desired had failed when he resigned from the position within the Seal Office that the Duke of Grafton had found for him. On 27 May 1803, shortly before he resigned, he wrote to George Bloomfield that another four months in the position would 'drive ... [him] mad' (Add. MS 28 268, fol. 126). Like John Clare, Bloomfield also complained to correspondents about the notoriety that accompanied his success: 'Extreme publicity begins to be more and more disgusting to my feelings'(30). Later, in a letter to Isaac Bloomfield dated 16 July 1807, he remarked that he was beset by 'the unseasonable and impudand visits of the vain, and the interested, and the curious, taking up my time, inviting me to Dinner', and linked these intrusions to his 'suffering in mind, and consequently in body' (Add. MS 28 268, fol. 230). As a result of these conflicting demands upon his emotions and time, the days upon which he could escape into the countryside might well have represented a period of 'stolen liberty' (24).

The speaker in 'A Visit to Whittlebury Forest' seeks to penetrate the deepest recesses of the forest, but physical features of the landscape are, as in Coleridge's conversation poems, always the key to an abstraction. In 'Shooter's Hill' the material of nature is sought for its own sake, for its health-giving power. Bloomfield clearly believed that physical well-being could be found in nature's secret sensuous places. He seeks health where 'with all his might, / The joyous bird his rapture tells, / Amidst the half-excluded light, / That gilds the fox-glove's pendant bells' (9–12), and later proceeds to 'nestle in the honied leaves' (23). This is both a performative and a symbolic expression of desire to access the tangible healing power present in nature. Amongst the labouring poor there was an enduring popular belief in natural herbal remedies, knowledge of which was passed down through the generations by word of mouth. The lines are also suggestive of natural holism, an approach to health which was popular towards the end of the eighteenth century, and was disseminated in advice and self-help books written by figures such as the Behmenist James Graham. Ginnie Smith argues that medical advice books reached an audience that included all but the very poorest, but this is debatable because little evidence is available. There was, however, an interaction between oral and literate culture in the dissemination of the ideas and information that medical advice books contained, because many confirmed and consolidated pre-existing oral culture (Smith 1985, 269). In *A Short Treatise on the All-cleansing, – all-healing, – and all-invigorating Qualities of the Simple Earth* (1790) Graham recommends 'bathing in naturally good and well situated Earth' (18). This regimen is in some respects echoed by Bloomfield's apparent desire to be physically immersed in the stuff of nature.

Bloomfield's search for health not only involves a physical response to nature, it also depends upon a particular way of seeing the landscape that accounts for detail and what it signifies. 'Shooter's Hill' reworks the eighteenth-century prospect poem which responded to landscape in a way that obscured detail. This was partly a consequence of early eighteenth-century demands that, in its representations of rural life, pastoral should 'let the Tranquility of that life appear full and plain, but hide the Meanness of it' (*Guardian*, no. 22, 6 April 1713). The prospect from a hilltop incorporates more of the countryside, but at the same time avoids uncomfortable glimpses of the hardship suffered by the rural poor. In *Grongar Hill* (1726) by John Dyer, there are numerous descriptive passages which offer such a detail-free vision of rural England: 'Ever charming, ever new, / When will the Landskip tire the View! / The Fountain's Fall, the River's Flow, / The woody Vallies, warm and low: / ... / The Town and Village, Dome and Farm' (103–11). In the introduction to his edition of Dyer's poems John Goodridge suggests that *Grongar Hill* offers a 'hilltop survey of the landscape' (xi). In fact Dyer occasionally pauses in his circular sweep of the countryside to focus upon particular detail. But when he does so, the speaker's observations generally give way to abstract and sententious moralization. Thomson rarely represents the detail of the landscape in *The Seasons*, and when he does so he simply lists general categories of landscape features: 'Heavens! What a goodly prospect spreads around, / Of hills, and dales, and woods, and lawns, and spires, / ... / Happy Britannia! Where the Queen of Arts, / ... / ... scatters plenty with unsparing hand.'(II: 1438–45) Ann Yearsley's 'Clifton Hill' disrupts the comfortable masculine prospect (Landry 1990, 130–33). But it does so in a way that likewise fails to take account of significant detail because it generates 'fragmentary female perspectives' without reference to the landscape itself (Landry 1990, 131).

The title 'Shooter's Hill' suggests that what follows will be a conventional prospect poem, but the speaker does not view the countryside only from an elevated perspective. Although the poem does contain descriptions of the view from an elevated point in the landscape, as in *Grongar Hill* they are usually juxtaposed by a representation of the kind of detail that such a panorama obscures. In stanza four the poet's eye ranges from the distant horizon to the traces of human lives found on gravestones: 'I start, with strength and hope renew'd, / And cherish life's rekindling fire. / Now measure vales with straining eyes, / Now trace the church-yard's humble names' (27–30). In the following stanza he concentrates on more of the details that would be hidden within an elevated prospect: 'I love to mark the flow'ret's eye, / To rest where pebbles form my bed, / Where shapes and colours scatter'd lie, / In varying millions round my head' (33–6). Then in stanza six the perspective becomes more general again, and is demarcated as being from an elevated location as the speaker's eye scans 'the smiling dales below' (42).

'Shooter's Hill' is different from the typical prospect poem (including *Grongar Hill*) because, although the speaker responds imaginatively to what he sees, he does not do so in such a way that his meditation ceases to be grounded in the people and things that exist in the landscape. In stanza five, in lines that echo Gray's *Elegy Written in a Country Churchyard* (1751), he imagines what is hidden by the impression of prosperity that a distant prospect can often generate. He discovers that plenty is not in fact scattered 'with unsparing hand'. Imagination and reason tell the speaker that lost and silenced within the landscape there will be: 'Gigantic talents, Heav'n's pure light, / And all the rays of genius [will] glow / In some lone soul, whom no one sees / With *power* and *will* to say "Arise," / Or chase away the slow disease, / And want's foul picture from his eyes' (43–8). In the countryside that the speaker sees, figures like the poet's young alter-ego in *The Farmer's Boy* are oppressed by poverty, and talent is wasted in this 'Happy Britannia'. In the context of late eighteenth-century beliefs about the power of natural genius, it is the purest and most uncorrupted talent that is ground down by the 'slow disease' of poverty. A few individuals, like Bloomfield himself, are given an opportunity to realize their potential by a patron with the '*power* and *will*' to help them, but most spend their lives in obscurity.

The account of the wasted talent in the region of 'Shooter's Hill reflects ironically upon the later description of the area as being one made up of 'smiling dales' (42). For many male eighteenth-century poets, the landscape reflected just this kind of complacent image of the British nation. For Romantic poets, nature as a general phenomenon reflects, or is implicated in fashioning the inner world of the observer. A number of critics have noted that through the eighteenth century and into the Romantic period, the ability to properly view a prospect was regarded as dependent upon the ability to see relationships between objects. It was considered necessary to be capable of abstract thought; an ability which women and the labouring poor were not thought to possess (Labbe, 1–35). It is necessary to investigate the ideological implications of dominant ways of seeing the landscape, but just as important to look for different ways of responding to it. For the rural labouring poor, the land was there to be worked, as it was for those interested in the practicalities of farming like William Cobbett or Arthur Young, but the poor also responded imaginatively to the landscape. The physical details of the land on which they lived and worked, had a direct impact upon the way they saw themselves both as individuals and collectively. Things which were not important to others were important to them, and Bloomfield was the first English poet to articulate their view of the landscape.

Those passages in which the speaker is attracted away from the actual landscape of Shooter's Hill draw attention to the potential danger of an insufficiently grounded imagination. In stanza ten the narrator remarks: 'Of Cambrian mountains still I dream, / And mouldering vestiges of war; / By time-worn cliff or classic stream / Would rove, — but prudence holds a bar' (73–6). It is not clear whether he means that it would be imprudent to visit Welsh mountains, or whether it is dream visions of this kind that he should avoid. But in the following lines, the speaker's health is explicitly linked to an ability to keep both sight and intellect focused on the countryside before him, and avoid imaginative flights of 'fancy': 'Come then, O Health! I'll strive to bound / My wishes to this airy stand; / Tis not for me to trace around / The wonders of my native land' (77–80). This is a critique of the kind of abstract associative thought process that occurs repeatedly in the poetry of Wordsworth and Coleridge, and in Bloomfield's 'A Visit to Whittlebury Forest'. Immediately after voicing his statement of intent, however, the tone of which is more resigned than enthusiastic, the speaker again acknowledges the power of fancy even as it clearly unsettles his mind: 'Yet Grampian hills shall Fancy give, / And, towering in her giddy seat, / Amidst her own creation live' (82–4). The poet in Bloomfield is drawn to imaginative fancy, but if he is to speak of the countryside as it is seen by the labouring poor and remain in contact with his origins, he must avoid this kind of response to the landscape.

It is significant that Bloomfield expresses solidarity with a particular type of poet: 'I would not that such turrets rise / To point out where my bones are laid; / Save that some wandering bard might prize / The comfort of its broad cool shade' (93–6). The bardic traditions of the Celtic cultures were increasingly appropriated by writers and painters during the late eighteenth century because they spoke of a society in which the creative and imaginative life held a position of some primacy (Smiles, 49). The ancient bards of pre-Norman Wales, like their Irish counterparts, were bound up within the elaborate social system of the Gaelic aristocracy. They would have been attached to a particular figure within a particular court, and could not survive without the patronage derived from this connection. In the Irish courts the relationship between king or lord and bard was so close that they would often share the same bed. Much of their poetry would have been written in order to serve the ends of their patron, eulogizing him or denigrating his enemies. When they were moved to write personal lyrics, they were often driven to do so by a grudge against their patron arising out of his failure to look after them properly, or to follow the code which regulated the relationship between prince and bard (Chadwick, 121). Bloomfield's apparent rejection of worldly vanity is apparently therefore an invocation of a world in which the poet had a social status eclipsed only by those who held positions of the highest rank, and which cherished and promoted the bard as the means of celebrating and perpetuating its own virtues. Bloomfield's casual expression of solidarity with his fellow poets is complicated by the fact that the figure is described as a 'wandering bard' because the bard of Celtic culture did not travel from place to place. It is therefore more likely that he was thinking of minstrels who would have wandered the countryside plying their trade. Thomas Percy had visualized the ancient English minstrels – whom he believed were responsible for the older poems within his *Reliques of Ancient English Poetry* (1765) – performing poems, which they held in their memories, at the seats of great aristocratic families. As Nick Groom remarks, this act of cultural engineering was driven by a desire to create a 'Gothic tradition' (Groom, 103). It was a vision that influenced many during the second half of the eighteenth century, but was justly criticized by, amongst others, Joseph Ritson who, in *Ancient English Metrical Romances* (1802), correctly argued that the minstrel was an altogether different kind of figure (I: 58).

In the past the word 'minstrel' had been a general designation for 'any one whose profession was to entertain his patrons with singing, music, and story-telling, or with buffoonery or juggling' (*OED*). Itinerant performers of ballads and songs had existed and might have been referred to as minstrels, but they would have been of humble stock. Bloomfield may have wished to register a fellow feeling with such figures. They shared the day-to-day lives, and perhaps more importantly the talk of the poor, and, as wanderers through the countryside, they would also have known the landscape like the labouring poor. In tales and songs that drew upon the material and imaginative lives of the rural labouring poor, wandering minstrels helped them to make sense of their existence. Bloomfield's search for reconciliation between his poetic vocation and his status as a labouring man appears to reach its apotheosis in the life of the minstrel. So it is strange that in the closing lines of 'Shooter's Hill' the speaker should apparently reject 'the moral songster's meed, / An earthly immortality' (99–100) and turn again to the kind of prayer that typically concludes the prospect poem: 'O let me, from the past / Remembering what to man is given, / Lay virtue's broad foundations fast, / Whose glorious turrets reach to Heav'n' (101–104).

In most other respects 'Shooter's Hill' reworks the prospect poem and there is not necessarily a contradiction between poetry and virtue. Indeed, Bloomfield had suggested elsewhere that in his own work the two were linked. In the preface to *Rural Tales* he had remarked: 'I feel peculiarly gratified that a poor man in England may assert the dignity of Virtue, and speak of the imperishable beauties of Nature, and be heard, and heard, perhaps, with greater attention for his being poor' (iv). Perhaps it is a kind of vanity to wish for what could not be; although he was occasionally able to 'steal' a moment of 'liberty' as on the day of his visit to Shooter's Hill (24), Bloomfield was not in general free to explore the countryside in this way. More importantly, as a leisured wanderer through the landscape, the speaker in 'Shooter's Hill' resembles the kind of Wordsworthian figure that he explicitly distances himself from in *The Farmer's Boy*. The first chapter of this study explores the way in which Bloomfield's sense of self-worth, and his poetic vocation were rooted in his status as a farmer's boy and then as a London shoemaker. 'Shooter's Hill' does not finally work through the feeling of dislocation that afflicts the speaker in 'A Visit to Whittlebury Forest' because Bloomfield's poetry was produced in very different circumstances from those described in the poem.

The ability of a labouring-class poet to write was affected to a much greater extent by the material circumstances of their life than was generally the case in respect of more fortunately positioned writers. Labouring-class poets often had to combine a physically demanding and poorly paid manual occupation with their vocation for poetry. Apparently Coleridge 'liked to compose in walking over uneven ground, or breaking through the straggling branches of a copse wood; whereas Wordsworth always wrote (if he could) walking up and down a straight gravel walk' (Hazlitt XVII: 119). But Bloomfield's poetry did not generally take shape in such an outdoor setting, and he often had to work on it whilst making shoes in the confined and noisy space that he shared with a number of other shoemakers. Wordsworth's famous definition of poetry in his 'Preface' to *Lyrical Ballads* (1800) as taking 'its origin from emotion recollected in tranquility' can hardly be said to apply to Bloomfield's poetry (266). 'To My Old Oak Table' is an account of Bloomfield's endeavour to prevent the creativity and artistic inspiration inside him from being drained by very basic cares. It is about Bloomfield's physical struggle to write poetry, and then retain control of his work within the literary marketplace. For this reason it is Bloomfield's most important lyric, and one of the key poems by any labouring-class poet. It is also central to any study of Bloomfield because in it he writes about the period immediately before May 1796 when he began to work on *The Farmer's Boy*.

'To My Old Oak Table' is a creative autobiography, like *The Prelude*, Coleridge's 'Dejection: An Ode' (1802) or 'Epipsychidion' (1821) which Shelley later described as 'an idealized history of ... [his] life and feelings' (*Letters* II: 434). But when Wordsworth and Coleridge write about the loss of their ability to produce poetry, their creative powers are generally restricted by a kind of emotional or intellectual 'writer's block'. *The Prelude* has been described as a poem about the growth of a poet's mind, and more recently, by Clifford Siskin, as an 'ongoing struggle for self-improvement' (Siskin, 117). In Book XI, Wordsworth links a temporary pause in his development to a flirtation with 'idolatry' (75) in the form of the picturesque movement, and the associated 'tyranny' (179) of the eye in his response to nature. In his 'Letter to Sara Hutchinson', written in April 1802 but not published during the poet's lifetime, Coleridge attributes the decline of his creative powers to the complexity of his love life. In 'Dejection: An Ode', the published version of 'Letter to Sara Hutchinson', the same problem is couched in quasi-philosophical terms. Most of the references to his personal life are removed, and, as in *The Prelude*, the failure of the speaker's 'shaping spirit of imagination' (86) is linked to his inability to relate properly to nature: 'those thin clouds above, ... / ... / Those stars, that glide behind them or between, / ... / Yon crescent moon, ... / I see them all so excellently fair, / I see, not feel how beautiful they are' (31–8).

It was quite courageous of a poet in Bloomfield's situation to write even a short poem like 'To My Old Oak Table' in such an explicitly autobiographical mode. In a letter to Capel Lofft, he confessed that he was sensitive about the fact that as a labouring-class poet he was seen as something of a novelty: 'I feel my situation to be novel; the world looks at me in that light; I am extremely anxious on that account' (12). This very personal poem can only have increased his readers' awareness of the fact that he was a particular kind of poet, very different from figures like Wordsworth and Coleridge. It is the only one of Bloomfield's published poems in which the reader gets an insight into the hardships associated with his trade:

> I shared thy sympathy, Old Heart of Oak!
> For surely when my labour ceas'd at night,
> With trembling, feverish hands, and aching sight,
> The draught that cheer'd me and subdu'd my care,
> On thy broad shoulders thou wert proud to bear.
> Oe'r thee, with expectation's fire elate,
> I've sat and ponder'd on my future fate:
> On thee, with winter muffins for thy store,
> I've lean'd, and quite forgot that I was poor. [6–14]

It is not difficult to see how Bloomfield might have struggled to compose and write verse at the end of the day, let alone whilst working at his cobbler's bench. We often look back on cobbling as a sedentary trade, but in Bloomfield's time everything had to be done manually, and after a day's labour a shoemaker might well have had very tired forearms and hands. Bloomfield also worked in a poorly lit garret, possibly having only very small windows or a skylight, and this would have had an effect upon his sight as he strained to see small details. But the poem also recalls the small pleasures which he associated with the table's support; the table was 'proud to bear' 'the draught that cheer'd' him and helped him cope with hardship.

Bloomfield is better able to explore the implications of the fact that he is a 'labouring-class' poet by directing his meditation into an apparently unrelated channel of thought. He imagines a lack of pedigree for the table, but at the same time appears to associate its origins with his own: 'Where dropp'd the acorn that gave birth to thee? / Can'st thou trace back thy line of ancestry? / We're match'd, old friend, and let us not repine, / Darkness o'erhangs thy origin and mine' (15–18). It may be tempting to read into these lines some self-consciousness about his ancestry. In *Views in Suffolk, Norfolk and Northamptonshire; Illustrative of the Works of Robert Bloomfield* (1806), published in the same year as *Wild Flowers*, E.W. Brayley remarks that 'From the little that can at present be ascertained of the family of Bloomfield, it appears that the great-grandfather of the Poet, both on the male and on the female side, is the most distant ancestor whose relationship can *regularly* be traced' (20). Brayley goes on to suggest a possible connection between Bloomfield and William Blomefield, a sixteenth-century author of at least two tracts on the subject of 'occult sciences'. In the end he concludes that 'the author of the Farmer's Boy requires no adventitious lustre to be reflected upon his name from a connection with literary ancestors', and suggests that Bloomfield 'is convinced that individual worth must arise from individual merit' (25). It is certainly true that Bloomfield did not have much time for artificial distinctions. He believed that honour was derived from merit and that virtue was dependent upon an individual's conduct. Bearing this fact in mind, it is hardly surprising that he suggests the circumstances surrounding birth are of no real consequence, and makes a kind of pact with the table:

'Both [our origins] may be truly honourable: yet, / We'll date our honours from the day we met' (19–20).

It would none the less have been particularly important for a poet like Bloomfield to keep in mind the idea that merit is more important than social class. Largely because of his origin within a subjugated social group he found his dealings with the literary marketplace bewildering, and remarked in a letter to Capel Lofft: 'I do not pretend to know how strong a negative ... my author's prerogative ought to give me' (12). Both Wordsworth and Coleridge received gifts, but neither lost control of their work to a patron or publisher, as was often the case in respect of poets from a labouring-class background. Bloomfield himself was unable to find a publisher for *The Farmer's Boy*, and it was eventually published only after the intervention of Capel Lofft. By the time he began work on 'To My Old Oak Table' he had experienced the way in which 'interest' dominated the literary marketplace in London. He had become embroiled in a bitter dispute between Lofft and his publisher Thomas Hood, a struggle which Bloomfield knew was for effective editorial control of his work. In a letter to his brother, he admitted that he had produced a second fair copy of *The Farmer's Boy* so that 'something in ... [his] own hand may be found hereafter' (17), and subsequently remarked of Lofft and Hood: 'they place me awkwardly in their quarrels: Genious is not wanted to work my extrication, but Jockeyship, constitutional vigour, and impudence' (Add. MS 28 268, fol. 75r).

Despite the considerable interest in 'natural' genius at the turn of the eighteenth century, Bloomfield also had to contend with prejudice against labouring-class writers. As William Hazlitt points out, there was at the time 'such a thing as an aristocracy or privileged order in letters' (VIII: 205). On a number of occasions, particularly after his initial popularity began to wane, Bloomfield himself was reminded of this fact in reviews of his poetry. The *Eclectic Review* praised *The Farmer's Boy*, but also argued that it was marred by 'homeliness of feature, rusticity of accent, and inelegance of manners', and had soon been 'eclipsed' by the work of 'higher born and higher gifted rivals' (7 (1811), 1104). The literary reviews were important cultural forums, and the fact that they approached Bloomfield's poetry with preconceptions about the ability of 'low'-born writers would have influenced their readers. The *Eclectic Review* also criticizes the qualities that distinguish the work of labouring-class poets like Bloomfield and John Clare from that often produced by 'higher born ... rivals'. In a letter to his brother, Bloomfield himself expressed considerable irritation at '*grammarians*, who judge more of points and constructions than of sense and spirit and animation', and remarked of 'Old Kate and Her Children' ['Richard and Kate'], 'if they were to set about labouring them into elegance, I doubt they would rub off their polish, the same polish that you see when you break a flint—its natural colour' (18).

Bloomfield clearly disliked the kind of political manoeuvring or 'jockeyship' that he believed was necessary in order to negotiate the literary scene in London. He found it difficult to be firm or 'impudent' in his dealings with Lofft because he felt gratitude, but also because of a habitual deference that he found difficult to overcome. His association with the oak table linked him to a time when life was simpler: 'When, of my worldly wealth the parent stock, / Right welcome up the Thames from Woolwich Dock / Thou cam'st, when hopes ran high, and love was young' (21–3). In a letter written during October 1801, Bloomfield observed that the people he had to deal with as a published poet were motivated by partisan 'interest', or were competing for 'fame' and 'money' (15). The 'rough' and 'rude' (107) old table evoked very different qualities. Bloomfield saw it as a 'substantial friend, / Whom wealth can never change, nor int'rest bend' (1–2). It is suggestive of these qualities at least in part because it results from the labour of an 'honest' tradesman. It was rooted in a value system that Bloomfield, as a shoemaker, found much easier to comprehend than the literary establishment in London. The table clearly had a symbolic resonance for Bloomfield, and it also anchored his poetic vocation to his life as an artisan shoemaker because he sat at it to make both poetry and shoes.

The way in which the table links the threads of his life performs an important poetic function for Bloomfield because the 'domestic' affairs of a labouring-class poet would have been more likely to impinge upon the creative process. The physical struggle for survival within the single room that Bloomfield shared with his growing family would not have been experienced in such an immediate way by a writer with greater material resources at his disposal. Following the opening passages of 'To My Old Oak Table' that focus upon the 'sympathy' between Bloomfield and the table, there is a forty-six-line embedded poem of family life. It is an account of the Bloomfield family's struggle to overcome repeated and confusing periods of ill-health, and illustrates the kind of precarious situation in which they often found themselves. As with most other hardships of the age, and as is still true today, the poor were usually affected to a greater degree by illness than more fortunate members of society. Within Georgian society: 'pain was ... hierarchically sorted and entirely construed in relation to social class ... [and] the suffering an earl or duke could expect in this life hardly amounted to that of persons of lower ranks' (Rousseau 1993, 96). A poor man and his family might not have had access to medical practitioners or medicine. And in the absence of sick-pay and a welfare state, the illness of those who generated income would have had an immediate affect on the economic stability of a labouring-class family.

In 'To My Old Table' Bloomfield recalls the way that ill-health affected him and his family during the period immediately before he began work on *The Farmer's Boy*: 'Then, midst the threat'nings of a wintry sky, / *That cough* which blights the bud of infancy, / The dread of parents, Rest's inveterate foe, / Came like a plague, and turn'd my songs to woe' (26–30). The illness suffered by the child was probably the croup or whooping cough, the principal symptom of both being a very loud, racking and apparently unstoppable cough that would sound like an 'undulating blast'. Whooping cough had a very high mortality rate, and a fear of tuberculosis would have added to the despair of the parents who could only watch their child's suffering and hope for the best. The child recovered, however, and 'To My Old Oak Table' provides an account of the way in which death 'Withdrew his jav'lin, and unclench'd his hand' (42). The pleasure that the Bloomfields feel at this release is short lived because the poem also reveals that the poet himself became ill soon afterwards: 'The creeping Dropsy, cold as cold could be, / Unnerv'd my arm, and bow'd my head to thee' (49–50). The dropsy or oedema involves a build-up of fluid in the cavities or tissues of the body, and could be a severely debilitating illness. Enid Porter cites a nineteenth-century account of one individual who was so ill 'that he could only just waddle about'. After doctors had failed to help him, he was eventually cured by a dietary regime which was the suggestion of a 'local' woman (Porter, 80). 'To My Old Oak Table' indicates that Bloomfield was worried about his child's health, but the 'anxiety' that precipitated his own illness could also have been caused by financial problems because he struggled to provide for his family throughout his life.

In a footnote to 'Shooter's Hill' Bloomfield notes the connection between illness and creativity: 'Sickness may be often an incentive to poetical composition; I found it so; and I esteem the following lines only because they remind me of past feelings, which I would not willingly forget' (75). Today, art therapy is a growing force in so-called alternative approaches to medicine, but like Bloomfield many believed that there was a link between ill-health and creativity in the eighteenth century too. The medical historian G.S. Rousseau has written about the 'intrinsic value of self expression for the ailing person and its complex relation to healing and curing', but assumes 'educated, talented patients ... who are members of an upper-, or at least a middle-class culture' (96). For the poor, the link between illness and creativity was somewhat different. Richard Greene argues of the labouring-class poet Mary Leapor: 'ultimately her own expectation of an early death caused her to approach her writing with greater urgency than might be expected in a young poet' (186). 'To My Old Oak Table' reveals that Bloomfield's ill-health and that of his family had a negative impact upon his practical capacity to write, but, as in 'Shooter's Hill', it is the 'delight' associated with returning health that provides inspiration.

In 'To My Old Oak Table' Bloomfield seems initially to attribute his recovery to his own resignation in the face of fate, and a determination to overcome: 'Resignation was my dearest friend, / And Reason pointed to a glorious end; / With anxious sighs, a parent's hopes and pride, / I wish'd to live — I trust I could have died!' (59–62) But it soon becomes apparent that the coming of spring is responsible because March brought sunshine with the 'length'ning day', 'And bade my heart arise, that morn and night / Now throbb'd with irresistible delight. / Delightful 'twas to leave disease behind, / And feel the renovation of the mind!' (65–8). Despite the fact that, as a shoemaker, Bloomfield spent most of his time indoors, either working in a crowded garret or within the single room in which he and his family lived, he can still feel the approach of the new spring. Indeed, unlike Wordsworth and Coleridge who periodically complain of an inability to 'feel' the beauty of nature, as an urban labouring-class poet, Bloomfield can only respond in this manner. Particularly before the publication of *The Farmer's Boy*, he was rarely free to wander the countryside. In a sense, and appropriately, the passage echoes the opening lines of *The Farmer's Boy*: 'O Come, blest Spirit! whatsoe'er thou art, / Thou kindling warmth that hovers't round my heart' (1–2). In *The Farmer's Boy* itself though, it is not spring that is the source of this 'kindling warmth'.

The return of health is also attributed to God in 'To My Old Oak Table' within one of the most religiously enthusiastic passages to be found anywhere in Bloomfield's *oeuvre*. The poet and his family are fixated at 'the centre of the chequer'd floor' of St Paul's, beneath the dome 'that lifts its flaming cross above the cloud', as the 'pealing organ' reverberates around the building (75–9). Although the encounter prompts him to 'worship God', Bloomfield is physically revived too: 'The strong sensation boiling through my blood, / Rose in a storm of joy, allied to pain' (80–81). Spiritual enlightenment can manifest itself in this way, but the sensation that Bloomfield seems to experience is not unlike that caused by the approach of spring. None the less, coming as it does immediately before his account of the genesis of *The Farmer's Boy*, the passage mystifies the origin of that poem. It suggests that *The Farmer's Boy* might be God's reward for the poet's faith because he feels 'amidst the fervor of ... [his] praise, / The sweet assurances of better days' (83–4).

Irrespective of the true cause of his recovery, the old table is implicated in the process of creation in 'To My Old Oak Table'. Both symbolically and in a sense physically, it links the various aspects of his life in space and time:

> In that gay season, honest friend of mine,
> I marked the brilliant sun upon thee shine;
> Imagination took her flights so free,
> *Home* was delicious with my book and thee,
> The purchas'd nosegay, or brown ears of corn,
> Were thy gay plumes upon a summer's morn,
> Awakening memory, that disdains control,
> They spoke the darling language of my soul:
> They whisper'd tales of joy, of peace, of truth,
> And conjur'd back the sunshine of my youth:
> Fancy presided at the joyful birth,
> I pour'd the torrent of my feelings forth;
> Conscious of the *truth* in Nature's humble track,
> And wrote "The Farmer's Boy" upon thy back! [85–98]

The table transports the new spring into the confined space in which Bloomfield is forced to spend most of his life as a shoemaker. In fact it represents the season in a way that spring itself might not have done had the poet been standing outside, able to view the conurbation of London. The spring sunshine that has such an impact upon Bloomfield is reflected by the surface of the table. The table also brings about a transport of memory that 'conjur[s] ... back the sunshine of [his] ... youth'. The 'purchas'd nosegay', and particularly the 'brown ears of corn' are evocative of the agricultural landscape of east Suffolk, and enable Bloomfield to make an imaginative connection with the springs of his boyhood on Mr Austin's farm. The table acts as a kind of poetic facilitator in a way that might have been even more important to Bloomfield in the years after the publication of *The Farmer's Boy*.

The opening passages of 'To My Old Oak Table' labour over the association between Bloomfield and the table in order to demonstrate that his poetry originates in a particular way of life. He is able to write the kind of poetry that he does precisely because, like the 'rough' and 'rude' table, he lacks the elegance and social finesse that might have enabled him to develop an easier relationship with the literary marketplace. The imaginative association that Bloomfield makes between the course of his own life and the table helps him to remain in contact with his origins, even when as a published poet he is being courted by figures like the Duke of Grafton: 'The sight of thy old frame, so rough, so rude, / Shall twitch the sleeve of nodding Gratitude; / Shall teach me but to venerate the more / Honest Oak Tables and their guests — the poor; / Teach me unjust distinctions to deride, / And falsehoods gender'd in the brain of Pride' (107–12). The poor have always been blamed for their inability to overcome difficulties that would crush many of those situated in circumstances of plenty, and this was especially true at the time that 'To My Old Oak Table' was written. During the early decades of the nineteenth century the previously generous parochial 'relief' for those living at the margins became increasingly punitive (Snell, 104–37). The Poor Law Amendment Act (1834) finally discontinued outdoor relief for the 'able bodied poor' who were thereafter incarcerated in the workhouses 'that loomed large in the … [lives] of the poor in mid-nineteenth-century England' (Thomson 1950, 69–72). The table operates upon the poet's memory in a way that reminds him of his own struggle to overcome poverty and illness. It guards him against the 'littleness of soul' (106) that would make him unable to empathize with the poor, and, crucially, continue to develop a distinctive labouring-class communitarian poetics. For Bloomfield the old oak table was truly a guardian and 'monitor' of his mind and soul, 'Sacred to Truth, to Poetry, and Love' (125–6).

The relationship between speaker and landscape in 'A Visit to Whittlebury Forest' and to some extent 'Shooter's Hill' makes it difficult for Bloomfield to reconcile his poetic vocation and his status as an artisan shoemaker. The speaker in the latter poem responds to what he sees in a way that is very different from other Romantic poets, but he is still a leisured wanderer rather than a worker in the landscape. The leisured 'outdoor' location in which the 'Romantic' lyrics of figures like Wordsworth and Coleridge are typically set is less appropriate for a shoemaker-poet. Although he fails to take account of poems written by figures like Bloomfield, Abrams' definition of the 'Romantic' lyric, indeed the lyric in any period, is correct in so far as such poems are generally driven by the speaker's desire to bring order to his experience. In 'To My Old Oak Table' Bloomfield reconciles the various threads of his life through his response to the table in a way that recalls the widow's address to her hour-glass in his first published lyric poem. He is able to do so because the table has the same kind of personal and cultural associations for him as the hour-glass has for the widow. Bloomfield's relationship with the table is easier than with the landscape in the earlier poems because his poetry is rooted in his life as a working man, and to explore better the implications of this fact he had to come indoors.

CHAPTER FOUR

Betwixt and Between Patrons, Publishers and Readers

Bloomfield remained a client of patronage until the end of his life, but it did not affect the presentation and publication of his work to the same extent after the appearance of *Wild Flowers* in 1806. Chapter Four therefore interrupts this study of Bloomfield's major poetry in order to give a clearer sense of the way his negotiations with various patrons impacted upon his career. Bloomfield repeatedly engages with the question of patronage in poetry and prose, but his writings reveal a degree of uncertainty both about its value, and how it should work in practical terms. He was willing to accept gifts from patrons; the Duke of Grafton awarded him an annuity of £15 in 1801, and later that year he wrote that if the Duke or some 'kind patron' would find him a position that generated £80 a year, he would soon establish his independence (Add. MS 28 268, fols 55–7). The third Duke of Grafton had held various government positions between 1763 and 1783, and, between September 1767 and December 1769, performed the role of prime minister due to Chatham's ill health (during this period the ministry was known by his name). Although he disagreed with the ministry over their policy in the American colonies, in general he was a loyal supporter of the government. Like Capel Lofft he was a Unitarian, but he would not have shared many of Lofft's more radical views.

In the preface to *Rural Tales* Bloomfield acknowledges his debt to the Duke, 'all his immediate and unknown friends', and his 'first great friend' Capel Lofft, of whom he remarks 'his private life is a lesson in morality; his manners gentle, his heart sincere' (v). But there are indications elsewhere in the volume that he was not entirely comfortable with this kind of dedicatory flattery. When the poetry engages indirectly with the question of patronage, it does so in a manner which suggests that Bloomfield did not think displays of deference and gratitude should be necessary. He never made any reference to particular patrons in his poetry, unlike so many labouring-class poets before him. But at the same time he endeavoured to maintain relationships with patrons; Capel Lofft, the Duke of Grafton and Edward Jenner being the three most important. Bloomfield continued to juggle his apparent, and in a sense contradictory, commitment to both patronage and artistic independence until the end of his life. *May Day* clouds the issue of whether labouring-class writers are best served by the survival of traditional patronage, or by the continued development of the literary marketplace, to which they would ideally have independent access.

Bloomfield's confusion is perhaps simply a reflection of the changing dynamics of literary production at the end of the eighteenth century. Most critics agree that patronage became less important, but there is not so much consensus regarding the nature and extent of this change. In a recent study, Linda Zionkowski argues that between the middle of the seventeenth century, and the end of the eighteenth a change took place in the way writers and writing were conceptualized. At the beginning of this period members of the aristocracy and the gentry believed that 'making a career out of poetry' and 'the widespread display ... allowed by the commercial press' threatened masculine identity (Zionkowski 2001, 9). Pope had to respond to criticism regarding the emasculation involved in his status as a 'professional' poet who endeavoured to please his reading audience. His enemies often derided him as 'the Ladies Play-Thing' and charged him with 'effeminacy for the sweetness or smoothness of his verse, his fragile body, and his appeal to women readers' (Thomas, 13; Zionkowski 2001, 99). Later in the eighteenth century this essentially Renaissance-based conception of masculinity and authorship was challenged. Zionkowski argues that Johnson's *Lives of the Poets* (1781) consolidated a tendency to view the intellectual labour involved in professional authorship as a marker of masculinity: 'Johnson's dismissive treatment of aristocratic poets and his omission of women poets ... strengthened a cultural practice that was not, at the time inevitable – the practice of defining poetry as the exclusive province of male writers engaged in commercial literary production.' (2001, 172) For Johnson, the experience of Richard Savage demonstrated that reliance upon patronage obstructed a poet's ability to function properly within the new literary marketplace: Savage's 'participation in two opposing systems of value leads to his failure in each' (Zionkowski 2001, 186).

Zionkowski's account of the way gender is implicated in different constructions of the 'author' during the eighteenth century is convincing. Her conclusions regarding patronage are less so because her examples are selected to demonstrate that 'by 1750, living upon the profits of their commodified intellectual labour was a definitive feature of professional authorship for men. [and that] Women, by contrast, were relegated to the residual economy of non-commercial literary production' (2001, 200). Dustin Griffin's reading of Johnson's *Lives of the Poets* is more nuanced: 'Thomson's story (like Fenton's) happens to be a story of success [and] ... their stories need to be set against those better-known stories of Savage and Dryden in order for us to arrive at Johnson's assessment of patronage as a whole' (1996, 226). In Griffin's account, Johnson does not condemn patronage as destructive or outdated; he merely warns 'against ... its perversions and its "particular dangers"' (1996, 222). Griffin also points out that many male writers still relied on literary patronage at the end of the eighteenth century: 'Few writers were more cosseted than Cowper in the rural refuge provided for him by Mrs Unwin ... [and] through the efforts of William Hayley, a pension of £300 a year was granted to ... [him] in 1794' (1996, 261). George Crabbe also relied heavily upon patronage; his most important patron being Edmund Burke who 'provided several of the traditional benefits, including extended hospitality at Beaconsfield and introductions to booksellers (Dodsley) and minister (Thurlow)' (Griffin 1996, 222). As was the case in most spheres of life, women writers did not have the same opportunities as men, but it is not true that as a class they were 'relegated to the residual economy of non-commercial literary production'. There are several examples of semi-independent women writers who achieved commercial success during the second half of the eighteenth century. Charlotte Lennox and Frances Burney relied upon patrons during the early part of their careers, but they were later able to establish themselves as independent writers within the expanding literary marketplace.

The late eighteenth century represents a transitional period in the dynamics of literary production. To be successful, writers had to negotiate with both patrons and increasingly powerful independent publishers. But labouring-class poets present a special case. Throughout the eighteenth and into the nineteenth century, they were unable to publish their work without the active and often self-interested support of patrons (Rizzo, 144–62). William Christmas shows that during the second half of the eighteenth century the patronage offered to labouring-class writers was also qualitatively different: 'Subscribers [to the works of poets like William Brimble, John Bennet, John Lucas and John Frederick Bryant] were, in effect, giving alms in exchange for a volume of poetical effusions' (2001, 212). Even on the small number of occasions when such poets were able to free themselves from the controlling influence of patrons, the question of patronage continued to dominate their literary output. Ann Yearsley and James Woodhouse are the most well-known examples of labouring-class poets who published independently. But in *Norbury Park* (1804) and *Crispinus Scriblerus* (1814), written between ten and twenty years after he parted company with Elizabeth Montagu, Woodhouse is still exercised by her poor treatment of him. *Poems on Various Subjects* (1787) might in some respects represent Ann Yearsley's 'mark of cultural independence' (Ferguson, 15). But as Christmas notes: 'Although there are no overt references to "Stella" in this volume [containing new poetry written after her quarrel with More], More hovers everywhere over it' (2001, 251). *The Rural Lyre* (1896) is not so dominated by the poet's relationship with More. But as Mary Waldron suggests, poems like 'Address to Friendship' and 'Paroxysm of the Moment' do connect the volume with 'the bitterness of the 1780s' (242). In fact an exegetic footnote to the former poem makes an explicit comment upon More's patronage.

The case of Robert Bloomfield can be said to represent an important shift in the way labouring-class poets negotiated with patronage. Ann Yearsley's dispute with Hannah More concerned the latter's attempt to control the earnings generated by *Poems on Several Occasions* (1785). Notwithstanding Christmas's argument that 'artistic autonomy, and control of public representation' were at stake in Yearsley's quarrel with More (2001, 237–55), it was as Donna Landry points out an argument about 'a business arrangement' (1990, 155). It became acrimonious because both parties felt that the other was questioning their honesty and honour. Yearsley suspected that More believed she was not a fit mother for her children and would not be able to manage the income from the sale of her poetry. More felt she was being accused of bad management and self-interest (Landry, 1990, 153; Waldron, 67). Bloomfield's dispute with Capel

Lofft might not be so interesting in terms of the animosity that it generated, but it is as, if not more, important in poetical terms. It seems that Yearsley was not overly concerned that her work would be read within the frame of her relationship with More because it continued to dominate her poetry after their quarrel. Bloomfield scrupulously avoided any explicit reference to literary patronage or patrons in his poetry. He quarrelled with Lofft because of the impact that he believed Lofft's editorial material was having on the reception of his poetry. In other words, Bloomfield was concerned to assert his artistic independence, whereas Yearsley was primarily concerned to achieve financial independence from her patrons. Just as Johnson believed that "indecent or promiscuous" dedication degraded literature, Bloomfield came to believe that both his poetry and his reputation were being degraded by Lofft's preface and notes.

Before examining some of the reasons for Bloomfield's concerns, it is necessary to provide an account of Capel Lofft. He now has marginal status in narratives of literary history, but at the time that he received the manuscript of *The Farmer's Boy* he was a figure of some renown. He was born in London on 14 November 1751, and was educated at Eton and Peterhouse, Cambridge. He left university in 1770 without graduating, became a member of Lincoln's Inn, and was called to the bar in 1775. When his uncle died in 1781 he inherited the family estates at Troston and Stanton near Bury St Edmunds. His political orientation was Whig, he took part in the agitation against the slave trade and the American war, and was also a strong supporter of parliamentary reform. He was a member of the Revolution Society, an honorary member of the Anti-Slavery Society in Philadelphia, and founder member, with Major Cartwright, Christopher Wyvill, John Horne Tooke and Tom Paine among others, of the Society for Constitutional Information. His support for such causes was not restricted to the membership of organizations, and on a number of occasions he spoke at radical county meetings at Stowmarket.

Lofft knew Samuel Johnson, and in his *Life of Johnson* (1791) Boswell gives an account of a dinner at which the two men were present:

> On Monday ... I dined with him [Johnson] at Mr Dilly's, and Mr Capel Lofft, who, though a most zealous Whig, has a mind so full of learning and knowledge, and so much exercised in various departments, and withall so much liberality, that the stupendous powers of the literary Goliath, though they did not frighten this little David of the popular spirit, could not but excite his admiration. [278]

Boswell's description suggests that Lofft was held in grudging admiration by those with more power and influence, and confirms that he was known as a defender of the weak and the poor. He had wide-ranging interests as is demonstrated by the number and diversity of his correspondents. During his lifetime, he engaged in correspondence with political figures including Charles James Fox and Thomas Green; the abolitionists Granville Sharpe, Thomas Clarkson and William Wilberforce; Unitarians such as John Jebb, Richard Price and Joseph Priestley, and literary figures such as William Godwin, William Hazlitt, William Roscoe and Henry Crabb Robinson.

Lofft had a reputation as a minor literary figure himself, and by 1798 had already published several volumes of poetry in his own name including *The Praises of Poetry, a Poem* (1775) and the epic *Eudosia, or a Poem on the Universe* (1781). He had also produced an edition of Milton's *Paradise Lost* (1792). His writing was not restricted to poetry, and he published works on various aspects of the law and on political issues that were of concern to him. His publications include *Elements of Universal Law* (1779), *Three Letters on the Question of Regency* (1788), *An Investigation of the Corporation and Test Acts, with an Investigation of their Importance* (1790) and *An Essay on the Effect of a Dissolution of Parliament on an Impeachment by the House of Commons for High Crimes and Misdemeanours* (1791). Many of his works directly and explicitly link Lofft with the radical and reformist causes that were initially reinforced by the events which had occurred in France. In *Remarks on the Letter of Mr Burke to a Member of the National Assembly* (1790), published before Tom Paine's *The Rights of Man* (1791), he defends Rousseau against Burke's criticisms, and argues that the *Reflections on the Revolution in France* (1790) tendentiously foregrounds the positive aspects of the British Parliament and the negative aspects of the French National Assembly. His most explicit declaration of radical sentiments was a one-page fly-leaf detailing the benefits of the revolution in France and entitled *To the FRIENDS of LIBERTY of MANKIND met to commemorate the ANNIVERSARY of the REVOLUTION of FRANCE* (1791).

It seems that Lofft's radical sentiments eventually earned the displeasure of the authorities. In 1800 he attempted to prevent the execution of Sarah Lloyd, a young servant girl from the Bury St Edmunds area, who had been sentenced to death for capital larceny. Sarah Lloyd had been seduced by a man called Joseph Clarke, who, on 3 October 1799, gained entrance to her mistress's house, persuaded her to steal various items, and then set fire to the house in four places. She was caught with stolen items in her possession, but there was no direct evidence against Clarke who had abandoned her after the crime, taking most of the valuable articles with him. Lofft, and a number of other individuals who were active in her cause, including her mistress Sarah Syer, managed to delay the execution and drew up a petition for her pardon that was signed by both the Duke of Grafton and the Duke of Gloucester. Despite this opposition, the execution was carried out on 23 April 1800 after an impassioned speech by Lofft. At first the local parson refused to give the girl a proper burial service, and in a letter to the Duke of Portland dated 29 April 1800, Edward Mills reports that Lofft inflamed 'a very great mob' so that:

> In the hearing of many – [they] grumbled "down with the parson" (this previous to the offer of service). "The Rich have every thing the poor have nothing – the Farmers are rich –. She was legally hanged. But as the man escaped she should not have been hanged –. Lofft is the poor man's friend – we will do what Lofft bids us." [MS E1/20/6.1, fol. 3]

Following representations from a number of Lofft's opponents in Suffolk, the Duke of Portland wrote to the Lord Chancellor on 6 May 1800 to recommend that Lofft's name be struck off the roll of magistrates because of his 'unbecoming' conduct in the affair (MS E1/20/6.1, fol. 5). It is clear from one of his autobiographical sketches in the *Monthly Mirror*, however, that Lofft believed it was more general concern about his association with radicalism that had resulted in the loss of his post as magistrate (9 (1800), 245). Lofft was therefore a somewhat controversial figure when he first became associated with *The Farmer's Boy* because the poem was published at a time when the dispute over the fate of Sarah Lloyd was at its most virulent.

Lofft's name was linked to *The Farmer's Boy* throughout Bloomfield's lifetime. That he believed his position as patron or editor to be threatened by the poem's success is clear from both the quantity and the nature of the editorial matter that accompanied the various editions. The first edition contained Lofft's preface of fifteen pages as well as Bloomfield's endnote regarding the nature of Otaheite society. Lofft introduced a seven-page supplement to the preface into the second edition, together with Bloomfield's 'On Revisiting the Place of my Nativity' and a second endnote in defence of the Rooks 'defamed' in Book I of the poem. A laudatory sonnet was added to the third edition along with a twenty-five-page appendix containing, amongst other material, assorted critical remarks in praise of the poem. It is in the fourth edition that the ever-increasing paratextual apparatus reaches its high point in terms of both quantity and intrusiveness. The fifth and sixth editions contain only minor variations, and although the arrangement of the material is slightly different in the seventh edition no extra matter was added.

In some respects the way Bloomfield is introduced in the first edition of *The Farmer's Boy* reflects the manner in which numerous other labouring-class poets had been presented. Like the prefatory material in *Poems on Sundry Occasions* (1764) by James Woodhouse and *Poems on Several Occasions* by Ann Yearsley, the preface to *The Farmer's Boy* provides an account of Bloomfield's impoverished circumstances. The bulk of the preface is taken up by a letter from Bloomfield's brother to Lofft providing a brief account of the poet's life. Lofft's editing stresses Bloomfield's struggle to overcome his limited education in a way which suggests that, like John Frederick Bryant and 'his handlers', Lofft was 'aware of contemporary theories of "original genius" circulating in the period' (Christmas 2001, 224). In *An Essay on the Genius and Writings of Pope* (1756) Joseph Warton argues that genius depends upon inborn inclination rather than learning and education. He goes on to say that 'in no polished nation, after criticism has been much studied, and the rules of writing established, has any very extraordinary work appeared' (200). In *Conjectures on Original Composition. In a Letter to the Author of Sir Charles Grandison* (1759) Edward Young remarks that genius is 'the power of accomplishing great things without the means generally reputed necessary to that end' (26). James Woodhouse's patron Elizabeth Montagu, who was clearly influenced by Warton, asserts that 'Heaven-born Genius acts from something superior to Rules, and antecedent to Rules; and has a right to appeal to Nature herself' (7). These writings served to promote the patronage of poets like Bloomfield, and helped to generate polite interest in their poetry. It would have been surprising if in his preface Lofft had not attempted to take advantage of this pre-existing market.

At the same time as showcasing Bloomfield's 'original genius', Lofft makes some effort to reassure polite readers that any success Bloomfield might achieve as a poet will not prove disruptive of the social order: 'the Author ... seems far less interested concerning any Fame or Advantage he may derive from it [*The Farmer's Boy*] to himself, than in the pleasure of giving a printed Copy of it, as a tribute of duty and affection, to his MOTHER' (1800, xv–xvi). Lofft also draws attention to Bloomfield's 'amiable' spirit, a phrase which suggests that despite having a considerable intellectual capacity, the poet will prove easy to manage and contain. By presenting Bloomfield in this way, Lofft is repeating the containing strategies of other patrons and editors of labouring-class poets (Zionkowski 1989, 91–108). Although she had ceased to represent a threat because she died before the publication of *Poems on Several Occasions* (1748), Mary Leapor was described as 'courteous and obliging to all, cheerful, good natured and contented in the station of life which Providence had placed her' (ii). The readers of *Poems on Sundry Occasions* were reassured that James Woodhouse did not let poetry interrupt his 'useful' work:

> He generally sits at his work [as a shoemaker] with a pen and ink by him, and when he has made a couplet he writes them down on his knee; so that he may not, thereby neglect the duties of a good husband and kind father; for the same reason his hours of reading are often borrowed from those usually allotted to sleep. [ii]

Despite Lofft's obvious attempt to construct Bloomfield as reassuringly 'humble' both through the preface and his editorial emendations to the poem, Bloomfield later expressed broad approval for the account of his early life incorporated into the first edition. In the preface to the 1809 edition of his poems he remarks that it had 'interested thousands in ... [his] favour, and spared ... [him] painful feelings which must have arisen from a perpetual recurrence of the same questions in all companies, and from a perplexing wish to comply with the natural curiosity of strangers' (I: ii).

It is likely that the representation of Bloomfield as a contented 'peasant' was a marketing ploy. It is inconsistent with other material within the preface which might have been less comforting for polite readers at the end of the 1790s. Lofft includes George Bloomfield's account of the poet's attendance at a series of lectures given by the radical dissenting minister John Fawcet, and of his participation in a '*Debating Society* at *Coachmaker's-hall*' (1800, vii). This suggests that Bloomfield was perhaps not so manageable, and did trouble reviewers. The *British Critic* expressed concern that Bloomfield might have 'received some impressions ... of a questionable kind' at the debating society (15 (1800), 602). That Bloomfield's patron was Capel Lofft, a known supporter of the French Revolution and the 'popular spirit', might in itself have been an issue for some readers. Lofft does announce his inclusive credentials early in the preface, commenting upon the rejection of the manuscript by certain 'persons' in London he remarks: 'With some a person must be rich, or titled, or fashionable as a literary name, or at least fashionable in some respect, good or bad, before anything which he can offer will be thought worthy of notice.' (1800, i) Lofft's statement might represent a relatively innocuous announcement of his belief in 'original' genius. But it might also have reminded readers of his political beliefs, particularly in view of the contemporaneous and politically charged controversy surrounding the trial and execution of Sarah Lloyd. In *Remarks on the Letter of Mr Burke* (1791) Lofft had expressed his commitment to the dismantling of artificial social barriers in a passage that finds an echo in his condemnation of prejudice in the preface to *The Farmer's Boy*:

> It should be the effort of philanthropy and of public wisdom ... to soften all harsh and debasing prejudices, all injurious impediments, to expand the gates and enlarge the avenues to the Temple of Honour and of Public Council, and to encourage the probability of not losing, by exclusive attentions to the mere *presumptions* of merit, one spark, wheresoever latent of animating virtue. [36]

This passage could be taken as an expression of support for the extension of suffrage to at least some amongst the labouring poor. It is certainly an endorsement of the poor man's 'natural Right' of entry into every field of human endeavour.

In Bloomfield's preface to the 1809 edition of his poems he approves the 'remarks from Mr Lofft as to the promiscuous gifts which God has bestowed on his creatures, without regard to worldly rank' (I: ii). Together with his approval for the account of his early life, this suggests that Bloomfield read the preface to the first edition as a relatively neutral introduction. And notwithstanding his concession to the expectations and insecurities of polite readers, Lofft does generally engage with both Bloomfield and his brother as social and political equals. He downplays his own role, and, unlike the patrons of Woodhouse and Yearsley, does not signal his relationship with the poet to be that of patron and client. He rejects George Bloomfield's address to the 'Writer of this Preface' with the remarks: 'I must not take praise to myself for having neglected or suppress'd such a Work when it came into my hands. And I have no farther merit than that of seeing what it was impossible for an unprejudiced Mind not to see, and of doing what it was impossible not to do' (1800, xiv). He provides limited commentary upon George Bloomfield's letter, but generally allows him to speak for himself. In respect of the poem itself, he admits that he had made 'occasional corrections with respect to Orthography, and sometimes in Grammatical construction', but confirms that 'not a line is added or substantially alter'd through the whole poem' (1800, xv). Lofft presents *The Farmer's Boy* to its first readers in a way that reflects his belief that it was necessary to 'expand the gates and enlarge the avenues to the Temple of Honour'.

In the preface to the first edition, Lofft had apparently shown himself to be a different kind of patron from Elizabeth Montagu and Hannah More who assumed a kind of proprietary interest in their clients. But material which he included with the second edition suggests otherwise. In the first edition the construction of Bloomfield as a humble peasant poet might have been justifiable on the grounds that there was a niche in the literary marketplace for such writers. By the time that the second edition was being prepared for the press such a ploy would not have been necessary because Bloomfield had become a successful published poet. But it seems that Lofft was more concerned to present Bloomfield as a helpless and even slightly comical figure at this stage in their relationship. The supplement to the preface includes an anecdote concerning Bloomfield's arrival in London, supposedly based upon information provided by George Bloomfield. According to his brother, Bloomfield 'strutted before us, dress'd just as he came from keeping Sheep, Hogs, &c ... his shoes fill'd full of stumps in the heels. He, looking about him, slipt up ... his nails were unus'd to a flat pavement' (1800a, xxiii). Lofft's representation of Bloomfield echoes the way in which Hannah More and Elizabeth Montagu endeavoured to confine Ann Yearsley 'rhetorically to a state of permanent pathos and inferiority' by repeatedly referring to her work with cattle and swine (Landry 1990, 129–30). For readers of the second edition, it might also have brought to mind the kind of figure who had been in receipt of charity through subscription during the second half of the eighteenth century (Christmas 2001, 210–26).

This anecdotal material appears to cut against the representation of Bloomfield as an educated and aspiring artisan in the first edition. It is possible Lofft felt that the unprecedented success of *The Farmer's Boy* had initiated a shift in the relations between him, a gentleman intellectual and relatively successful man of letters, and his labouring-class protégé. Although the reading public was fascinated by the spectacle of Bloomfield the labouring-class poet, the poem itself generated more interest than any previously published by such a figure; some reviews questioned the subject matter, but on the whole the response was very positive. The *Monthly Mirror* remarked that the work 'under existing circumstances ... [has] never been equalled, and never will be surpassed' (13 (1802), 23) Notwithstanding the fact that he had expressed his intention to make 'some farther and more particular CRITICAL REMARKS' upon the poem, it could be argued that there was no real necessity for Lofft's involvement in the production of the second edition (1800, iii). He was not providing Bloomfield with financial support in the way that patrons had traditionally done in the past, and the supporters of William Cowper and George Crabbe were still doing during the 1790s (Griffin 1996, 261–2). Bloomfield did receive financial assistance from the Duke of Grafton in the form of an annuity and later a place in the Seals Office. Nor was Lofft providing Bloomfield with introductions, another form of assistance traditionally provided by patrons. Bloomfield's own celebrity status brought him direct invitations from the Duke of Grafton, from other individuals of rank and status, and from literary figures like Dr Nathan Drake (Lawson, 26). In addition, Vernor and Hood had made money out of *The Farmer's Boy*, and notwithstanding the fact that they might have required some persuasion to publish the first edition, they required none to publish further editions. They had an interest in the poem, an interest that Lofft would come to distrust and resent. If Lofft wished to signal the need for his continued involvement with the poem, the rhetorical emasculation of Bloomfield in the supplement to the preface might have been the only means available to him.

Bloomfield disliked the way in which he was represented in the second edition of *The Farmer's Boy*. In the 1809 edition of his poems, he felt the need to correct George's recollection of the events surrounding his arrival in London:

> Now the strict truth of the case is this; that I came (on the 29th of June, 1781) in my Sunday Clothes, such as they were; for I well remember the palpitation of my heart on receiving his proposals to come to town, and how incessantly I thought of the change I was going to experience: remember well selling my smock frock for a shilling, and slyly washing my best hat in the horse pond, to give it a gloss fit to appear in the meridian of London. [I: xviii]

The matter did not, however, precipitate a quarrel with Lofft in May 1800, when the second edition was published. This is perhaps because Bloomfield was unsure of the nature and extent of the authority that he possessed over his own work. But it could also be due to the fact that, although the material might have impacted upon the way readers saw Bloomfield, it would not necessarily have affected the reception of *The Farmer's Boy* itself. Just one year later he showed himself willing to question Lofft's conduct when he thought that the latter's 'editorial' apparatus was likely to affect the critical reception of his poetry.

Despite the fact that in many respects his attitude towards Bloomfield did not resemble that of a traditional patron, Lofft did retain some outdated assumptions regarding patronage. As Griffin notes, by the end of the eighteenth century, in their successive rulings on literary copyright, the courts had established 'more firmly that the originator and the owner of a literary work – until such time as he sells his rights to it – is the author' (1996, 282). Lofft probably did not see himself as the 'true author and only begetter' of the work, as did many late seventeenth- and early eighteenth-century patrons (Griffin 1996, 30–31). But the way in which he conducted his relationship with Bloomfield during the months before publication of the first edition suggests that as a patron he believed he had a considerable degree of authority over *The Farmer's Boy*. The poet was not consulted over the presentation of his poem or over its preparation for publication. In his 1809 preface Bloomfield remarks:

> At length, in March 1800, my brother Nathaniel ... called to say that he had seen, in a shop window, a book called *The Farmer's Boy*, with a motto. I told him I supposed it must be mine; but I knew nothing of the motto: and I the more believed it to be mine, having just received through the hands of Mr Lofft a request to wait on the Duke of Grafton, in Piccadilly. [I: xxxiii]

It appears that he did not ask to examine the proofs or call 'to enquire after' progress towards publication despite the fact that 'during the fifteen months which elapsed before publication ... [he] felt much anxiety' (I: xxxii). The poet might well have held himself back from making any inquiry with Lofft because of his confusion over the extent of his own authority. He would later confirm that this was the case in a letter to Lofft: 'I do not pretend to know how strong a negative in any case my author's prerogative ought to give me' (12).

Bloomfield's uncertainty is illustrated by the fact that he did not feel able to express his opinion despite the fact that there were aspects of Lofft's preface that he did not like. In the first edition there are two footnotes to the preface which clearly identify Lofft's politics as oppositional, and which he saw fit to include irrespective of whether they corresponded with the views of the author. The first note is a criticism of the government's restrictions upon the 'circulation of *Newspapers*, and other means of *popular* information' (1800, vi). Then a few lines later he expresses concern over the fettering of debating societies which he believes were 'no useless Schools to some of our very celebrated speakers at the Bar and in Parliament: and, what is of infinitely more importance ... contributed to the diffusion of Political knowledge and Public Sentiment' (1800, vii). In introducing the Treasonable and Seditious Practices Act (1795) and the Seditious Meetings Act (1795), or the two 'Gagging Acts', to which Lofft clearly refers, the intention of the government had been to restrict the ability of radical sympathizers to communicate their views and win converts to their cause. In the context of the political climate that existed in the 1790s his comments might have been received as provocative. It is certain that Bloomfield strongly disapproved of their inclusion, as was to become apparent in 1805 when he suggested revisions to the preface and other paratextual matter for the eighth edition of *The Farmer's Boy*. He does not say whether he sympathizes with the sentiments expressed. He criticizes figures like Henry Hunt and William Cobbett in correspondence, but in the 'Harvest-home' passage of *The Farmer's Boy* itself he comes close to an expression of sympathy for some of the concerns of radical thinkers and activists. In the end Bloomfield regarded the question of whether the footnotes were right or wrong to be beside the point. He argues optimistically that the matters being addressed are probably no longer relevant, and asserts that such overtly political material should not in any case appear in a volume of poetry (1803, MS C.61.a.3, loose leaves attached to viii and ix).

Some of the editorial material incorporated into later editions would have added to Bloomfield's uncertainty because Lofft began to use the space around the poem to discuss his personal affairs. Lofft had an outdated understanding of the way in which literary works achieve distinction, and this is the probable reason for what some might regard as the most inappropriate element of new editorial apparatus in the third edition. He includes material which is apparently part of his campaign against those responsible for his removal from the roll of magistrates. In the 'appendix' he highlights the selfless and benevolent manner in which he had performed the role of Justice, and declares his continuing commitment to the public good (1800b, 105–107). Bloomfield did not explicitly comment upon the remarks, but a letter from Lofft to the poet indicates that Vernor and Hood did not appreciate them: 'My remarks on my removal as a Justice were treated, I must say, neither with delicacy nor, I think, with good judgment' (13). The publishers also disliked Lofft's expanding preface: 'More than sufficient fault was thought necessary to be found with a considerable part of that preface. I was there supposed to have said more than was proper' (13). Publishers had not in general previously challenged the authority of patrons: Yearsley's publishers found the poet's attempt to establish control over the publication of her work to be an irritation (Waldron, 76). The dispute over the presentation of *The Farmer's Boy* is illustrative of the changing dynamics of literary production, and reveals a shift in power from patrons to increasingly influential publishers like Vernor and Hood (Griffin, 1996, 282). In a new footnote for the fifth edition Lofft responds to the criticism of his appendix: 'As to what is personal to myself, I should have passed it entirely here, if that also did not concern the PUBLIC; and if it did not concern the FARMER'S BOY on account of the relation in which I stand to it as *Editor*' (1801, 106). Lofft believed that it was his reputation rather than the literary or indeed the 'commodity' value of the poem itself that interested potential readers in *The Farmer's Boy*. His response is based upon an adherence to the dynamics of cultural production that prevailed before writing poetry became a commercial activity; when it was only by drawing on the authority that the patron possessed as a consequence of 'birth, education, taste, and leisure' that 'the client-writer' could speak (Griffin 1996, 23). This might have been the case earlier in the century, but on the basis of available evidence it was not the case in respect of *The Farmer's Boy* in 1800. The publishers probably believed that the editorial apparatus was beginning to have an adverse impact upon sales. They would have been concerned to protect their economic interest in *The Farmer's Boy*. For the publishers the issue was not, as it was for Lofft, one of personal reputation and honour.

Bloomfield felt considerable irritation as a consequence of the dispute between Lofft and Hood and, in a letter to George Bloomfield written in November 1801, remarked: 'they place me awkwardly in their quarrels: Genious is not wanted to work my extrication, but Jockeyship, constitutional vigour, and impudence' (Add. MS 28 268, fol. 75r). He was awkwardly placed because in some respects he agreed with his publisher's criticisms, but not sufficiently to offend his patron. This is all the more surprising given that, like his publishers, Bloomfield would have been concerned to maximize the monetary return from *The Farmer's Boy*. It was one of his principal sources of income: B.C. Bloomfield estimates that over his lifetime he received £4000 in royalties or similar payments from sales of the poem (93). Bloomfield clearly had considerable respect for Lofft. Despite his dislike of the editorial apparatus, he persuaded the publishers not to remove anything from the sixth edition, and in a letter to his brother suggested that he had done so because 'the blame [Lofft's] would have fallen' on him rather than them, and because a quarrel with Lofft might have an effect on his 'public character' (17). He only sided with his publishers when persuaded that it was in fact his patron's editorial material which was potentially damaging to his 'public character' and the critical reception of his poetry. This was something which, as the prefaces to *Rural Tales* and *Wild Flowers* demonstrate, Bloomfield wanted to control for himself. Although Hood was the first to express concern, the poet worried that the notes which Lofft wished to include after each piece in *Rural Tales* might invite the displeasure of reviewers and readers. In a letter to Lofft written on 22 October 1801, he expressed his opinion in uncharacteristically blunt terms: 'In the notes of approbation which you have attached to each piece in the volume now printing, a praise too direct, if not premature, is made to meet the public eye. These notes, sir, will be disapproved, I know they will' (9). The contentious notes consist of a brief statement of the qualities and strengths of each piece, located at the end of the poem and signed 'C. L.'. In the note to 'The Widow to Her Hour-Glass' for example Lofft remarks: 'There is something very pleasing in the lyric stanzas here used. It is a very harmonious and characteristic form of versification: which ... is here happily revived. The turn of thought is natural, affecting, and poetic.' Bloomfield was very uncomfortable about such presumptive praise, and may also have believed it to be unnecessary in view of the fact that *The Farmer's Boy* had been so successful. In the same letter he goes on to inform Lofft that he felt his readers should be left to judge the poetry for themselves:

> If it is asked, What possible detriment can it be to the author? I answer, that if it be known that he saw the proofs, and permitted such *direct praise* to pass him, it may and will be said, that 'He is not very averse to flattery, if he can deceive himself into a belief of the justness of such applause *before the public has seen this second attempt*.' [9]

With the benefit of hindsight, it is clear that the poet was entirely justified in his concern because reviewers did criticize the notes, and for the very reasons that he suggested in his letter. The *Poetical Register*, in an otherwise positive review of the collection, remarked of the notes: 'Lofft has, with great kindness, given a sort of direction to the reader what opinion he must form on what he has just read. This impertinence of commentary cannot be too severely reprobated. We recommend to Mr Bloomfield to expunge ... this obtrusive nonsense' (1802, 427).

There are a number of reasons that Lofft may have wished to include endnotes with the poems in *Rural Tales*. He might have wanted to reassert the cultural authority derived from 'birth, education, [and] taste' that he believed Bloomfield's publishers were endeavouring to undermine. Lofft's letter of 24 October 1801 reveals that he was already upset because Bloomfield had expressed a desire to write his own preface: 'I was excluded from any other part in this volume at your own express desire ... I do not mean to write either note or essay to any future edition of any poems you may publish in my lifetime' (10). In view of the fact that the publishers disliked his preface to *The Farmer's Boy*, Lofft may have believed they had suggested to the poet that he write his own for *Rural Tales*. He certainly believed that they were ultimately responsible for Bloomfield's criticism of the notes: 'I imagine all this is from Mr Hood, who ... wishes ... to exclude my name from every part of your works, and to make you believe that my judgement of approbation is greatly to be dreaded' (10). The fact that he particularly expresses concern about his 'name' being excluded from Bloomfield's 'works' is suggestive of the way that cultural authority was at stake for Lofft. Nevertheless the fact that he was prepared to correspond with Bloomfield is another indication that he did not view the poet as an inferior and subservient client of patronage in the same way as patrons of earlier labouring-class poets. Hannah More refused any further communication with Ann Yearsley following their dispute over her financial arrangements; she apparently believed that to defend her position in a letter to her labouring-class client would be beneath her (Christmas 2001, 237).

There are indications in the correspondence exchanged between patron and poet that the notes might have been present for other less egotistical or class-bound reasons. In his letter of 28 October 1801, Lofft informed Bloomfield: 'Perhaps I know what is called the public better than you as yet know it. I know that the public is just to authors after their deaths, but is commonly too careless to be just to them in their life, unless its attention be called to a new author.' (13) It appears that Lofft felt Bloomfield was in need of some kind of protection from critics; this is another 'service' that patrons had traditionally provided for their clients (Griffin 1996, 20–22). It is true that Bloomfield was not a new author, and the critical reception of *The Farmer's Boy* had been broadly favourable. But the poetry within *Rural Tales* is very different from that within *The Farmer's Boy*. Perhaps Lofft sensed that 'the public' might require some guidance in reading the kind of poetry that they would encounter in the new volume. The poet himself appeared to realize the necessity for this when he came to write the preface to *Wild Flowers*.

Lofft may have had in mind the tendency of contemporary reviewers to criticize labouring-class poets for their lack of originality. Ann Yearsley was condemned as an imitator, or at best as being unable to translate her conceptions into poetry: 'Milton and Young are evidently her models: but she is not infrequently obscure. Her mind appears to be bewildered, lost in the immensity of its own conceptions' (*Monthly Review* 77 (1787), 484). In *The Lives and Works of the Uneducated Poets* (1831) Robert Southey was simply echoing a common view of labouring-class poets when he remarked:

> A process, indeed, is observable, both in the verses of Woodhouse, and Stephen Duck, which might be looked for, as almost inevitable: they began by expressing their own thoughts and feelings, in their own language; all which, owing to their stations in life, had a certain charm of freshness as well as truth; but that attraction passes away when they begin to form their style upon some approved model, and they then produce just such verses as any person, with a metrical ear, may be taught to make by a receipt. [118]

Southey's remarks give a clue to what might have been Lofft's thinking because they encapsulate a way of responding to labouring-class poets that in the late eighteenth and early nineteenth centuries became almost *de rigueur*. Poets like

Duck, Woodhouse and Bloomfield were regarded as capable of an initial burst of inspiration 'owing' as much to 'their station in life' as their talent, but a decline in the quality of their poetry was seen as 'almost inevitable'. It was a way of responding to them that had an influence on successive generations of readers; in *The Rural Muse* (1954) Rayner Unwin firmly locates Bloomfield within this narrative of decline: 'Like Duck, Bloomfield's limited powers made him a one-poem man' (106). The positive critical reception that greeted *The Farmer's Boy* would not therefore have guaranteed a similar reception for *Rural Tales*. Indeed it might have predetermined readers to expect a decline in originality and quality in the new volume. In the notes Lofft attempts to counter any predisposition to apply this kind of narrative to Bloomfield's new poetry.

When he describes Bloomfield's poetry as 'simple' (14) and 'natural' (62) in the endnotes to 'Richard and Kate' and 'The Widow to Her Hour-Glass', Lofft is again invoking the kind of qualities that late eighteenth-century treatises on genius had identified as signifiers of originality. He is apparently exploiting polite interest in uncultivated poets whose imagination is less fettered by civilization and learning. In focusing upon the 'natural' and simple' qualities of Bloomfield's ballads and tales, Lofft also connects them with the demotic and primitive origins of English poetry, and the so-called Gothic revival which probably owed its greatest debt to Percy's *Reliques of Ancient English Poetry* (Groom, 19–105). But it is possible that Lofft wanted the reader to make other associations too because William Duff's *Critical Observations on the Writings of the Most Celebrated Geniuses in Poetry* (1770) controversially connected these qualities with iconographic figures in the history of literature. Both Homer and Shakespeare are associated with seemingly spontaneous natural processes because they apparently wrote independently of any rules of art by means of a kind of inspired enthusiasm (1–63, 126–96). The process of creation is simple in that it is not bound by complex and artificial human rules, but this simplicity veils a more profound level of complexity because it is inscrutable in the same way as the primary causes of natural phenomenon.

Lofft makes another attempt to offset the tendency to view labouring-class poets as hostages to the established literary fashions of the day when he describes Bloomfield's poetry as 'characteristic' in the endnotes to 'Richard and Kate' and 'Market Night' (14, 69). In a recent study Deirdre Lynch has explored the way in which during the late eighteenth century, fiction 'offered a framework ... for exploring what made personal effects, or characteristics, personal' (86). The debate, which implicated numerous discourses in addition to fiction, the most important being political economy, centred on the endeavour to define those qualities that enabled an object or individual to resist categorization. The manner in which Lofft uses the word represents another attempt to show that Bloomfield's new poetry is not imitative, even though it might owe a debt to various strands of literary tradition. In other words it is characteristic, not in the sense that it is part of a particular tradition, for example the self-taught tradition, but because of its own unique and distinctive qualities.

Lofft was aware of the way the apparently positive qualities that he identifies in his notes could be implicated in criticism of labouring-class poets. Poetry which could be described as 'simple' and 'natural' could just as easily be labelled commonplace or trite, particularly if written by an 'uneducated' labouring-class poet. Lofft makes sure the reader knows that this is not the case in respect of Bloomfield whose poetry is both 'animated' and 'lively' (34, 105). As Deirdre Lynch notes, during the late eighteenth century the question of when a character became sufficiently singular or eccentric to be considered something, or someone else, was also a matter of some debate (102–19). Poetry could be labelled 'characteristic' for the wrong reasons; for its lack of sophistication or because it had breached good taste. Again this is perhaps more of a danger in respect of poetry produced by a poet recently come 'from keeping Sheep, Hogs, &c'. Bloomfield's poetry was considered singularly grotesque by one reviewer who described his language as 'the corrupt and clownish dialect of an obscure county' (*Annual Review* (1806), 526). Most reviews of Bloomfield's early poetry were positive, but this does not alter the fact that labouring-class poets did encounter attitudes of this kind. Lofft points out that, notwithstanding the connection with the vernacular roots of English poetry, the diction in Bloomfield's ballads and tales is both 'graceful' and 'beautiful' (34, 58).

Perhaps Lofft did not consider it sufficient merely to state the positive qualities that he saw in specific poems. The notes suggest that he believed the kind of poetry produced by Bloomfield needed some form of authentication or validation from another layer of culture. At the same time he wanted to remind the reader of Bloomfield's technical skill as a poet, a quality which might have been obscured by his unaffected style. This is clear from the comparisons between Bloomfield's poetry and that of Dryden. There was a revival of interest in Dryden towards the end of the eighteenth century, and Lofft's desire to compare Bloomfield with him might simply have been some kind of marketing ploy (Amarasinghe, 9–34). But if attention is paid to the reasons for this renewed interest, the possibility that Lofft made the comparison for a particular purpose must be considered. Samuel Johnson had praised Dryden for his ability to 'chuse the flowing and the sonorous words; to vary the pauses and adjust the accents; to diversify the cadence, and yet preserve the smoothness of his metre' (*Lives of the Poets* I: 466). Wordsworth and Coleridge also admired Dryden, and Walter Scott, who produced an edition of Dryden in 1808, believed that the poet 'first shewed that the English language was capable of uniting smoothness and strength', and that his 'poetry was gifted, in a degree, surpassing in modulated harmony that of all who preceded him, and inferior to none that has since written English verse' (*Works* I: 483). It is the strength of the language, its appropriateness to the subject, and the smoothness of the verse that are admired in Dryden. And these are the features of Bloomfield's verse that Lofft points out for his readers. According to Lofft's note 'Walter and Jane' 'has much of the clear, animated, easy narrative, the familiar but graceful diction, and the change of numbers so interesting in DRYDEN' (34). In respect of 'The Miller's Maid' he remarks: 'I believe there has been no such

Poem in its kind as the MILLER'S MAID, since the days of DRYDEN, for ease and beauty of language; concise, clear and interesting narrative; sweet and full flow of verse; happy choice of the subject, and delightful execution of it' (58). The reader is also reminded that the 'modulated harmony' that Johnson and Scott find in Dryden is also there in Bloomfield, although Lofft calls it a 'change of numbers'. The themes treated by the two writers might have been different, but as Lofft remarks, the manner in which they handled this differing subject-matter is comparable.

There is evidence Lofft also believed that, despite its success, *The Farmer's Boy* required authentication from another layer of culture. In the supplement to the preface included with the second edition he includes remarks of approbation from rich, titled and fashionable figures, and provides details of favourable literary reviews (1800b, xxiv–vi). In the appendix, which he included with the third edition, he cites a lengthy extract from Dr Nathan Drake's review of *The Farmer's Boy* for *Literary Hours* which, like the notes for *Rural Tales*, draws attention to the originality of the poem and the beauty of the versification and diction (1800b, 113–21). Lofft also includes his own 'Critical Remarks' on the literary echoes to be found in *The Farmer's Boy* (1800b, 122–8). It is possible that Bloomfield was aware of the classical works to which Lofft refers. Although he had not received a classical education, like John Clare he read every kind of printed matter, and during the second half of the eighteenth century many translations of the Greek and Roman classics appeared in periodicals and journals. The publishers did not like this material, but it did not figure prominently in the dispute between patron and poet. This fact begs the question why was Bloomfield concerned about brief notes appearing after each poem in *Rural Tales*, but not worried about similar and more extensive material in the editorial apparatus to *The Farmer's Boy*? Remarks that he made when sketching out his own ideas for revisions indicate that for Bloomfield the issue was as much the location of the material as what Lofft says. In the seventh edition Lofft had moved the critical material to the front of *The Farmer's Boy*, a change which Bloomfield did not approve: 'I never cordially liked the setting of criticism before any matter or book, and I think that this would look best in the appendix'(1803, MS C.61.a.3, loose leaf attached to xliv). That Bloomfield felt the material would be best dispensed with altogether is clear from the fact that he omitted it from the 1809 edition of his poems.

The reason he took a stand regarding *Rural Tales* in 1801 might be the fact that at the turn of the eighteenth century the appearance of notes before or after literary ballads or tales would have been suggestive of antiquarian ballad scholarship. Collections of old ballads often included a critical introduction, which might explain Bloomfield's dislike of setting criticism before the text, and head or footnotes with each piece. Percy's *Reliques of Ancient English Poetry*, and many of the numerous ballad collections that appeared during subsequent decades, had adopted this format. The poetry that accompanied the notes was authenticated by them, and Bloomfield might have felt that Lofft's critical material was providing a similar kind of authentication for his poetry. The notes usually consisted of comments upon the antiquity and authenticity of the version of the ballad included in the collection, together with background historical information concerning the incidents described. The editor would sometimes make remarks concerning the construction of the ballad itself, and adopt a critical stance with respect to the piece. The recovery of popular poetry for a cultivated readership seems, in the ballad collection as it does in Bloomfield's poetry, to provide scope for the editor to speak with superior judgement, sometimes in the language of high culture. In a head note to 'Auld Maitland' in his *Minstrelsy of the Scottish Border* (1803) Walter Scott remarks: 'The incidents are striking and well managed; and they are in strict conformity with the manners of the age in which they are placed' (232). His comments are similar to many of Lofft's remarks in praise of Bloomfield's poems, for example when he comments upon the 'delightful execution' of 'The Miller's Maid'(58).

It is true that Lofft's notes are different in scope from those included within ballad collections which often occupied several pages of the text, but even an oblique link with ballad scholarship could potentially have had an impact upon the reception of Bloomfield's poetry. At the end of the eighteenth century poetry was still an art form with a restricted audience. As Richard Altick indicates in his study of English reading audiences, at this time most of the labouring classes in England would have been unable to read. Reading had made its greatest gains amongst the commercial middle classes, and in the towns where only a minority of the total English population lived. Although the expansion of circulating libraries had done much to make books available to more people, reading matter was still too expensive for all but a minority to purchase outright (Altick, 65; Sutherland, 1–48). Bloomfield's poetry would have been read by an audience consisting of members of the aristocracy, the gentry and the growing commercial and professional middle classes. These social groups would have been highly receptive to the kind of presentational engineering to which Lofft had subjected Bloomfield's poetry. They would have enjoyed being able to share in the sense of cultural superiority that his manner of presentation involved. Bloomfield was aware of this as he remarked in a letter to Lofft: 'I feel my situation to be novel; the world looks at me in that light; I am extremely anxious on that account' (12). The association of his new volume of poetry, even obliquely, with ballad antiquarianship can only have increased his anxiety that he was being constructed and read as a kind of anthropological curiosity which was the subject of scholarly commentary and approving critical judgement.

Lofft's editorial apparatus is in some respects more about his relationship with Bloomfield's readers than it is about the poetry with which it is published. He cannot have been unaware of the fact that some of the 'critical' material incorporated into later editions of *The Farmer's Boy* and the notes in *Rural Tales* construct Bloomfield as an object for social and anthropological inquiry, and impose a reading of the poetry that privileges its origins. But this was the only way in which he could continue a dialogue which the commercial and critical success of Bloomfield's poetry had the potential to disrupt. When

Bloomfield expressed confusion in his correspondence over the extent of the authority that he possessed, Lofft replied: 'you have undoubtedly the full right of an author over your works' (13). Notwithstanding his apparent commitment to democratic inclusiveness, however, he expected Bloomfield to defer to his decisions about presentation. He informed the poet that this was because he knew the reading 'public better than you as yet know it' (13). He is perhaps referring to the fact that because he had been a published author for several years he knew the literary marketplace better than Bloomfield. But in view of the success achieved by *The Farmer's Boy*, Bloomfield clearly knew what the 'public' wanted. It is more likely that it is a reference to Lofft's social status which was closer to that of Bloomfield's readers: as a result he could communicate with them in a way that the poet could not. Lofft was 'hurt' by Bloomfield's conduct because in criticizing the editorial apparatus, his client was interrupting a dialogue to which he was in a sense not a party.

Lofft felt his authority as a patron to be threatened by Bloomfield's publishers and by the poet himself, but there is a sense in which it was also threatened by changing conceptions of authorship. There is some evidence that Lofft himself was made aware of the need to demonstrate the authenticity of *The Farmer's Boy*. In a supplement to the preface for the eighth edition, presumably in response to criticism, he defends his emendations to the text of the poem. He incorporates a list of variations between the original MS copy and printed version of *The Farmer's Boy* (originally published in the *Monthly Mirror* for January 1802). It is not at all clear that Bloomfield agreed with Lofft's characterization of these emendations as 'insubstantial', and the actual effect of them upon *The Farmer's Boy* is considered in the first chapter of this study. Like Ann Yearsley, Bloomfield wanted to make money from his poetry, but he was more concerned about his artistic integrity. This is perhaps best demonstrated by the poet's reaction on being offered money by a person signing himself 'B. C.' to ghost-write an elegy on the death of a prominent Royal Navy captain. In the past there had been no stigma attached to writing occasional poetry for a specific social or political purpose in exchange for money (Griffin 1996, 32–3). But Bloomfield expressed considerable anger and indignation in his letter to B. C.: 'the return of your note [£10] gives me the opportunity to assure you that the offer of Mr B. C. is not accepted on the part of R. B. only as a novel and strange kind of indignity, to which my situation renders me liable, but which I could wish to prevent the repetition of if it was in my power' (36). For Bloomfield, in relation to his poetry, income as well as acclaim was to be had directly from the public rather than from or through patrons. He hoped that he might be in the vanguard of a new more democratic age of writing, and in his 1809 preface expresses a desire that his own example might 'teach men in [his] ... own station of life not to despair if they feel themselves morally and intellectually worthy of notice; and at the same time teach them not to *rely* on an untried and brittle support, by throwing away the honourable staff of mechanic independence' (I: xx). In this respect he was a man of his age because, during the nineteenth century, artistic authenticity and independence would become increasingly important markers of value in literature.

In the end the contentious notes were incorporated into the small octavo version of the first edition only, and were omitted from all subsequent editions of *Rural Tales*. As a consequence of the dispute over the presentation of *Rural Tales*, Bloomfield also gained more control over the way in which *The Farmer's Boy* was presented. He was invited by Lofft to suggest revisions to the editorial apparatus for the eighth edition. Bloomfield retained the bulk of the original preface, but excluded most of the supplement to the preface and the appendix. It is certain that Lofft made this concession reluctantly because he added a number of rather petulant footnotes to the ninth edition of the poem, a typical example of which reads: 'In the seventh Edition I inserted Dr Drake's Analysis of The Farmer's Boy [in fact this was first included with the third edition]. And it is not agreeably to my wish that it has since been omitted' (1806, xxxii). Bloomfield further corrected Lofft's preface to *The Farmer's Boy* when preparing the preface for the two-volume edition of his collected works published in 1809. This was the first time that he had more or less complete control over the editing and presentation of his work for publication. He excluded all of the editorial matter that had accumulated since the first edition, but again retained narrative of his early life, originally provided by his brother (Add. MS 29 869). As will have become clear, he also attempted to correct some of the wrong impressions that might have been generated by Lofft's preface and appendix. Despite the difficult nature of his relationship with his first and most important patron, Bloomfield did not reject patronage outright; he even managed to maintain a relationship with Lofft. But he did take steps to ensure that his future patrons should have no influence upon the creative process and little or no involvement in the way the text was presented. In this respect he was no different from Wordsworth and Coleridge who both accepted gifts from patrons, but passionately defended their artistic independence. It is not possible to say when Bloomfield first came to know Edward Jenner, but they met on several occasions and entered into correspondence with each other. From the beginning the poet's association with Jenner was more evenly balanced than his relationship with Lofft. Jenner and his discovery needed the kind of positive publicity that a famous poet like Bloomfield could provide. Bloomfield, on the other hand, felt himself under an obligation to offer assistance in the campaign to achieve the universal acceptance of smallpox vaccination. His father had died of smallpox, and in the 'Advertisement' to *Good Tidings; or, News from the Farm* (1804), he dwells upon the personal debt which he owed to vaccination: 'I have, in my own, insured the lives of four children by Vaccine Inoculation, who, I trust, are destined to look back upon the Small-pox as the scourge of days gone by' (2). The death of his brother's child whilst he was working on the poem clearly increased the intensity of this feeling, as he reveals in a footnote: 'I had proceeded thus far with the Poem, when the above fact became a powerful stimulus to my feelings, and to the earnestness of my exhortations' (16). Bloomfield was, nevertheless, unsure how to approach his relationship with Jenner, and a letter to George Bloomfield dated 21 July 1802 reveals just how irritating he found his interventions: 'This moment a letter from Dr. Jenner invites me to tea this evening. What shall I do – leave 150 lines of an unfinished subject in his hands? ... [It] is hard to say *no* in such cases as this. I wish he would suspend his curiosity six months, and I would take my chance' (29). Bloomfield must have been concerned that Jenner would attempt to control the manner in which he defended smallpox vaccination. Jenner later asked Bloomfield if he could preface the poem with an essay by Dr Drake promoting vaccination and demanding the prohibition of inoculation. Lofft could see no objection to 'Dr Drakes's essay being prefixed', but in a letter to the poet recommended that the 'prohibitions and injunctions' be omitted on the grounds that compulsion would prove counter-productive (31–3). In the end Bloomfield decided not to include the essay, perhaps because experience had taught him to dislike the way material provided by patrons could affect the presentation and reception of his poetry. But he also wanted to defend vaccination in his own way, in a manner that both reflected and distinguished his labouring-class origin, and, at least in part, located the practice within the healing power of nature (White 141–54).

Bloomfield's later editions of poetry are introduced by his own prefaces in which he makes an effort to defend his labouring-class communitarian poetics. But his ability to do so was sometimes compromised by his relationships with patrons. In March 1806 the Earl of Buchan wrote directly to Bloomfield's publishers enclosing an address to 'THE READERS OF BLOOMFIELD'S "WILD FLOWERS"', and suggested that they incorporate it into the new book along with a letter from Bloomfield written in 1802. He also suggested that the poet's letter should appear under the heading 'ROBERT BLOOMFIELD, THE POETICAL SHOEMAKER, TO THE EARL OF BUCHAN, ON BEING INVITED TO DRYBURGH ABBEY' (39). The fact that Buchan did not consult the poet before writing to Longman & Co indicates that he saw himself as a traditional patron who did not necessarily have to consider Bloomfield's wishes. Buchan wanted to 'promote the sale of "Wild Flowers"' (38), but the manner in which he wished to introduce it, and the letter itself, which is full of 'condescension', suggest that Bloomfield is a humble and subservient client of patronage. This would have undermined Bloomfield's growing confidence, and cut against his own representation of himself as an independent author in his preface to *Wild Flowers*. He had to resist the overtures of both Buchan and Lofft who in a letter to the poet suggested that to 'disappoint his [Buchan's] wish' would be 'liable to be considered as pride, or unkindness, or injustice' (42).

Between 1807 and 1810 when his dispute with Lofft was behind him and he was working on *The Banks of Wye*, Bloomfield had to remain sensitive to the expectations of his 'friends'. It is possible that he was asked by Mrs Lloyd Baker to produce some kind of record of their tour in Monmouthshire. If this was the case, and in view of the fact that they arranged and paid for the tour, he would have been sensitive to the question of whether the Lloyd Bakers regarded themselves as patrons, and whether they viewed any record which he had agreed to produce as owing to them as part of some kind of patronal agreement. Bloomfield and Mrs Lloyd Baker continued to correspond regularly for a period of three years. In letters written during the year immediately after the tour it seems that she repeatedly asked him about the progress he was making on his 'triple-paged journal. Drawings, prose, and rhime' (Add. MS 28 268, fol. 242). His responses indicate that he saw himself as in some way committed to her and to other members of the party. On 2 October 1807 he wrote: 'Do be so good as to make my respects to them [the other party members], and say that I have not forgot any of my promises to them' (Add. MS 28 268, fol. 242). By April 1808 he felt the need to apologize for his lack of progress:

> I am rather ashamed, not of my progress in the journal, but of my promise, for I have not completed my task! I certainly shall *in time*, but I find much to say, and that the subject is worthy of attention if it be only for the amusement of the individuals of the party, and with no other aim. [Add. MS 28 268, fol. 254]

The fact that he felt the need to emphasize the words '*in time*' indicates that he was beginning to feel a degree of pressure. From December 1808 to July 1810 his letters are dominated by accounts of his own ill-health and by family matters. No mention is made of the journal, but he does make some general statements about his 'muse', possibly in response to Mrs Lloyd Baker's enquiries. On 21 December 1808 he writes: 'I have not budged an inch after the Muses since April, but I have a strong notion that we shall be friends again in the Spring' (Add. MS 28 268, fol. 261r). In May 1810 Bloomfield wrote that his son Charles had broken his thigh in two places during a fall, but Mr Lloyd Baker still asked to see the journal at the beginning of July, forcing the poet to find more excuses: 'tell him [Mr Lloyd Baker] that I am going over it again and he must have patience until the Autumn' (Add. MS 28 268, fol. 288). Eventually the Lloyd Bakers began to become impatient for some tangible evidence that he had fulfilled 'his promise'. This represents the strongest evidence that they saw Bloomfield as under some kind of obligation to them. They seem to have pressurized the poet in the same way as Edward Jenner had done seven years before.

At some point between mid-July 1810 and mid-January 1811, it is not clear precisely when, Bloomfield let the Lloyd Bakers see a manuscript version of his poem. Then on 16 January 1811, in his longest letter to them, he wrote announcing his decision to publish. In this letter there are further indications that he regarded the Lloyd Bakers as having some kind of interest in his poem. He clearly felt the need to justify himself, and informs them that various influential figures including Thomas Park, Samuel Rogers and Capel Lofft had seen the work and agreed that it ought to be published. As a successful poet with three previous volumes behind him, it is strange that he felt the need to defend his decision in this way. It seems that he was still unsure about the nature of his relationship with the Lloyd Bakers, and felt that any objection they had to the publicity involved in publication might be countered by the fact that these literary figures of standing had approved his decision. He was certainly conscious of the possibility that Mrs Lloyd Baker might be put out by the fact that his sketches, rather than her own, were to appear with the poem, and remarks with emphasis: 'This, I fear, may appear strange to you; but not surely if you recollect that *their* [the publishers] object is to lay hold of everything which can *interest* or *bias* in the *sale*' (50). Finally he informs her emphatically that the matter is now out of his hands: 'I know of nothing which can *now* retard its ultimate appearance before the world' (50). Although they did not correspond so frequently after the appearance of *The Banks of Wye*, there is nothing to suggest that the Lloyd Bakers were in any way unhappy about the fact that the poem had been published.

Bloomfield was uncertain in his dealings with various 'friends' because the dynamics of literary production were changing during the second half of the eighteenth century. The modern literary marketplace in which authors and publishers more or less independently enter into contractual agreements to publish had not fully emerged. The authority of the patron had, however, been undermined by changes in the way authors and readers saw themselves, and by the increasing financial and cultural power of large publishing houses. Dustin Griffin and Linda Zionkowski both take account of these changes, but the case of Bloomfield and Lofft is of particular significance because it focuses on the relational implications. Literary production had become a somewhat chaotic contest for authority involving poet, patron, publisher, and, at least to some extent, readers; all of whom had differing ethical, social and financial interests in literary texts. As a result, both writers and patrons operated in a world in which neither was really sure of the extent of their authority, or of the role that they performed in the process. In view of his inevitable social clumsiness and insecurity, the fact that Bloomfield did in the end take a principled stand can be regarded as heroic. The example of Bloomfield (and *May Day*) might even have assisted John Clare during his struggle to resist the domineering influence of patrons, publishers and readers.

CHAPTER FIVE

'History from Below' on *The Banks of* [the] *Wye*

The Banks of Wye was the product of an act of patronage, but ironically it was also the first new work over which Bloomfield managed to retain control of both presentation and publication (he controlled the presentation and publication of *The Poems of Robert Bloomfield* (1809) but this did not contain any new work). If the poem can in some ways be viewed as marking Bloomfield's arrival as an independent poet within the literary marketplace, it also represents a significant shift in his poetics. In *The Banks of Wye* he writes for the first time about an episode in his life that is not related to his experience as a farm-worker or a shoemaker. Jonathan Lawson argues that he 'loses his authentic voice' as a consequence of this fact (123). *The Banks of Wye* was certainly not as successful as his earlier work in either commercial or critical terms, but this chapter demonstrates that the Wye trip was an opportunity for Bloomfield to engage with a new landscape in a different and more sophisticated manner that takes into account the literary, political and social history of Monmouthshire. In the process he attempts to recover 'the Banks of the Wye' for those who live and work in the landscape, people who are largely absent from Wordsworth's response to the region. In fact it can be argued that the poem adds to, rather than detracts from Bloomfield's status as a poet, and lends an added dimension to the body of his work. This was acknowledged by some contemporary reviewers. The *Eclectic Review* remarked that the poem has a 'thousand faults', but that 'those who will take the pains to be pleased will not be disappointed; they will find the faults diminishing, and the beauties multiplying, the more patiently these pages are examined' (7 (1811), 1118).

In a letter written during the summer of 1807, Mr and Mrs Lloyd Baker invited Bloomfield to accompany them on a tour down the Wye valley. The precise date on which the Lloyd Bakers had written to Bloomfield is not known, but the poet wrote accepting the invitation on 6 August 1807. At the time he was still experiencing the health problems that had affected him when writing 'Shooter's Hill' and 'To My Old Oak Table'. The preface suggests that this is so, and in the invocation at the beginning of Book I he makes a direct connection with the lines in 'Shooter's Hill' that had prompted his 'friends' to propose the tour: 'When sickness weigh'd thee down, and strength declin'd / When dread eternity absorb'd thy mind, / Flow'd the predicting verse, by gloom o'erspread, / That "Cambrian mountains" thou should'st never tread' (I: 7–10). Bloomfield might have believed that his fragile health would prevent him from visiting the Wye, but it is not because of his health that he had 'never dar'd to sing' of the region (I: 6). He knew that in doing so he would be inviting comparison with the work of other writers, and the preface reveals his awareness that the Wye would have been familiar to his readers:

> Should the reader, from being a resident, or frequent visitor, be well acquainted with the route, and able to discover inaccuracies in distances, succession of objects, or local particulars, he is requested to recollect, that the party was out but ten days; a period much too short for correct and laborious description, but quite sufficient for all the powers of poetry which I feel capable of exerting. [vi]

This remark explicitly distances his poetical vision of the Wye from William Gilpin's *Observations on the River Wye* (1782), a series of observations on picturesque beauty. Many of Bloomfield's readers would have experienced the Wye through the lens of Gilpin's book, indeed references to Gilpin in *The Banks of Wye* reveal Bloomfield's own knowledge of it. Moreover, Bloomfield and his party followed more or less the same route that Gilpin did in 1770. They travelled south down the river from Ross-on-Wye to Chepstow, stopping at Goodrich Castle, New Weir and of course Tintern Abbey. From Chepstow they travelled directly to Raglan Castle, whereas Gilpin had returned to Monmouth before turning west to Raglan. Both parties then journeyed to Brecon via Abergavenny and Tretower Castle. From Brecon Gilpin had turned south-west to Neath, and then east along the coast via Bridgend, Cardiff and Newport to Caldicot, where he took a ferry across the channel to Bristol. Bloomfield and his party travelled north-east from Brecon, returning to their point of departure at Uley via Hay-on-Wye, Hereford, Cheltenham and Gloucester.

Notwithstanding Bloomfield's attempt to distance *The Banks of Wye* from picturesque guides to the region, the poem is surely indebted to *Grongar Hill* (1726) by John Dyer, often described as one of the 'godfathers' of the picturesque movement (Griffin 1981, 457-69). Bloomfield adopts the octosyllabic couplet used in the published version of *Grongar Hill* nearly a century before, as well as Dyer's prosopopoeia. But there is another more significant way in which both 'Shooter's Hill' and *The Banks of Wye* echo Dyer's response to the countryside. The speaker in Dyer's poem does not survey the countryside from a single elevated location as in the typical prospect poem. Like the speaker in Bloomfield's poems, he is clearly passing through, and as a consequence is able to respond to the landscape in a way that takes account of both the 'distant' prospect and some of the features that are often hidden within such a view. In fact it is this attention to apparently commonplace detail that connects Dyer, and it could be argued Bloomfield, with late eighteenth-century picturesque sensibility. There is, however, an important difference between Dyer's response to the landscape and that of Bloomfield. Dyer discovers more in the landscape, but he does not explore the significance of what he sees. Observations in *Grongar Hill* generally give way to sententious moralization. The speaker in *The Banks of Wye* explores the landscape for evidence of the experience of those who live, and have lived in it.

Bloomfield may have had *Grongar Hill* or *The Fleece* in mind when he began work on *The Banks of Wye*, but Dyer was by no means an influential figure in English poetry at the beginning of the nineteenth century. Other literary associations would, however, have both stimulated and intimidated Bloomfield. He had read 'Tintern Abbey', and had expressed concern that his own work should not be read as derivative of Wordsworth's poetry. But it could be argued that in one sense Bloomfield's attempt to find inspiration in the Wye valley actually mirrors a typical response to features in the landscape in 'Tintern Abbey' and *The Prelude*. Bloomfield had apparently become weary of the kind of landscape in which he had spent much of his life: 'The verse of gravel walks that tells, / With pebble-rocks and mole-hill swells, / May strain description's bursting cheeks, / And far out-run the goal it seeks' (II: 194–7). He never wrote poetry about the kind of artificial landscape which he seems to have in mind here, and his descriptive passages are rarely if ever bathetic. On the other hand his previous poetry had generally been marked by a certain domestic restraint, and he had developed an appropriately low-key manner of responding to the gentle countryside of Suffolk and the area around London. Bloomfield believed that the sublime landscape of the Wye could stimulate his imagination in a different way: 'Here sight may range, and hearts may glow, / ... / As youthful ardour shouts before: / Here a sweet paradise shall rise / At once to greet poetic eyes' (II: 201–206). Wordsworth also saw the sublime landscape as a catalyst for the imagination as is clear from one of the key passages in his *oeuvre*. In Book VI of *The Prelude* he describes his journey through the Alps, but the place matters only in so far as it stimulates 'Imagination' and becomes a physical and metaphorical channel for his thoughts. The features of the gorge though which he passes are the 'workings of one mind ... / ... / The types and symbols of eternity' (568–71). The fact that the landscape seems to be irretrievably bound up with his own consciousness, as well as his conception of the 'one mind', is the reason that Keats famously described Wordsworth's poetry as a manifestation of 'the egotistical sublime' (*Letters*: 157). Keats' remark highlights the important difference between the two poets' conception of a properly functioning imagination.

For Bloomfield the imagination appears to have been simply a faculty of the mind, not so bound up with his sense of who he was as a man and a poet. In *The Banks of Wye* a properly functioning imagination helps the poet to understand the historical significance of particular landscape features. In 'Tintern Abbey' the detail of the landscape and what it signifies are secondary, because the poem is principally about Wordsworth's response to recent European history and the development of his own poetic sensibility. There is no reason to doubt that his memory of other 'forms of beauty' in the Lake District or elsewhere served the same kind of palliative function for Wordsworth when in 'lonely rooms, and mid the din / Of towns and cities' (26–7). The fact that he uses the term 'form' in his account of the scene is also significant because his description is suggestive rather than concrete; it represents an outline sketch that could refer to a number of different places. *The Banks of Wye* is about the development of poetic sensibility; in this sense the poem resembles 'Tintern Abbey', but the particular landscape and culture of the region are implicated in the process for Bloomfield.

The different ways in which both Bloomfield and Wordsworth respond imaginatively to the 'bards of yore' (III: 5), reflects the latter's apparent lack of interest in the specific cultural associations of place. Wordsworth made numerous references to the bards in his early poetry, and, notwithstanding the fact that no direct allusion is made to them in 'Tintern Abbey', Richard Gravil has argued that 'an admirer of Iolo's bardic triads would have found the poem's philosophy both cogent and familiar, an apotheosis of liberal druidism, that fashionable blend of Unitarianism and nature feeling' (116). Gravil does not fully investigate the implications of this association because during the 1790s Edward Williams [Iolo Morganwg] had used his 'elaborate pseudo-antiquarian Bardic discourse as a vehicle for his Jacobin sympathies' (Davies 2002, 135–7). For example, from 1789 the members of the London Gwynedddigion Society, which included a number of Welsh radicals including Williams, organized a 'series of seminal eisteddfodau – formalized and radically charged reinstitutions of ancient bardic competitions' (Davies 2002, 145). The key point in terms of the comparison with Bloomfield, however, is that both Wordsworth and Williams made use of the eighteenth-century Welsh renaissance to formulate their response to the events of the 1790s. Bloomfield was more concerned with the bards as historical figures, and with the ways in which they might have been important to the people of Monmouthshire.

Early in the poem Bloomfield makes an explicit connection between the bardic tradition and the region through which he had travelled: 'where / The foes of verse shall never dare / Genius to scorn, or bound its power, / ... / ... / Till time forgets "the Bard" of GRAY' (I: 39–44). The historical bards possessed power, but it was a secular and regulated form of power, constrained by the intricate structure of ancient Celtic society. In this passage, however, Bloomfield is apparently invoking a different kind of figure, like that suggested by Gray's Pindaric ode 'The Bard' (1757). In Gray's poem the bard is a more mysterious figure: 'On a rock, whose haughty brow / Frowns o'er old Conway's foaming flood, / ... / With haggard eyes the poet stood / (Loose his beard and hoary hair / Streamed like a meteor to the troubled air)' (15–20). The nature of his power is enigmatic and impenetrable. Gray's poem inspired many writers and artists during the second half of the eighteenth century. In early illustrations such as Richard Bentley's *The Bard* (1757), the bard remains rooted in the historical context of the conflict with Edward I. The sublime potential of the theme was gradually realized, however, in paintings like Thomas Jones's *The Bard* (1774) which 'concentrates on the bard and his sublimely primitive domain as opposed to his haranguing of Edward I and his army' (Smiles, 52). In later pictorial representations of Gray's poem such as Richard Corbould's *The Bard* (1807) or John Martin's *The Bard* (1817), the bard becomes even more mysterious and his link with the sublime landscape greater. Sam Smiles remarks of Martin's painting: 'The bard is now a creature of the mountains, the genius loci of that wild, untamed landscape which stands in opposition to the urban lowland culture bent on subduing it' (57). Even the lowland Druid bard in Thomas Love Peacock's *The Genius of the Thames* (1810), published just one year before *The Banks of Wye*, is sublime in appearance: 'His grey hair, gemmed with midnight dew, / Streamed down his robes of sable hue: / His cheeks were sunk: his beard was white: / But his large eyes were fiery-bright' (417–20).

Bloomfield is attracted to the Wye valley because of his desire to draw upon the energy of the bards through their apparent connection with the sublime landscape. On many occasions in the poem passages expressing wonder at features in the landscape lead into an invocation of the creative potency of the bards. In Book I the narrator remarks upon the latent power of Coldwell Rocks which 'Boast ... o'er man in proud distain, / A silent, everlasting reign' (293–4). The grandeur of the rocks causes the narrator to express the wish that 'Cambria's bards ... [had] here / *Their names engraven*, deep and clear', that they 'Might greet with shouts those sires of song, / And trace the fame that mortals crave, / To LIGHT and LIFE beyond the grave' (301–303). The narrator's vision physically connects the names of the bards with elements of the sublime landscape. Later on the summit Pen-Y-Vale, of which Bloomfield remarks in the MS journal 'we had left beauty behind ... here was nothing but sublimity' (Add. MS 28 267, fol. 45), and which in the poem he describes as the 'heights of inspiration' (III: 252), he invokes the memory of Burns: 'SPIRIT of BURNS! The daring child / Of glorious freedom, rough and wild, / How have I wept o'er all thy ills, / ... / How almost worship'd in my dreams / Thy mountain haunts, – thy classic streams! / How burnt with hopeless, aimless fire, / To mark thy giant strength aspire / In patriot themes!' (III: 145–53). In January 1802 Bloomfield had observed in a letter to the Earl of Buchan: '*I do remember Burns*; but I am not Burns, neither have I his fire to fan nor to quench, nor his passions to control' (40). This passage suggests that by 1807 he was ready to share in the very same 'fire' and 'passion', the lack of which he had earlier felt in himself. At the turn of the eighteenth century, Burns lived on in the cultural memory as an epitome of natural genius. Like Bloomfield's bards, he was linked to both the working countryside and the power of nature. By journeying to 'bleak mountain' regions it seems that Bloomfield felt he could draw upon the same 'rough and wild' forces that had inspired Burns.

Bloomfield seeks 'inspiration' from 'sublimity' for a particular purpose: 'O for the fancy, vigorous and sublime, / Chaste as the theme, to triumph over time! / ... / To speak new transports to the lowland youth, / ... / When his [heart] who strives to charm them beats no more!' (I: 27–32). It is debateable whether either the historical bards, with their fate so completely bound up with that of their patron, or the detached and mysterious bard of early-Romantic culture, communicated with the people in this way. Bloomfield is able to maintain the belief that by sharing in the power of the bardic tradition he would be able to communicate better with ordinary people because the kind of bard he has in mind is different in some important respects from the high-tragic figure of Gray. As he does in 'Shooter's Hill', the bard of *The Banks of Wye* probably owes something to the more demotic figure of the wandering minstrel. Rather than standing aloof from the people, Bloomfield's bard lives amongst the rural labouring poor and regulates their lives. He provides a kind of moral guidance which the written word could not replace for an audience of limited education. In the invocation at the beginning of Book III Bloomfield expresses the wish that the 'Great spirits of her bards of yore' might teach the people of Monmouthshire to value simple but irreplaceable gifts: 'Train her young shepherds, train them high / To sing of mountain liberty: / Give them the harp and modest maid; / Give them the sacred village shade' (7–10).

The bard's capacity to guide the people is linked to his ability to understand the relationship between past, present and future; to 'triumph over time' (I: 28). This phrase apparently links Bloomfield's bard to the prophetic strain that was present in popular culture during the eighteenth century; circulated in broadsheets, almanacs and other kinds of street literature, and became a vehicle for radicalism during the 1790s (Perkins, 89–122). Wordsworth negotiates the radical associations of prophetic enthusiasm to fashion his safe prophetic persona in certain key passages of *The Prelude* (Mee, 82–128, 214–56). But for Bloomfield the ability to guide the people into the future is not dependent upon the possession of prophetic powers, it is dependent upon a knowledge and understanding of the past. While the natural landscape of the region was important to him, his poetic response is shaped to a great extent by its history. Bloomfield's principal source when researching the poem appears to have been not one of the various picturesque guides to the region, but William Coxe's *An historical tour of Monmouthshire* (1800). The party took a copy of the book with them on their tour, and on his return to London the poet wrote to Mrs Lloyd Baker asking if he could borrow the volume (Add. MS 28 268, fol. 257). The MS journal of the tour also reveals an interest in Welsh history and the ancient Britons, and includes one passage drawn from a Welsh-language text and translated into English in Bloomfield's hand. He was one of a number historians, antiquarians, artists and writers who at the turn of the eighteenth century were interested in the ancient Britons (Smiles, 26–45).

In the only other extended study of *The Banks of Wye* so far undertaken, Tim Burke argues that the poem is to a large extent driven by Monmouthshire's status as 'disputed territory' (100). His essay focuses on Bloomfield's interest in 'cultural and political differences between Wales and England', and his attempt to recover the suppressed voices of the Welsh in the region through which he was travelling (Burke, 100). In *An historical tour in Monmouthshire* (1801) Coxe suggests that Monmouthshire 'unites the scenery, manners, and language' of both England and Wales (1). It is indisputable that from a geographical perspective it was and still is border country, although culturally it is, and was in 1807, predominantly Welsh (Sylvester, 381). But the 'Norman overprint' left its mark in four places: the town of Monmouth; the coastal levels; the eastern fringes of the county; and, significantly, the Monnow and Wye valleys (Sylvester, 377). Bloomfield's tour therefore encompassed first one of the more anglicized parts of the county, and then in the western mountains one of its more inhospitable and uninhabited areas. He did not spend much time in the predominantly Welsh central uplands which extend north into Herefordshire; the largest and most fertile area of the county, celebrated in georgic poems like John Philips' *Cyder* and John Dyer's *The Fleece*. But he was primarily interested in the way in which the rural workers; whether Welsh or English, and village communities in the region remembered the past.

In a letter written to Mrs Lloyd Baker in January 1811, Bloomfield states that the four songs interspersed through *The Banks of Wye* had been added to relieve 'the sameness and length of the tale' (50). This remark belies the fact that the songs perform an important function in that they represent a key to the relationship between the popular culture and the history of Monmouthshire. As Tim Burke notes 'Mary's Grave' is of Welsh provenance, being a reworking of one of the poems that Iolo Morganwg claimed were lost works of the fourteenth-century bard Daffyd ab Gwilym. These poems were not the work of the bard, but this fact was not discovered until some considerable time after their publication in 1789 (Burke, 100). Many songs were 'recovered' during the eighteenth-century Welsh renaissance, but the old 'flame' could never be rekindled because the 'poetry [of the renaissance] was ... the hobby of amateur enthusiasts, not the recognized craft of a profession [the bards] central to society' (Morgan, 64). The other three songs in *The Banks of Wye* – 'The Maid of Llandogo', 'Gleaner's Song' and 'Morris of Persfield' – are Bloomfield's own compositions. They are distributed within the poem so that they represent the living popular culture of the labouring poor, in a way that echoes Burns' use of 'Scottish song to create an alternative cultural economy to that of the "genteel [English] world"' (Davis, 196). They question the cultural discontinuity that is suggested by the concept of a 'revival', but they represent a tradition that would not have been shared by elite Celtic 'society' or by the educated intellectuals who were largely responsible for the renaissance. The singing of songs and the telling of tales helped the labouring poor to construct meaning in their lives, and perpetuate their world-view (Janowitz 1998, 79–80). As such, both practices helped to shape the cultural memory of the people.

The particular way in which Bloomfield responds to the numerous ruins in the region is implicated in the layering of meaning around the songs in *The Banks of Wye*. During the early part of the eighteenth century, ruins associated with past political turmoil had been pointed out in order to highlight the enduring and stable character of the Hanoverian order (Charlesworth, 70). Later in the century, observers were less interested in the human history of ancient architecture. In his *Three Essays; On Picturesque Beauty* (1794) Gilpin suggests that 'the ruined tower, the Gothic arch, the remains of castles, and abbeys ... are the richest legacies of art. They are consecrated by time; and almost deserve the veneration we pay to the works of nature itself' (1994a, 21). In 'Tintern Abbey' the ruin (only mentioned in the title to the poem), divested of its historicity, becomes a stimulus to individual reflection: 'So the solitary speaker in the landscape, the man speaking to men, is an abstraction of those men, an enabling image of the nation now formulated as personal, individual, and non-historical' (Janowitz, 1990, 81). By the beginning of the nineteenth century, visitors to Kenilworth Castle, for example, came 'not to see a place where the acts of history had really happened long ago but to see a place where deeds of fancy were fictionally recurring forever' (Mulvey, 18). In *The Banks of Wye* ruins are interpreted in a way that is quite different from either eighteenth-century observers, or other Romantic writers such as Wordsworth.

In 1798 and 1807, when Wordsworth and Bloomfield visited the Wye, the landscape around the ruin of Tintern Abbey would have been heavily marked and scarred by the Industrial Revolution which so altered Wales in general, and Monmouthshire in particular during the last three decades of the eighteenth century and the first half of the nineteenth century (Davies 1994, 319–97). This fact is lamented by Gilpin in his *Observations on the River Wye*: 'The country about Tintern-abbey hath been described as a solitary, tranquil scene: but its immediate environs are only meant. Within half a mile of it are carried on great iron-works; which introduce noise and bustle into these regions of tranquillity.' (1994, 256) Coxe also makes a reference to the existence of iron foundries near to the abbey (283). The condition of most people living in the area was desperate. The miner's houses were often of very poor quality, and the forest around the abbey was peopled by vagrants, many of whom survived through the marginal occupation of charcoal burning. Gilpin and Coxe both note that the ruins themselves provided a home for some of these people (Gilpin 1994, 255; Coxe, 283). Marjorie Levinson argues that Wordsworth's idealization of nature in 'Tintern Abbey' represents a calculated and guilty erasure of social and political contexts that is a consequence of the apparent reactionary turn in his politics (15–57). Although the assumptions upon which her reading is based have been questioned (Bromwich, 75), this does not alter the fact that Wordsworth was not interested in the day-to-day lives of those who inhabited the abbey and its environs. Both Bloomfield's journal and *The Banks of Wye* are also silent regarding the poverty and human suffering in the area around Tintern. But unlike Gilpin and Wordsworth, Bloomfield is interested in the historical associations of the ruin which despite its ability to produce a 'thousand raptures in [the] ... brain' and enchant the soul, 'Shall echo to the step no more; / Nor airy roof the strain prolong, / Of vesper chant or choral song' (II: 128–30) The introduction of 'Some rustic maiden's village song' (II: 90) into the account of Tintern is perhaps inappropriate in terms of the occupations of the people who inhabited the surrounding area. Although in the context of Bloomfield's interest in history, the song represents a kind of commentary upon the cultural significance of the ruin. The monk's 'vesper' or 'choral song' no longer sung was the property of a church which endeavoured to keep its culture beyond the understanding of the labouring poor, while this 'village song', passed down through the generations, has survived for the very reason that it is the property of the people.

Bloomfield further demonstrates the resilience of popular culture by introducing the 'Gleaner's Song' into his account of Goodrich Castle. The tale of Goodrich Castle is told early in *The Banks of Wye*: 'Twas here / LANCASTRIAN HENRY spread his cheer, / When came the news that HAL was born, / And MONMOUTH hail'd th' auspicious morn; / A boy in sports, a prince in war, / Wisdom and valour crown'd his car; / Of France the terror,

England's glory, / As Stratford's bard has told the story' (I: 155–62) The reign of Henry IV was disrupted by rebellion; Goodrich Castle itself was used during his protracted struggle against Owain Glyn Dwr. That of his son produced the short period of 'glory' told of by 'Stratford's bard', but his war against the French was not an unmitigated success. Historians keen to correct the legend of Henry V have argued that in the long term 'he won unity for his realm and glory for himself at the price of immediate misery for France and eventual confusion for England' (Myers, 122) Even those who have examined Henry's reign in the context of fifteenth-century standards of governance, argue that he was not politically astute and that he passed on a 'damnosa hereditas' to his son (Allmand, 442). Bloomfield does not specifically question the historical significance of Henry's reign, but the 'bold, impressive, and sublime' (I: 149) ruin does not inspire the kind of enthusiastic response that sublime features of the natural landscape do elsewhere in *The Banks of Wye*. And a change of tone half way through the passage transforms it into a lament for the instability of political power: 'Here KINGS shall dwell, the builders cry'd; / Here England's foes shall low'r their pride; / ... / Vain hope! for on the Gwentian shore, / The regal banner streams no more! / Nettles, and vilest weeds that grow, / To mock poor grandeur's head laid low, / Creep round the turrets valour rais'd' (I: 175–83). In a way that evokes Dyer's response to ruins in the landscape in *Grongar Hill* (71–92), the inability of the building to retain its physical integrity echoes the 'vain hope' of the builders and some of the most humble productions of nature usurp the place of 'kings' and 'suppliant nobles'.

Immediately after their encounter with the ruined castle, the poet and his party sit down to a pastoral lunch: 'Upon the sparkling stream we din'd; / As shepherds free on mountain heath' (I: 208–209). As Tim Burke points out, they are confronted by a group of gleaners at precisely the location where Gilpin in his *Observations on the River Wye* had 'rejoiced in their absence' (1994, 98). Gilpin was, however, making the quite correct observation that 'The banks of the Wye consist, almost entirely, either of wood, or of pasturage', and asserting that according to the demands of picturesque beauty, if a landscape be marked by agriculture it is best that it is pasturage (1994, 253). At the turn of the eighteenth century Monmouthshire was, as it still is, 'overwhelmingly a grazing county', although there was some arable farming especially on the coastal levels (Sylvester, 384). Furthermore, below Monmouth the hinterland of the Wye was particularly unsuited to arable farming. Both banks of the Wye at Coldwell, the point where Bloomfield supposedly encountered the gleaners, were and still are very steep, heavily wooded and therefore completely unfit for arable farming (Ordinance Survey Old Series Map 43; Sylvester, 379). No mention is made of gleaners in the journal (Add. MS 28 267, fols 12–20), so the reason for the inclusion of this passage at this point in the poem deserves some attention. Whether or not it is a poetical contrivance, however, if Bloomfield's interest in the past is kept in mind the appearance of the gleaners suggests a distinctive kind of history that is quite different from the history represented by Goodrich Castle.

The manner in which the gleaners are announced is curious: 'A troop of gleaners chang'd their shade, / And 'twas a change by music made; / For slowly to the brink they drew, / To mark our joy, and share it too' (I: 219–23). The musical imagery suggests that the 'troop' approach the river in a regimented or trance-like fashion. It is as if they come forward from the past, like the chorus in a classical Greek tragedy, in order to sing their tale to the party. The reader could be forgiven for asking the question, are the gleaners real, or are they a pageant passing through the narrator's memory? The vision does draw his mind to the past: 'How oft, in childhood's flow'ry days, / I've heard the wild impassion'd lays / Of such a group, lays strange and new, / And thought, was ever song so true?' (I: 223–6). This is another peculiar passage because it is not at all certain that gleaners, living on the edge of extreme poverty, would have sung as they worked, and certainly not as a group. The atmosphere of improbability is reinforced by the fact that the gleaners by the river also burst into song, providing the party with a kind of impromptu cabaret. The coherence of the plot is not, however, what is important here; the rural labouring poor did sing songs about their lives and their labour.

The 'wild' and 'impassion'd' nature of the gleaners' song is suggestive of a tradition, the origin of which is in some way primeval, unknown to the singers, and lost in the mist of time. The customary practice of gleaning did have biblical provenance, and figures like Capel Lofft argued that it was a legitimate activity because it was 'a custom founded in benevolence' and 'ascertained by immemorial usage' (1788, 220). Although the question of whether this fact legitimized the practice at the turn of the eighteenth century was the subject of some debate. The kind of traditional world-view represented by customary practices like gleaning has increasingly been the subject of enquiry over recent decades by historians concerned to rescue 'the past experiences of the bulk of the population from either total neglect by historians or from what [E.P.] Thompson calls the "enormous condescension" of posterity' (Sharpe, 27). Gleaning was certainly part of a whole network of customary usages that structured the world-view of the labouring poor, and which they struggled to preserve during the drive for agricultural 'improvement' (Thompson 1993, 97–184; Neeson, 185–293). The 'truth' inherent in their world-view is represented and sustained by the gleaners' songs. The 'truth' told by the ruin of Goodrich Castle, however, 'dies the while' (I: 152) it tells its tale because it is not sustained by the living culture of the labouring poor.

As Bloomfield proceeds along the Wye and out into the Black Mountains he repeatedly comments upon the political history associated with ruins in the landscape. Raglan Castle is associated with the history of the closing stages of the English civil war: 'Majestic RAGLAND! Harvests wave / Where thund'ring hosts their watch-word gave, / When cavaliers, with downcast eye, / Struck the last flag of loyalty' (III: 19–22). It is a history that still has the power to move, and provide 'Food for reflection till we die' (III: 56). Like Goodrich Castle, this monument to political dispute is gradually being reclaimed by nature and obliterated by time as '... ivy, creeping year by year, / Of growth enormous, triumphs' and '... years and storms prevail, / And spread ... its dust upon the gale' (III: 31–40). The meditative observer's thoughts must be directed once again to the futility of war, and to the thought that, as in England's civil war, both sides are generally the losers in internecine strife. Bloomfield's most explicit condemnation of political ambition occurs when the narrator turns his attention to Brunless Castle where Owain Glyn Dwr 'Left war's attendants, blood and tears, / And spread their terrors many a mile, / And shouted round the flaming pile' (IV: 102–103). In England Glyn Dwr had always been regarded as a destroyer of Welsh towns and traitor to the English crown. In Wales he was a popular if morally ambiguous figure in folklore, but during the seventeenth and eighteenth centuries, Welsh intellectuals often reproduced English views of him (Henken, 89–145). Towards the end of the eighteenth century, however, Glyn Dwr was rehabilitated as a 'Welsh hero' by figures like Edward Williams (Henken, 166). Bloomfield's source for this passage is not Coxe who is neutral in so far as Glyn Dwr's status as villain or hero is concerned. He clearly went out of his way to unearth the details of Glyn Dwr's connection with Brunless Castle, and to present his career in such negative terms. Bloomfield condemns greed for power, whatever its source, and corrupt government which can create the kind of vacuum that is often filled by individuals like Glyn Dwr: 'May heav'n preserve our native land / From blind ambition's murdering hand; / From all the wrongs that can provoke / A people's wrath' (IV: 105–108). The attentive observer is, however, able to see that political history is not the only kind of history suggested by ruins in the landscape.

By the summer of 1807, when Bloomfield encounters Raglan and Brunless, they have been reshaped by country people, and re-absorbed into the peaceful agricultural landscape. The ruin of Raglan Castle is surrounded by the new harvest, one of the most important symbols of the seasonal renewal that shapes and sustains the lives of rural communities. A footnote, an extract from Coxe, also reveals the manner in which the actual fabric of Raglan Castle has been transformed by the labouring poor: 'In addition to the injury the castle sustained from the parliamentary army, considerable dilapidations have been occasioned by numerous tenants in the vicinity, who conveyed away the stone and other materials for the construction of farm-houses, barns, and other buildings' (71). The fabric of Brunless Tower that once provided a refuge for ambitious men of violence now protects the plough-horse and other humble farm-yard animals: 'Lone tower! though suffer'd yet to stand, / Dilapidation's wasting hand / Shall tear thy pond'rous walls, to guard / The slumb'ring steed, or fence the yard' (IV: 95–8). The tower itself has become a storehouse for the 'full-dried hay' of local farmers (IV: 91).

The contrast between the two histories that dominate *The Banks of Wye* is at its most explicit in the account of Brunless Tower. The poem focuses on the countless workers that figure in the landscape around the ruin, enacting a kind of mock conquest of the castle: 'And every mile was but a change / Of peasants lab'ring, lab'ring still, / And climbing many a distant hill' (IV: 86–8). This is a generalized, naturalized vision of the agricultural worker; an initial reading brings to mind John Barrell's work on the representation of the labouring poor in eighteenth-century poetry and painting. It is clear, however, that Bloomfield was never driven by the kind of politically motivated moralistic considerations that caused other writers simply to brush the rural worker into the physical landscape, 'to represent the work, its effects and circumstances, but ... keep the worker out of sight' (Barrell 1992, 215). At the same time he is not concerned, as he had been in *The Farmer's Boy*, to represent the lives and work of the labouring poor in detail. The labourers that appear before the eye of the narrator in *The Banks of Wye* are representatives of all those workers who have appeared in the same countryside through time. The poor were 'lab'ring' in the time of Glyn Dwr's bloody conflict with Henry IV, and are 'lab'ring still' as Bloomfield's party pass through on their way to Hay-on-Wye, when the history of that conflict has faded from the common memory.

The ruins are reconfigured by the labouring-poor in other ways that are perhaps more important because they question both the manner in which the past is remembered, and its value and meaning. The study of history as a discipline endeavours to investigate diverse records of past events and to bring some rational order to those events. In this way history is concerned with 'truth'. Bloomfield displays knowledge of the 'truth' in terms of the significant individuals and political history associated with the various ruins that he visits. But he also reveals sensitivity to the truth that inheres in the 'myth', 'tradition' and custom of the labouring poor in the region; although he cannot share those truths in quite the same way that he shares similar truths relating to rural Suffolk. Bloomfield understands the importance of the mythical 'truths' that peoples have 'found necessary to preserve as essential for their entire social existence' (Mali, 4). Myth and legend are not less true than political history, it is just that they speak of a different kind of truth: 'However legendary a myth may be, it does not signify fabrication or pure fiction, because it usually contains or refers to certain crucial issues in the history of the community, such as those that concern the common ancestry or territory of the community' (Mali, 4; see also Vasina, 129). Indeed some contemporary historians have argued that because myths 'impart meaning to history,' without an attempt to understand the traditional world view of a people there can be no access to the past (O'Flaherty, 27).

The cultural memory of a people develops out of their 'historical gossip' as it is passed from generation to generation (Vasina, 17–21). A footnote to the passage relating to Raglan Castle suggests how 'truth and tradition' become a 'mingled stream' as the significance of the ruin is transformed in the popular culture of the poor: 'A village woman ... desired us to remark the descent to a vault ... in which she had heard that no candle would continue burning; "and," added she, "they say it is because of the damps; but for my part, I think the devil is there"' (73–4). The men and women that have worked, and continue to work in the environs of Brunless Castle reconfigure history both through their labour and through their talk: 'Perhaps they told / Tradition's tales, and taught how old / The ruin'd castle? False or true, / They guess it,— just as others do' (IV: 91–4). The precise history of the castle and its role in Glyn Dwr's revolt does not appear to be important to the rural labouring poor, but 'tradition's tales' will live on in popular culture. These 'tales' do not often fit into 'the highly sophisticated, highly abstract scientific conception of time, as a measurable continuum' but then this is 'a conception which is largely meaningless for ordinary human purposes' (Finley, 23; see also Tonkin, 66–82). For the labouring poor, the old castle is both a hay barn and a stimulus for the creation and embodiment of a popular culture that both informs and is informed by their day-to-day lives. The alternative belief systems of the labouring poor that result from this kind of 'historical gossip' represent 'a shared understanding of the world around them' rather than 'an irrational response to their experiences' (Bushaway 1995, 198). Indeed, as Victor Turner has argued, 'tradition's tales' might have been especially important during periods of political turmoil: 'Where historical life itself fails to make cultural sense in terms that formerly held good, narrative and cultural drama may have the task of *poesis*, that is of remaking cultural sense' (Turner 1981, 164).

In respect of Clifford Castle, Bloomfield explores in greater detail the manner in which the selection and interweaving of historical truth and tradition occurs. A recent history of Wales has argued that the March was 'a central element in the history of Wales for four hundred years and more' (Davies 1994, 109). In Davies's account other ways of remembering the past are implicitly subordinated to the political history of the region. The people that Bloomfield encounters remember the past differently, they choose to remember the story of 'Fair Rosamond' (IV: 188) rather than the history of the March Lordships of Clifford. Rosamond is believed to have been the daughter of Walter de Clifford of the Fitz-Ponce family, and, as a footnote to the poem remarks, to have been born circa 1140 at Clifford Castle (116). It is thought that she was a secret mistress of Henry II for several years, but he openly acknowledged her only after he had imprisoned his wife Eleanor of Aquitaine in punishment for having encouraged her sons during the rebellion of 1173–74. At some point Rosamond retired to a nunnery, she died circa 1176 and was buried in the nunnery church of Godstow. The body was removed in 1191 by order of St Hugh, the Bishop of Lincoln, and apparently re-interred outside the church. This is all that is known about Rosamond and so represents the historical truth concerning her life. Tradition gradually transformed this history into a tale of passion, jealousy and the desire for revenge, universal emotions which most of us feel to some degree at some stage of our life. According to 'tradition' Henry built Rosamond a beautiful bower within a labyrinth in a park at Woodstock, which could only be found with a 'clue of silk'. The jealous Queen Eleanor discovered the secret of the clue and appeared before her rival with a dagger and a cup of poison, offering a choice between two deaths. After shedding tears and offering many useless prayers to the Queen, the 'Fair Rosamond' took the poison and fell dead in the midst of the bower while the birds continued singing all around her.

The story that she was poisoned by Queen Eleanor first appears in the fourteenth-century French Chronicle of London. Further details were added later by other story-tellers, possibly in the many traditional ballads and broadsides that treated the theme, for example *The Life and Death of Fair Rosamond, Concubine to King Henry the Second, Shewing how she was poisoned by*

Queen Eleanor (undated) or *A Mournful Song on the Death of Fair Rosamond, the Unhappy Daughter of Walter Lord Clifford, and concubine to Henry the Second, for which she was poison'd at Woodstock by Queen Eleanor* (1755). That the story had entered into the nation's consciousness is also revealed by the fact that Samuel Daniel published 'The Complaint of Rosamond' with his sonnet sequence *Delia* (1592); Dryden produced a version of the story in *Henry the Second, King of England; with the Death of Rosamond. A Tragedy* (1693); Joseph Allison wrote an opera on the subject; and Sir Walter Scott introduced the character Rosamond Clifford into *The Talisman* (1825) and *Woodstock* (1826).

The labouring poor not only remember the past in a particular way, they often choose to remember events in the day-to-day lives of individuals that would not generally be registered by historians. History records the often violent political maneuvrings of the propertied classes, while the poor celebrate the benevolent acts of the rich in songs like 'Morris of Persfield'. Morris is remembered because he 'listen'd to pity's soft sigh ... / ... gave with a spirit so free, / And fed the distress'd at his door' (II: 244–6). When he announces the song, Bloomfield locates it within the bardic [minstrel] tradition: 'Hark! 'tis some hoary bard complains! / The deeds, the worth, he knew so well, / The force of nature bids him tell' (II: 238–40). The song arises out of the Romantic connection between the bard and the sublime landscape. But unlike the heroic versions of the bard derived from the history of the region or from Gray's poem, Bloomfield's more low-key bard remembers gentle acts of human kindness in his song. Bloomfield acknowledges Coxe as his source for Morris's story, but he is somewhat selective in order to present him as a type of the 'Man of Ross', selflessly devoted to the needs of the labouring poor. Coxe relates that the 'embarrasment' felt by Morris at being forced to sell Persfield resulted from a variety of causes including: 'an expensive style of living, numerous benefactions, imprudent management of his West India estates, a succession of unfavourable seasons in the Island of Antigua, inattention to his accounts, but, above all, an unfortunate propensity to gaming' (312). Bloomfield's song alludes to these failings, but asserts that because his claim to fame (for the labouring poor) is so strong he is deserving of such a living monument: 'If ever man merited fame, / If ever man's failings went free, / Forgot at the sound of his name, / Our MORRIS of PERSFIELD was he' (II: 277–80).

In providing Morris with this fictional monument Bloomfield is responding to another literary connection with Monmouthshire. The passage recalls Pope's 'unsung' hero in his *Epistle to Allen Lord Bathurst: Of the Use of Riches* (1733). Pope's 'MAN of ROSS' relieves the suffering of the poor whenever he can, just like Morris of Persfield: 'Behold the Market-place with poor o'erspread! / The MAN of ROSS divides the weekly bread: / ... / Is any sick? the MAN of ROSS relieves, / Prescribes, attends, the med'cine makes, and gives' (263–70). In Pope's poem though, the 'Man of Ross' does not receive a memorial of any kind; he was buried with 'no monument, inscription, stone ... / His race, his form, his name almost unknown' (283–4). It is possible that Bloomfield felt the ingratitude in this, and that it is partly to put right a perceived wrong that Morris does receive a monument. It is not, however, an imposing stone monument, the lack of which Pope laments. The memorial that Morris receives in *The Banks of Wye* is more valuable than this. It is a self sustaining monument in that he is remembered by the people and lives on in the songs and 'hearts of the poor' because he endeavoured to improve the quality of their lives.

In an important passage in Book I, Bloomfield had expressed the wish that his journey along the Wye might enable him to 'hear the Twick'nham bard again' (I: 85). In fact he is able to 'hear' what Pope does not; that an individual like the 'Man of Ross' would never be remembered in the way envisaged in the *Epistle to Allen Lord Bathurst*, but at the same time would not remain 'unknown'. 'Morris of Persfield' also suggests a way in which, through *The Banks of Wye*, Bloomfield achieves his desire, expressed early in the poem, to emulate in his own life and poetry that of the bard or wandering minstrel. Like the songs that appear in the poem, two of which he explicitly attributes to a bard or 'sage', the account of his journey is a monument to the values and simple way of life of the labouring poor. Bloomfield becomes, like the bard, but in a less mysterious way, the voice of the people he encounters in the landscape. He is eventually able to see and hear what is missed by other Romantic adherents to the 'bardic tradition' such as Edward Williams, Thomas Love Peacock and William Wordsworth. It is not the impression generated by the figure of the bard, or even necessarily what he says that is important. The impact made by the bard is dependent upon whether his 'songs' speak of and to a living culture.

Wordsworth's 'Tintern Abbey' is a monument to the poet's own mind, to his own particular way of responding to the sublime landscape. The ability to hear 'the still, sad music of humanity' (92) and feel the 'sense sublime' present in nature is an exclusive faculty that can be possessed by only a few (96). It is a 'gift' which derives its distinctive quality from the very fact that it is not widely shared. There is a sense in which Wordsworth's response to the Wye mirrors that of the war lords whose history Bloomfield traces in his poem. Both desire to impose their own vision upon the Wye, and for different reasons consider the world-view of the people who inhabit the region to be irrelevant. In *The Banks of Wye*, however, it is the forgotten labouring people who are ultimately able to impose themselves upon the landscape. The world-view of the labouring poor has survived because it develops and adapts to new circumstances as it is passed from generation to generation through communitarian customs reinforced by traditional ballads and songs. It is not linked to the world-view of 'significant' individuals, and it is sustainable because it has a broad foundation, unlike the predatory moral code of warlords like Glyn Dwr. In Bloomfield's version of the history of the Wye, the labouring poor, represented by the old village woman 'Jane Edwards', are the real 'conquerors' (III: 357–60) of time.

CHAPTER SIX

Community Labour and Poetry in *May Day with the Muses*

May Day is the ideal consummation of Bloomfield's career as a poet because it reasserts many of the grand themes of his *oeuvre*: that humanity prospers within mutually supportive communities; that labour is the stimulus for a particular kind of poetry; and that genius exists in all social situations. It is his most direct statement of a kind of Romanticism that stands in opposition to the elitist transcendental poetics of figures like Wordsworth and Coleridge. Although it is not possible to say whether Bloomfield was directly influenced by the 'second-generation' Romantics, there are also ways in which the poem can be said to acknowledge and respond to developments in the discourse of Romanticism. *May Day* is marked throughout by the kind of playful tone that is found in much of Byron's poetry, particularly *Don Juan*. The first two cantos of *Don Juan* (1819) were published whilst Bloomfield was working on *May Day*, and generated such notoriety that he cannot have been unaware of the work. *May Day* also makes reference to contemporary events on several occasions through the kind of complex allusion and allegory that Bloomfield had not previously written, but which is common in the poetry of Byron and Shelley. The poem reveals that Bloomfield was aware of the social, economic and political difficulties faced by the British people during the second decade of the nineteenth century. He was concerned to engage with issues of this kind in a way that he had not done before, but at the same time reassert the labouring-class poetics that differentiates him from Byron, Shelley and Keats as much as from Wordsworth and Coleridge.

It is possible that *May Day* is a riposte to a passage in *English Bards and Scotch Reviewers* (1809). In view of the fact that the passage contains a personal attack it is likely that Bloomfield was aware of it, but because he makes no reference to the poem in correspondence or elsewhere, this cannot be established with certainty. Byron's poem echoes an often repeated eighteenth-century view articulated most famously by Samuel Johnson. According to Boswell, Johnson apparently remarked of the shoemaker-poet James Woodhouse: 'it was all vanity and childishness: ... such objects were, to those who patronised them, mere mirrours of their own superiority. "They had better (said he,) furnish the man with good implements for his trade, than raise subscriptions for his poems"' (*Life of Johnson*, 127). *English Bards and Scotch Reviewers* is also strongly critical of the popular interest in poets from a labouring-class background: 'When some brisk youth, the tenant of a stall, / ... / St Crispin quits, and cobbles for the muse / Heavens! how the vulgar stare! how crowds applaud! / How ladies read, and literati laud!' (765–

70). The passage makes an explicit, and less than flattering reference to both Bloomfield and his patron Capel Lofft. Lofft is held up satirically as a reliable judge of the poetry produced by labouring-class poets: 'Genius must guide when wits admire the rhyme, / And Capel Lofft declares 'tis quite sublime' (773–4). Bloomfield and his brother Nathaniel are implicated in Byron's ironic rallying-call for more such poets: 'Swains! quit the plough, resign the useless spade! / Lo! Burns and Bloomfield, / ... / Then why no more? ... / ... Why not brother Nathan too / Him too the mania, not the muse, has seized; / Not inspiration, but a mind diseased' (776–84). *May Day* could be described as a direct response to Byron's rallying-call, and a rebuff to the sentiment expressed in this passage; that individuals of humble origin do not possess the talent to produce poetry worthy of serious notice. It is a long poem consisting of a frame and several embedded shorter poems. The frame is an account of the May-Day celebrations on the estate of Sir Ambrose Higham, and the shorter poems are the compositions of his tenants, tendered in place of rent.

Notwithstanding the fact that in some respects *May Day* represents a response to developments in Romantic poetry, in September 1819 Bloomfield expressed fears that it might be 'out of fashion from the taste of the times' (Add. MS 28 268, fol. 404). So it is surprising that he begins his preface with a statement which suggests that he did not feel the need to explain his conception:

> I AM of the opinion that Prefaces are very useless things in cases like the present, where the Author must talk of himself, with little amusement to his readers. I have hesitated whether I should say any thing or nothing; but as it is the fashion to say something, I suppose I must comply. [iii]

It soon becomes apparent, however, that these remarks merely establish the playful tone that reappears repeatedly in *May Day*. Bloomfield does go on to provide a preface, and taken as a whole it reveals him to be just as concerned as he had been in the past with forestalling criticism and directing in advance the way the book should be read. Although they had appeared many years before, he might still have had in mind the need to address reviews of *Wild Flowers* and *The Banks of Wye*. These had not been so uniform in their praise as had notices of his first two 'attempts at verse'. The *Critical Review* remarked of the former: 'There is a nerveless imbecility of conception which pervades the whole volume' (s.3, 8 (1806), 127). And the same journal felt that the latter contained 'no symptoms' of 'an increased intimacy with the machinery of poetry' and 'is little else than a journal in easy rhyme of an excursion in South Wales, with occasional apostrophes to objects, which excited more than ordinary attention' (s.4, 1 (1812), 376). There are features of *May Day* which suggest that Bloomfield might have had his critics in mind when writing the poem itself. The embedded shorter poems are more integral to the whole than those incorporated into *The Banks of Wye*, and several reveal a considerable command of 'the machinery of poetry'.

Bloomfield's preface proper begins with a quotation from Samuel Johnson's *The Rambler* (No. 82), as an apparent defence of the frame; this relates to a landowner who accepts butterflies from his tenants in place of rent. Then he remarks: 'my old Sir Ambrose stands in no need of defence from me or from anyone; a man has a right to do what he likes with his own estate' (iv). Both statements seem to represent a continuation of the dismissive and humorous tone that had been established in the first paragraph of the preface. But it is possible that the latter remark has a more subtle ironic meaning, especially if it is read in the context of Bloomfield's previous writings on rural life. During the early decades of the nineteenth century many men in a similar position to Sir Ambrose were doing exactly what they wanted with their estates. Rather than displaying a paternal care for their tenants, however, they were enclosing and improving them like Mr Parker in Jane Austin's *Sanditon* (1817) who turns a working village into a voyeuristic pleasure-ground for the rich. Like the majority of the labouring poor, Bloomfield believed that ownership of a landed estate was always accompanied by certain responsibilities. It was a common belief that a 'lord of the soil' like Sir Ambrose should 'reside in his manor house ... [and he] or his resident tenant was also firmly expected to work as much of the home farm land as possible, maintain a household-full of servants and keep up a table for the day-labourers' (Laslett, 78).

In the next passage Bloomfield turns his attention to rural poets and suggests that 'a cluster of poets is not likely to be found in one village' (iv). He goes on to cite a poem by his friend Thomas Park (1759–1834). Park trained as an engraver, but he abandoned this art in 1797, a year in which he also published a small collection of his verse entitled *Sonnets, and other small poems*. He was a respected antiquary and bibliographer, and a friend of William Cowper, William Hayley, Anna Seward, Robert Southey, Sir Walter Scott and several other figures who were eminent in the field of letters at the turn of the eighteenth century. He edited numerous works including John Dryden's *Fables from Boccaccio to Chaucer* (1806), Horace Walpole's *Royal and Noble Authors, Enlarged and Continued* (1806) and the *Harleian Miscellany* (1808–13). According to the *Dictionary of National Biography* he corrected and superintended the publication of various editions of Bloomfield's 'Poems', but there is no evidence that he was directly involved in the publication of the poet's work before Bloomfield's death. He did assist the poet in his effort to find a publisher for *May Day*, and the inclusion of his poem might have been Bloomfield's way of expressing his thanks. But in that it is a critique of English village life, 'Written in the Isle of Thanet, August, 1790' is also relevant to Bloomfield's remarks about rural poets: 'For sad experience shows the heart / Of human beings much the same; / Or polish'd by insidious art, / Or rude as from the clod it came' (5–8). Like Park, but unlike Byron, Bloomfield believed that, while working people could be 'boors', they could also possess ability. Those that attend the feast on Oakly Manor display both a degree of licentious and unruly behaviour, and a considerable amount of talent. Moreover Bloomfield generally chose for his theme the best, rather than the worst of country life and Park appears to approve such selection: 'Nature may form a perfect scene, / But Fancy must the figures draw' (19–20). *May Day* is clearly peopled with fanciful figures, but it is also marked by the poet's own practical experience of life in the countryside.

The fact that Bloomfield goes on to censure the kind of fancy that is inappropriate represents evidence that he wishes to define for his readers the role of imagination in pastoral or rural poetry. At the same time the playful tone that has thus far marked the preface is maintained. He comments upon the kind of fancy which characterized the pastoral songs that he was obliged to hear in his youth and which often described sleeping shepherds and shepherdesses. In another injection of humour he remarks of one song in which both characters go to sleep: 'if I understand any thing at all about keeping sheep, this is not the way to go to work with them' (vi). Like so many passages in this preface, at first sight these remarks appear to have little serious import. Considered in the context of poems like 'Shooter's Hill' or 'To My Old Oak Table', and the critical perspective that begins to take shape in statements made within the preface to *Wild Flowers*, they take on a much greater significance. Within the body of the poem itself Bloomfield engages further with the question of what constitutes good poetry, and makes his most explicit and didactic remarks regarding what he considers to be fit subject matter. In 'The Invitation' Sir Ambrose reminds his tenants, and of course Bloomfield's readers, of what constitute vulgar and unimaginative themes for poetry: '... harkye, bring / No stupid ghost, no vulgar thing; / ... surely fancy need not brood / O'er midnight darkness, crimes, and blood, / In magic cave or monks retreat' (94–103). This is clearly a reference to the sentimental Gothic vogue in both novels and verse that was popular during the late eighteenth and early nineteenth centuries. But it could also refer to the 'oriental tales' of Byron and Thomas Moore that appeared to unprecedented public acclaim between 1813 and 1817. For Sir Ambrose there is enough of interest in 'the bright world' for the poet of imagination, and it is not necessary to follow flights of sensational fancy. Sir Ambrose concludes these words of guidance with the following request: '... bring me nature, bring me sense, / And joy shall be your recompense' (111–12). He provides readers with a clear and unambiguous indication of the kind of poetry they can expect in *May Day*, and a direction that it should be read as both a representation of real life and a particular imaginative perspective upon it.

John Lucas asserts that *May Day* does not engage with the 'bright world' of early nineteenth-century rural life, rather it is 'set in the past' and is 'an implicit lament for days that are no more' (1994, 66; 2006, 125). The tone of lamentation in the opening passages of 'The Invitation' might also be a consequence of the fact that Bloomfield had been separated for nearly forty years from the rural Suffolk scenes that had inspired virtually all of his verse. Moreover, he had not produced a volume of poetry since *The Banks of Wye* in 1811. His lack of inspiration seems to result from the consequent decay of his poetic faculty: 'time creeps o'er me with palsied hand, / And frost-like bids the stream of passion stand, / And through his dry teeth sends a shivering blast, / And points to more than fifty winters past' (7–10). He returned to the country in 1812 when he moved to Shefford in Bedfordshire, but his small-minded neighbours irritated the poet, especially when they spread rumours about him.

In May 1821 he wrote to Mr Lloyd Baker: 'As to what you have heard of me from this vile little town. I can assure you that trade is so very bad, so very dull, that the people are obliged to seek new employments, or to improve the old ones, they therefore don't forget slander'(Add. MS 28 268, fol. 417). Apparently, and in a sense appropriately, it is Bloomfield's memory of the time when he was situated like Sir Ambrose's tenant-poets that provides inspiration: '"Remember Spring." / Stay, sweet enchantress, charmer of my days / And glance thy rainbow colours o'er my lays; / Be to poor Giles what thou hast ever been' (14–17). In any case, he was certainly successful in overcoming the languor that seemed to afflict him because, as John Lucas has remarked, the poetry that follows is some of his best, and taken as a whole *May Day* is perhaps his most original poem in overall conception (1998, 306).

In some respects life on Oakly Manor is simply an idealized representation of the old paternalist system. Like Herbert Brooks in 'The Broken Crutch', Sir Ambrose is a perfect paternalist landlord who takes an interest in what goes on in and around his estate. Perhaps more importantly he also represents a source of support during times of hardship: 'Where sickness raged, or want allied to shame, / Sure as the sun his well-timed succour came; / Food for the starving child, and warmth and wine / For age that totter'd in its last decline' (49–52). The majority of his tenants produce something that they can sell, and many are semi-independent cottagers or smallholders, as the beginning of Sir Ambrose's 'summons' makes clear: 'All ye on Oakly manor dwelling, / Farming, labouring, buying, selling' (83–4). Mutuality is also an important feature of the community as is clear from the description of the preparations for the feast. The whole of Sir Ambrose's large household is engaged in these preparations, and his workers appear to be long-term employees hired on a living-in basis. He does not view them as a resource to be used and discarded at will, and provides security for those that work the estate land that he retains for himself. This is the most explicit celebration of communal labour in Bloomfield's poetry:

> Some swung the biting scythe with merry face,
> And cropp'd the daisies for a dancing space,
> Some roll'd the mouldy barrel in his might,
> From prison'd darkness into cheerful light,
> And fenced him round with cans; and others bore
> The creaking hamper with its costly store,
> Well corked, well flavour'd, and well tax'd, that came
> From Lusitanian mountains, dear to fame. [204–11]

May Day represents a way of conceptualizing rural life that Bloomfield first developed in *The Farmer's Boy*, and was integral to his poetics throughout his career. It stands in opposition to a Wordsworthian countryside populated by sublime individuals, such as the figure of Michael, or the shepherd in *The Prelude*.

Lucas's account of the poem is correct as far as it goes, but he fails to notice the different levels of meaning that are present in *May Day*. It does not offer a straightforward nostalgic picture of eighteenth-century paternalism; of 'rural England as it perhaps once was, or can be imagined to have been, and as it might be again' (Lucas 2006, 130). Bloomfield reshapes paternalism to suit his own vision of an ideal community. Most importantly there is no deference and no formality on Oakly Manor. Displays of deference by the labouring poor were not always sincere, but they were an important part of the dialogic of 'theatre and counter-theatre' that characterized eighteenth-century paternalism (Thompson 1993, 71). But Bloomfield saw the way in which formality and deference reinforced distinctions between different groups within society, and regarded both as a 'dripping besom quenching nature's flame' (255). He disliked the way in which distinction undermined the communicative and social bonds that he believed were the foundation of a properly functioning community: 'Avaunt, Formality! / ... / Thou cankerworm, who liv'st but to destroy, / And eat the very heart of social joy' (254–7). Perhaps most importantly in terms of the schema of *May Day* itself, a formal hierarchical society also suppresses intellectual creativity. It keeps those amongst the labouring poor who possess fertile minds trudging along behind the plough or digging for turnips, and is a 'freezing mist around intellectual mirth' (258). The passage attacks the kind of haughty elitism that is expressed in *English Bards and Scotch Reviewers*, and argues that the very distinctions Byron appears to approve are themselves the product a 'cankerworm' or 'disease' within society.

Like the lines in 'Shooter's Hill' that concern the way genius is suppressed by 'want's foul picture' (48), Sir Ambrose's view represents an implicit call for equality of opportunity regardless of social class. In fact the passage connects the folk occasion and the apparently free, frank, loving and responsible character of life on Oakly Manor with the creative life in general and with the production of poetry in particular. Bloomfield reiterates the message of *The Farmer's Boy*; that social interaction within an inclusive community causes people 'to think who never thought before' (142), and produces both poets and poetry. Taken as a whole, *May Day* is Bloomfield's most sustained denial of Wordsworth's belief that poetic sensibility develops in isolation from 'the deformities of crowded life'. Bloomfield is saying something similar to John Clare in 'Dawnings of Genius' which had been published two years earlier within *Poems Descriptive of Rural Life and Scenery* (1820). 'Dawnings of Genius' does not make any reference to formality, but it is about the manner in which the budding, searching intellect of the rural labourer dies for want of nourishment: often will he witness 'with admiring eyes, / The brook's sweet dimples o'er the pebbles rise; / ... / Raptures the while his inward powers inflame, / And joys delight him which he cannot name; / Ideas picture pleasing views to mind, / For which his language can no utterance find' (21–8). It was the whole structure of society as well as deep-rooted attitudes at all social levels that prevented those within the labouring classes from fulfilling their creative and intellectual potential. As he indicated in the preface to the 1809 edition of his poems, Bloomfield felt that he was no longer accepted amongst labouring people following the success of *The Farmer's Boy* (I: xxxv). Twenty years later

Clare encountered considerable suspicion from other villagers in Helpston following the success of *Poems Descriptive of Rural Life and Scenery*.

Sir Ambrose's decision to hold the feast was made partly as a consequence of his interest in natural genius. Like the Duke of Grafton he had a desire to uncover 'the latent sparks of genius found / In many a local ballad, many a tale, / ... / Though unrecorded as the gleams of light / That vanish in the quietness of night' (70–74). His acceptance of poetry for rent could therefore be regarded as an example of the patronage which was an integral part of the traditional paternalist system. It is possible, however, to regard the exchange that takes place between Sir Ambrose and his tenants in a different way. The tenants who are chosen to recite their poetry at the feast can be seen as representatives of a new class of writer. All of them are peasant or labouring-class poets, but their poetry is brought to a marketplace and exchanged for one of their most basic needs. It is true that it is an imaginary marketplace, but it is one in which the kind of poetry that Bloomfield himself wrote, the 'local ballad' and the 'tale', is a marketable commodity. The arrangement which Sir Ambrose proposes appears to combine the security of patronage, and the paternalist structure linking landlord and tenant, with a degree of freedom in so far as the sale of his tenant's writings is concerned. As is supposed to happen within any free market, they receive recognition of, and payment for their individual talents. The tenants also appear to be extended complete freedom regarding choice of subject-matter (the significance of this will become clear when their poems are examined). This courtesy was not always extended to labouring-class poets. Hannah More informed Ann Yearsley's readers that she expected her to produce poetry which evinced a 'justness' of literary taste and familiarity with 'the opinions of the best critics' (1787, ix). Later Lord Radstock pressurized Clare to 'expunge certain highly objectionable passages' from *Poems Descriptive of Rural Life and Scenery* (Storey, 61): his wrath was directed at 'Dawnings of Genius' amongst other poems.

If *May Day* is an idyll recalling a lost or disappearing world, it is also a fiction marking the rise of the professional writer. Bloomfield himself struggled to retain his independence and earn a secure living from his writing throughout his life. Even taking into account his earnings from other sources he was never financially secure, and his situation deteriorated significantly in 1811 when his publisher Thomas Hood died. As he remarked in a letter to Mrs Lloyd Baker on 10 September 1812:

> ... the business came into the hands of a younger partner, who found himself involved, sold off his stock and copyrights, &c., when property of mine (which sold among the rest) was in his hands to the amount of four hundred pounds. And I have since the mortification to find him a bankrupt, by which I shall lose half that sum, and know not *when* I may get any. [55]

Bloomfield encouraged his children to find what employment they could, and linked his family's difficulties to the 'poetical revolution' that followed the death of Mr Hood. In a letter to his eldest daughter written in December 1815 he expresses his relief at 'the remotest prospect of [her] ... getting employment' even though it was '*much against the grain* of [his] ... affection'. He then informs her that he asks her to find work because: 'Up to this moment I cannot even guess what I shall get for my reversions of copy. If I get but a small sum I must make it larger by parting with half my share of the whole concern' (Add. MS 28 268, fol. 358r). The question of copyright was a matter of dispute at the time, and had been the subject of a House of Lords decision in *Donaldson* v. *Becket* (1774). This enforced the Statute of Anne 1709 which limited the author's copyright to fourteen years (a further fourteen-year copyright would be granted to authors still alive after the initial term). Although the poet had not explicitly sold his copyright to them, Bloomfield's publishers believed that in publishing his work half of the copyright became theirs, at least until it came up for renewal. In a letter dated 26 November 1800, addressed to Lofft but not sent, Hood had remarked: 'We should not have presumed to print a second, third and fourth Edition unless we had not been assured that one half of the copyright of the Farmer's Boy was ours' (Add. MS 28, 268, fol. 48r). Bloomfield did sell fifty per cent of the extended copyright in *The Farmer's Boy*, but it has not been possible to establish how much he received for this: it was, however, less than he expected. Presumably he also sold a percentage of the extended copyright in *Rural Tales* and *Wild Flowers*, but again it is not known how much he received. Like John Clare a few years later he had to contend not only with patrons, but also with a literary marketplace that he found confusing and felt had cheated him. Things got so bad that in September 1816 Sir Samuel Egerton Brydges and other friends issued a subscription on his behalf in an effort to 'secure independence and comfort to himself and his family during the remainder of his own sickly existence' (*Correspondence*, 58). Despite all of this, Bloomfield still saw himself as a professional writer, unlike earlier labouring-class poets such as James Woodhouse. Even after Woodhouse had ceased to be dependent upon patrons his experience of patronage continued to dominate his poetry.

The arena in which Bloomfield's labouring-class poets are invited to recite their work appears to provide an ideal opportunity for them to display their artistic independence. For the labouring poor, the feast or carnival had traditionally been a time when social distinctions were temporarily levelled, giving them an opportunity to engage in a degree of social and political criticism: 'it marked the suspension of all hierarchical rank, privileges, norms, and prohibitions. Carnival was the true feast of time, the feast of becoming, change, and renewal. It was hostile to all that was immortalized and completed' (Bakhtin, 10). May-Day was not an occasion on which rents were generally collected. Rents were customarily paid on Lady-Day – 25 March, Midsummer's-Day – 21 June, Michaelmas-Day – 29 September, and Christmas-Day – 25 December. But May-Day was at the time, as it still is today, associated with popular uprising and rebellion. In an article for *The Watchman* in 1796, Coleridge traces the origin of the May-Day festivities to a period of imagined freedom before the Norman Conquest:

> The vassals met upon the common green around the May-pole, where they elected a village lord, or king, as he was called, who chose his queen. He wore an oaken, and she a hawthorn wreath, and together they gave laws to rustic sports during these sweet days of freedom. The MAY-POLE, then, is the *English Tree of Liberty*! [*Works* II: 103]

There is an unfinished etching by James Gillray, provisionally entitled 'Lawful Liberty / Liberty Without Law' (1793), which may have been rejected by his loyalist employers because, although the image of French anarchy is satisfyingly shocking, the representation of British liberty is too suggestive of the May-Day festivities often associated with the liberty tree of the Revolution (Donald, 157).

The May-Day celebrations on Oakly Manor are divested of their traditional ritual elements, but in choosing an occasion with such associations Bloomfield must have had a particular purpose in mind. Having said this, although he tends to indulge the behaviour of the revellers, Sir Ambrose does endeavour to maintain a degree of control over the proceedings, and retains considerable paternal authority over those present. And the first poem to be recited appears to appeal for order and abstinence, rather than offer a critique of those in positions of authority. In the sentimental ballad 'The Drunken Father' Andrew is clearly failing in his responsibility to the community in general, and to the other members of his family in particular. The manner in which his behaviour disrupts and threatens their economic security is clear: 'He spent in muddy ale at night / The wages of the day' (11–12). His behaviour also exposes his children to danger when they are required to take over responsibility for the family. His nine-year-old son and even younger daughter are forced to leave the safety of their cottage at night in order to retrieve their father from the tavern. When Andrew finally returns to his cottage he is chided by his wife in melodramatic terms: 'This infant starves upon my breast— / To scold I am too weak. / I work, I spin, I toil all day, / Then leave my work to cry, / And start with horror when I think / You wish to see me die' (171–6). He is apparently shocked into a realization that his behaviour is wrong, and the poem ends on a redemptive note for the father, his family and, it seems, nature: '"I'll drink no more," —he quick rejoin'd,— / "Be't poison if I do." / From that bright day his plants, his flowers, / His crops began to thrive, / And for three years has Andrew been / The soberest man alive' (195–200).

The poem bears some resemblance to the kind of tale that would have appeared in tracts distributed with the intention of morally reforming the poor. At the turn of the eighteenth century, such material was not only, or even principally a response to fears regarding the spread of radical views amongst the labouring poor. Publications such as Hannah More's *Cheap Repository Tracts* were rather 'a broad evangelical assault on late eighteenth-century popular culture'; they represented an attempt 'to combat the "vulgar and licentious publications ... profane and indecent songs and penny papers" – in other words, chapbooks – sold by an army of 20,000 hawkers' (Pedersen, 87). Drink featured as one of the principal evils in More's tracts:

> Few of the tracts can be read without coming across some reference to the evils of gin, and, in several, drink plays a major role in ruining health, thrift and piety. Drink also destroys family life, and the tracts are peopled with countless patient wives suffering from their husbands' drunkenness. [Pedersen, 91]

More's ballad 'Robert and Richard; Or, the Ghost of Poor Molly who was drowned in Richard's Mill-Pond' (1796) is about a drunken libertine who abandons his pregnant betrothed. She then drowns herself and their baby in his mill-pond, but comes back to haunt him. 'The Carpenter; Or, the Danger of Evil Company' (1795) bears an even closer resemblance to Bloomfield's poem. It concerns a carpenter led astray by his drinking companions, but brought to his senses by his wife and children. On his return from the Inn one evening his wife gives him a knife and says: 'There lies thy babe ... / Oppress'd with famine sore; / O kill us both – 'twere kinder for, / We could not suffer more' (121–4).

The public house was also seen as one of the principal sources of indiscipline by supporters of agricultural "Reform" who demanded orderly temperance from workers. There was a growing 'bias against recreations which were public and in favour of domestic pleasures' (Malcolmson, 156). According to William Howitt, public amusements 'may indicate, in a certain degree, that a people [are] happy; but real happiness is a thing of a more domestic nature. It is a Lar [household God], and belongs to the household, or is to be found in the quiet and enclosed precincts of home gardens' (Howitt, II: 293). Even 'large assemblies of a better character' were the object of censure (Anon. 1827, 21). The new capitalist spirit of efficiency, to which such doctrines were linked, disregarded the fact that the lives of the rural labouring poor had previously been of a particularly social character. In the countryside traditional pastimes, like work, were often communal and were usually bound up with the different daily, weekly and monthly tasks associated with agricultural production: 'the irregularity of working day and week were framed, until the first decades of the nineteenth century, within the larger irregularity of the working year, punctuated by its traditional holidays and fairs' (Thompson 1993, 377).

This change in the way that the labouring poor were expected to behave is reflected repeatedly in the poetry of Wordsworth. All of his heroes, from Michael, or the shepherd in *The Prelude* to the wanderer in *The Excursion* (1814), are abstemious and withdrawn figures. In *Michael* the leisure time of the central character and his family is spent in 'endless industry' (97). When they have completed their evening meal Michael and Luke 'both betook themselves / To such convenient work, as might employ / Their hands by the fire-side; perhaps to card / Wool for the House-wife's spindle, or repair / Some injury done to sickle, flail, or scythe' (106–10). The only occasion on which Wordsworth describes a communal leisure activity is his account of Grasmere Fair in Book VIII of *The Prelude*. But even here there are limited entertainments on offer, and he foregrounds the sober commercial character of the event: 'Behold the cattle are driven down; the sheep / That have for traffic been culled are penned /... the chaffering [bargaining] is begun; / ... / Booths are there none: a stall or two is here' (19–25). In '[Benjamin] The

Waggoner' (1819) Wordsworth endeavours to understand the temptation of 'open house and ready fare', but unlike the hero of Burns's 'Tam O'Shanter' (1790) on which the poem is based, Benjamin loses his job and his place in the community through drink (Taylor 1999, 49).

Bloomfield also wished to say something about the suffering caused by over-indulgence in ale, but the meaning of 'The Drunken Father' is not quite as straightforward as it might seem to be. In fact the poem requires a delicate act of reading, and this becomes especially apparent if it is read within the context of the frame. There is no reason to suppose that the views of the farmer's son who composed the poem and recites it at the feast coincide exactly with those of Bloomfield, Sir Ambrose or the narrator of *May Day*. The speaker is described as 'Phillip, a farmer's son, well known for song' (269). The voice of the farmer's son might be a fictional echo of a number of the voices that could be heard in the countryside at the turn of the eighteenth century; the cold, dry voice of evangelical piety or what Bloomfield considered to be the selfish and ignorant voice of agricultural "Reform". The identity of Phillip's father and the extent of his wealth are not revealed by the narrator. He might be one of those farmers who, like Charles Musgrove in Jane Austin's *Persuasion* (1818), had converted the accommodation of those who used to 'live in' into part of his own private dwelling. If this were the case, he would need to join in the call for sobriety and discipline among the day or wage labourers that he would then require to work his land.

The nature of the audience and the communal character of the feast that brings them together could be said to represent a counterpoint to the moralizing point of view apparently expressed in the ballad. As soon as the poem is concluded, the ambiguous and playful tone that often marks descriptions of the festivities on Oakly Manor re-emerges. Sir Ambrose reminds his listeners of the need for moderation in their applause, but in terms that do not represent an attempt to curtail the exuberance of the gathering. Instead he is concerned with a democratic wish to ensure that all of the poets who speak receive a fair hearing: 'Neighbours we are, then let the stream run fair, / And every couplet be as free as air; / Be silent when each speaker claims his right' (7–9). In fact Sir Ambrose's speech appears to invoke the levelling sentiment that is traditionally associated with May-Day celebrations. As on other occasions Bloomfield may also have had the literary marketplace in mind when writing this passage. It is certainly consistent with a call for equal right of access to that marketplace irrespective of social origin.

In terms of alcohol consumption, the remarks of the principal narrator in the interlude that follows 'The Drunken Father' add to the ambiguity of the point of view expressed in *May Day*. When he describes the celebrations of those at the feast, the tone is one of toleration and shared joy. Bloomfield's empathy with the frailty of the human condition and his awareness of the fact that inflexible social mores often damage both individuals and communities is apparent. Even the reveller's response to signs of drunkenness is a humorous and ironic invocation of the ballad they have just heard: 'Thenceforward converse flow'd with perfect ease, / Midst country wit, and rustic repartees. / One drank to Ellen, if such might be found, / And archly glanced at female faces round. / If one with tilted can began to bawl, / Another cried, "Remember Andrew Hall"' (13–18). Bloomfield knew the value of mutuality within communities, and that the consumption of alcohol, frequently in the local tavern or public house, often accompanied the kind of 'converse' that reinforced it (Malcolmson, 71). The tenor of this passage resembles that of 'The Horkey', in which Bloomfield expresses broad approval for the 'rude' social activities of country people: 'Joint stock you know among the men, / To drink at their own charges; / So up they got full drive, and then / Went out to *halloo largess*. / ... / We follow'd them, we wor'nt afraid, / We'ad all been drinking ale' (97–104).

The reference to the paintings of David Wilkie at the end of the passage is significant in the context of both popular culture and attitudes to drink. Wilkie's *The Village Festival* (1811) depicts a village celebration outside a local tavern. It is possible that Bloomfield had this picture in mind when writing 'The Drunken Father' because within the central group there is a scene which might have been his inspiration. There is an inebriated, but apparently happy male figure whose wife, assisted by their child, attempts to wrest him from the grip of his companions in order to take him home. The moral message implied by this scene is undercut by the humour, but there is a scene in the bottom right-hand corner of the painting which apparently takes a more didactic position. Another male figure has apparently drunk himself into a stupor and collapsed beside an animal drinking trough. As in Bloomfield's poem, the point of view of the painting is ambiguous in respect of drink and drunkenness because this somewhat grotesque and critical scene 'is tempered somewhat by the comical juxtaposition' (Marks, 184). In general Wilkie's attitude could be said to mirror that of Bloomfield because 'the message, softened by the interjection of the comic passages and a general veneer of humour, is delivered very gently, and does not at all appear as a didactic lesson' (Marks, 183).

The author of the next poem to be recited is more in key with the relaxed and libertarian atmosphere of Oakly Manor than the apparently severe author of 'The Drunken Father'. In the opening stanzas of 'The Forester' a strong link is established between the keeper and nature. He was 'BORN in a dark wood's lonely dell, / Where echoes roar'd, and tendrils curl'd / Round a low cot, like hermit's cell' (1–3). Because he grows up close to nature, he is not corrupted by the complicated social relations and partisan interest that often dominate human relations: 'I felt no bonds, no shackles then, / For life in freedom was begun' (5–6). His experience mirrors the kind of primitive childhood described by Rousseau in the *Discourse on the Origins and Foundation of Inequality among Men* (1755) in which 'children toddled off into the wood at an early age to be cared for by nature' (Blum, 118). But his sense of freedom is also dependent upon the fact that, as it did for Rousseau's Emile (*Emile*, 80), nature has regulated his desires: 'Old Salcey Forest was my world' (4). He neither possesses nor is interested in the private property that would shackle him with the 'chains' that Rousseau found in eighteenth-century society (*Social Contract*, 65–8). It is likely that Bloomfield was aware of Rousseau's ideas which were disseminated widely in England during the second half of the eighteenth century. Rousseau's association with the French Revolution did, however, cause a decline in his reputation, if not his influence during the war years (Dart, 13–14).

The keeper enjoys a special relationship with nature, and through his work learns 'the wiles, the shifts, the calls, / The language of each living thing' (13–14). But unlike Wordsworth's detached heroes, he is interested in humankind too: 'I gloried in th' exploits of men' (7). He represents a kind of link between humankind and nature. As a huntsman he is a predator, but he is also the steward of nature in the forest. His relationship with nature is neither unthinkingly instrumental, nor unthinkingly pastoral. As Donna Landry remarks of Bloomfield's 'Hunting Song' (1802), 'Hunting, like georgic notions of cultivation as requiring conservation and stewardship rather than maximal extraction for the market, required both the consumption of resources and their safeguarding and replenishment.' (2006, 259) The keeper and others like him who work with rather than exploit nature, are the last representatives of a time before the human greed that reaches its rationalized apotheosis in capitalism began to destroy the natural balance of the world in which we live.

The fact that the author of 'The Forester' is a special kind of individual is apparent from the principal narrator's introduction. The keeper does not wait to be introduced, but like the Ancient Mariner holds the gathering with his eye and his voice: 'But who is he, uprisen, with eye so keen, / … / Short prelude made, he pointed o'er the hill, / And raised a voice that every ear might fill; / His heart was in his theme, and in the forest still' (25–33). The atmosphere of inscrutability that seems to surround the keeper is also reflected in the tone of his poem, which is much more intense than that of 'The Drunken Father'. The shorter iambic tetrameter adds rapidity and vigour to the lines, while the double ballad stanza avoids the sparseness of narration that often characterizes the ballad. The keeper's link with an increasingly rare way of responding to nature in general, and the forest in particular, apparently endows him with a mysterious power over those whom he addresses. In many cultures the forest or woodland has long been symbolic of mystery and of secret or hidden powers. It is also a favourite dwelling place of hermits and ascetics, and thus of localized spiritual power. The keeper, having been to a greater extent immersed in nature from childhood, has the ability to communicate some of its mystery. He appears to have established that link between his own poetic spirit and the genius loci of the forest which Bloomfield seeks to make in 'A Visit to Whittlebury Forest'.

May Day in general is a fictional monument to the poetic talent of the labouring classes. With the exception of the 'farmer's son', whose origin is not clear, all of the poets who speak are, like Bloomfield, labouring-class poets. But 'The Forester' reveals that labouring-class poets also have important things to say. Byron expressly denies that the life experience of the labouring poor has any intellectual worth: 'And now no boor can seek his last abode, / No common be enclosed without an ode' (785–6). Wordsworth does see a kind of value in the experience of shepherds, but he rarely allows the labouring poor to speak for themselves in his poetry. Their lives and experiences can be informative, but only when filtered through the consciousness of elite poets like Wordsworth who in *The Prelude* described himself as a 'chosen son' with 'holy powers' (III: 83–4). Bloomfield clearly believed that the poor were often capable of as much if not more insight than individuals of higher social status: 'I have heard more sense and truth in a tap-room, than I have often heard in better company; and there is nothing more striking to me, than the *total* ignorance of the *manner of living* among the poor ... of what they talk, and of what they think' (*Remains* II: 71–2). Moreover, he appeared to believe that rural workers have access to knowledge that only those who labour close to nature can possess, but which is characterized by an enigmatic quality that they might not fully understand.

There are many layers of meaning present in 'The Forester', and this becomes all the more apparent when the keeper's account of his own origin is suddenly interrupted as he recalls the fall of an oak tree during an autumn storm. It seems that Bloomfield's inspiration for this passage was a reproof from the Duke of Grafton in a letter dated 10 February 1817:

> The Duke of Grafton regrets that Mr. B.'s muse should have been so long silent. An occurrence such as was witnessed by several persons in a neighbouring forest (Salcey), might have roused her from her lethargy, if she had been within reach of surveying the remains of the largest oak in the forest, which fell with a prodigious crash, a few days ago, within a hundred yards of the principal lodge, of which it had been for an age the chief ornament. The noise attracted the notice of all, but of none more than the forest deer, which assembled and remained for some hours around it, as if to perform the funeral obsequies of a departed and reverend friend. At last they seemed mournfully to retire, their movements being silent and slow. [59]

It is significant that in the same letter the Duke advised Bloomfield that he had authorized payment of the annuity which the poet had been forced to remind him was in arrears. The third Duke of Grafton had been Bloomfield's principal aristocratic patron, but, unlike his father and Sir Ambrose, the new Duke did not seem so interested in labouring-class poets. It is not clear whether the Duke expected Bloomfield to make use of the description, but it is certain that he would not have approved the political tone of the passage within which it eventually appears.

The imagery in the keeper's poetic account of the incident turns it into an allegory for the fall of kings or governments: 'The shadowing oak, the noblest stem / That graced the forest's ample bound, / Had cast to earth his diadem; / His fractured limbs had delved the ground' (45–8). In the next stanza the fall of the tree becomes merged with English history: 'He lay, and still to fancy groan'd; / He lay like Alfred when he died— / Alfred, a king by Heaven enthroned, / His age's wonder, England's pride!' (49–52). It is not even clear whether Alfred or the tree is 'His age's wonder, England's pride', or whose name 'shall rouse the patriot's blood / As long as England's sons can feel' (55–6). Appropriately the keeper makes a link between the forest and the period of imagined freedom before the Norman Conquest that is traditionally recalled during May-Day celebrations. The connection represents an implicit criticism of the political state in 1822. It begs the question is the court of the George IV and by implication Lord Liverpool's government 'by Heaven [nature] enthroned'?

The allegory becomes potentially more seditious in stanza ten when the curious but affrighted deer gather round and explore the fallen tree: 'Some in his root's deep cavern housed, / And seem'd to learn, and muse, and teach, / Or on his topmost foliage browsed, / That had for centuries mock'd their reach' (65–8). The deer, representatives of the English people, learn from the tree which represents the kind of freedom that they enjoyed in the time of Alfred, but which by implication is now denied to them. But the keeper's imagery goes further and links the behaviour of the deer to the way in which labouring people had endeavoured to share their knowledge and opinions in the 1790s and during the second decade of the nineteenth century. In that they have ideas and pass on their learning to each other, the deer represent cooperative labouring-class organizations such as the London Corresponding Society and local Hampden Clubs. The stanza ends with a direct warning to those that govern England: 'Winds in their wrath these limbs could crash, / This strength, this symmetry could mar; / A people's wrath can monarchs dash / From bigot throne or purple car' (69–72) These lines establish an explicit rather than an allegorical connection between what nature can 'teach', and the Painite view that it is the people's natural right to remove a corrupt government.

The sentiment expressed in this passage is suggestive of Robert Southey's *Wat Tyler* (1794), a pirate version of which was published by Sherwood Neely and Jones in 1817, much to the embarrassment of the then Poet Laureate. It is quite possible that Bloomfield was aware of the play, both because of the publicity surrounding Southey's attempt to have it suppressed, and because it sold an estimated sixty thousand copies in pirated versions. He may not have agreed with the republican and levelling point of view expressed in *Wat Tyler*, but he would surely have felt sympathy for 'the honest, staid, hard working Tyler' (*Wat Tyler*, 75) and his companions, forced to revolt by the activities of a corrupt government. The tone and phrasing of Bloomfield's poem also make a connection with radical activists as it echoes the millenarian language often employed by them. Thomas Spence, for example, concludes his dream vision ballad 'The Propagation of Spensonianism' with the following lines: 'I beheld these Preachers were well understood, / When the People in all places arose like a Flood; / All ancient Oppressions were then swept away, / And virtue and Freedom for ever did sway' (41–4).

In view of the fact that the second decade of the nineteenth century was a troubled period for the English people, the keeper's allusive imagery would have made an impression upon contemporary readers. Many amongst the labouring poor did not feel that their interests were taken into account by the government or by others in positions of authority. The Corn Law of 1815 prohibited the import of corn until the price on the home market reached eighty shillings a quarter. This made bread so expensive that for much of the time the poor could not afford to buy other staple foods. The hardship caused by the Corn Law was exacerbated by the fact that there were a series of bad harvests between 1815 and 1822, further pushing up the price of food. At the same time, manufacturing industry declined after the boom that accompanied the Napoleonic Wars came to an end. This led to increased unemployment in towns and cities which were already struggling to cope with an influx of people from the countryside. One consequence of Enclosure and agricultural reform was the creation of an ever-larger class of landless labourers, many of whom were ultimately forced to migrate in search of more secure employment.

Popular outrage at the perceived injustice of this situation manifested itself in events like the Spa Fields riots of 1816, the Pentridge rising of June 1817 and the Cato Street conspiracy of 1820. In Suffolk there was considerable unrest resulting in the rise of the Luddite movement, and in machine-breaking and rick-burning during 1816 and 1822. In the latter year John Constable remarked that things in Suffolk were 'as bad as Ireland – "never a night without seeing fires near or at a distance", the Rector & his brother the Squire have forsaken the village [Brantham-cum-Bergholt] – no abatement of tithes or rents – four of Sir Wm. Rush's tenants distrained next parish' (*Correspondence*, 88). Resistance at grass-roots level was accompanied by the rise of a new reform movement under the leadership of politicians like Sir Francis Burdett and Henry Hunt, and journalists like Thomas Wooler in the *Black Dwarf* (1817–24), Richard Carlisle in the *Republican* (1819–26) and William Cobbett in the *Political Register* (1802–35). This was the first in a series of radical movements which drove reform during the nineteenth century. Both organized labouring-class revolt and the political reform movement were incompetently and ruthlessly repressed by the government. They were prepared to resort to any means at their disposal, including the infamous six Acts passed at the end of 1819 and the use of *agent provocateurs*. The outrageous massacre of a crowd which had gathered to hear Henry Hunt speak at St. Peters Fields in Manchester in the summer of 1819 was probably an accident that the government would rather have avoided, but it does indicate the level of panic felt by the more fortunate classes in society.

The behaviour of the deer is suggestive of organized labouring-class resistance, but the keeper has not so far made an explicit reference to events that occurred while Bloomfield was working on *May Day*. He does so in stanza ten in a way that both reinforces the subversive tone of 'The Forester' and reveals that *May Day*, when read as a cohesive single work, is not simply backward-looking or nostalgic for a lost paternalistic Golden Age. The keeper compares the grief felt by the deer with that felt by the English people following the death of Princess Charlotte Augusta at Castle Clermont in November 1817: 'When Fate's dread bolt in Clermont's bowers / Provoked its million tears and sighs, / A nation wept its fallen flowers, / Its blighted hopes, its darling prize' (73–6). The death of the princess did provoke an outpouring of public sorrow and grief, not unlike that which followed the death of Princess Diana. In the words of Henry Brougham: 'This most melancholy event produced throughout the Kingdom feelings of the deepest sorrow and most bitter disappointment. It is scarcely possible to exaggerate, and it is difficult for persons not living at the time to believe how universal and how genuine those feelings were.' (*Letters of Princess Charlotte*, 184) Because of her popularity amongst the population at large, and because she had Whig advisers, such as the Duke of Sussex, she was seen as a problem by many within Lord Liverpool's government. She also became a focal point for popular resistance to the hated conduct of her father following her refusal to marry the Prince of Orange. In the minds of the people the Prince Regent was responsible for the increasingly tyrannical and repressive measures with which the government attempted to suppress any disturbances amongst a hungry and discontented population. After her flight from Warwick House to Connaught Place following her father's attempts to curtail the extent of her social contacts, Brougham is reported to have remarked that were her dispute with the Prince Regent to become public 'I would have only to take you to that window, and show you to the multitude, and tell them your grievances, and they will all rise on your behalf.' (Hibbert I: 71)

The death of the princess was taken by others as an occasion for political commentary. During December 1817 Percy Bysshe Shelley wrote 'An Address to the People on the Death of the Princess Charlotte'. He argues that although women die in childbirth every day and each instance is equally tragic, 'it were well done … that men should mourn for any public calamity which has befallen their country or the world, though it be not death' because 'this helps to maintain that connexion between one man and another, and all men considered as a whole, which is the bond of social life' (*Prose Works*, 232). He suggests, however, that the death of the princess did not justify such a response because 'the accident of her birth neither made her life more virtuous nor her death more worthy of grief' and 'for the public she had done nothing either good or evil' (*Prose Work*, 233). On the other hand, he argues that the execution of Jeremiah Brandreth, Isaac Ludlam and William Turner for high treason because of their involvement in the Pentridge rising was an event which did justify public mourning. This was because they had been tempted to their ruin through the operations of the *agent provocateur* known as William Oliver, but also because the rising was a response to the government's misrule which left the people to choose between oppression and anarchy.

Bloomfield's response to the death of Princess Charlotte is more subtle than that of Shelley, perhaps making his commentary acceptable at a time when the latter's explicit criticism of the government would not have been. Shelley's publishers were certainly worried, and printed only twenty copies because they 'recognized some danger to themselves (if not to 'The Hermit of Marlow' [Shelley's pseudonym]) in printing and distributing a pamphlet which could well have irritated … the Ministry … by its use of the princess's death as an occasion for explicit anti-government propaganda' (*Prose Works*, 448). In 'The Forester' the keeper attributes the 'blighted hopes' of the 'nation' to the death of the princess. This could simply be a reference to the loss of the heir to British throne, but because the princess was associated with resistance to tyranny, it could also refer to the people's desire for just government. The people's desire for justice is not expressed in the dissimulating and corrupted language of a self-serving ruling class, but it does represent 'the voice of nature' (96). The will of the people represents natural right because they have not, like Lord Liverpool's government, been corrupted by power.

In the closing stanzas the keeper suggests that those with the ability to manipulate language for their own ends will be unable ultimately to resist nature and natural right: 'Who then of language will be proud? / Who arrogate that gift of heaven? / To wild herds when they bellow loud, / ... / I've heard a scream aloft, so shrill / That terror seized on all that fly' (81–8). In the final passage of the poem the 'language' of nature is equated with science, as it had been in *Good Tidings*. It seems that Bloomfield had in mind systematic rational enquiry as well as the experimental physical branches of science. The implication being that developments in science merely represent nature better understood, and that it is not possible to undo such developments whether in the physical sciences or the science of politics: 'Empires may fall, and nations groan, / Pride be thrown down, and power decay; / Dark bigotry may rear her throne, / But science is the light of day' (89–92). The keeper concludes his poem with a statement which reiterates the idea that the labouring poor are in a better position to 'learn' from nature than those who govern them: 'My joys shall pomp and power outlast— / The voice of nature cannot change' (95–6).

The ability, indeed the right of the labouring poor to decide the fate of humankind is epitomized in the person of the next speaker; the shepherd-poet John Armstrong. At least since Biblical times, the shepherd has been associated with the leadership of men or with the possession of prophetic powers, and the principal narrator suggests that John Armstrong might not be a typical 'peasant poet': 'He was a poet,— this Sir Ambrose knew,— / A strange one too' (22–3). Figures like Lord Radstock and, according to Lofft's letter of 1 March 1800, the Duke of Grafton liked to find 'untaught genius, starting from ... [their] neighbourhood' (4), but they also sought to control the kind of poetry that was produced by their protégés. Sir Ambrose does not appear to be so concerned about the content of his tenant's poetry. He makes no remark upon 'The Forester' so it seems that the subversive undercurrent did not concern him. And the shepherd is potentially a more threatening figure than the keeper. The carvings on his staff explicitly suggest that he is the possessor of special powers. It is decorated with carvings of birds, which in many cultures are regarded as symbols of the link between heaven and earth, and as embodiments of immaterial things, particularly the soul. There are also representations of animals, which for many peoples symbolize the incomprehensible nature of divine and cosmic forces. The apparently throw-away remarks made by the shepherd himself in the final stanza of his poem are even more disturbing because they suggest a belief that his words should hold sway over his audience. He describes his staff as 'my sceptre, my baton, my spear' and his dog as his 'prime minister' (66–7).

The narrator's description of the shepherd implies that he is a sombre individual, but the title of his poem, 'The Shepherd's Dream: or; Fairies' Masquerade', apparently suggests that it will be a light-hearted contribution to the proceedings. The way in which the poem is introduced also indicates that it will lighten the tone of the proceedings: 'No tragic tale on stilts;— his mind had more / Of boundless frolic than of serious lore' (25–6). But a masquerade is by definition not what it seems, and readers familiar with dream-vision poems would have known that they almost always have several layers of meaning. The tone of the opening passage immediately contradicts the somewhat frivolous title. More than any other part of *May Day*, it displays considerable command of 'the machinery of poetry' and as such reveals John Armstrong to be a technically accomplished poet. The unusual and difficult anapestic metre foregrounds the contrived nature of the syntax, and distances it from normal speech patterns. (During the Romantic period relatively few poems were written in anapestic metre, Byron's 'The Destruction of Sennacherib' (1815) being perhaps the most well-known example.) The language is also quite different from any that Bloomfield had previously employed in descriptions of nature:

> I loiter'd beside the small lake on the heath;
> The red sun, though down, left his drapery glowing,
> And no sound was stirring, I heard not a breath:
> I sat on the turf, but I meant not to sleep,
> And gazed o'er that lake which for ever is new,
> Where clouds over clouds appear'd anxious to peep
> From this bright double sky with its pearl and its blue. [2–11]

The imagery is suggestive of an otherworldly brightness because the sunset is usually a time that is characterized by its blending of subtle shades rather than contrasting primary colours like 'red' and 'blue'. Moreover words like 'drapery' and 'pearl' recall the surreal dream landscape of *Pearl* (1350–1400) and suggest that the place where the narrator falls asleep might not be entirely natural.

It is not only because of its technical sophistication that contemporary readers might not have associated 'The Shepherd's Dream' with a labouring-class poet. The supposedly simple poetry produced by such poets was regarded as somehow outside the 'mainstream' tradition of English literature, but John Armstrong's poem foregrounds the intertextual nature of virtually all poetry. In addition to the echo of *Pearl*, the opening lines make an explicit connection with John Langland's *The Vision of Piers Plowman* (1379); even as late as the nineteenth century, the most famous dream-vision poem in English literature. Bloomfield's narrator is a shepherd, the hero of Langland's poem dresses as a sheep, and both fall asleep by an uncannily strange stretch of water to dream of fairyland. The tone of the opening passage of 'The Shepherd's Dream' is also suggestive of Milton's Eden in Book IV of *Paradise Lost* (1667), a poem that ends with a prophetic vision on an epic scale, and the biblical resonances make a connection with what was considered the earliest of written records. The shepherd is clearly concerned to locate the idioms and concerns of his poem within a literary tradition that spans many centuries.

The kind of prophetic dream vision that occurs in 'The Shepherd's Dream' also had more recent analogues. The bridge between enthusiastic religion and the prophetic strain in radical Jacobin politics lent the latter a potential popular appeal (McCalman, 60). The upsurge in millenarian zeal following the French Revolution had particular personal resonances for Bloomfield because his wife was at one time a follower of Joanna Southcott. The millenarian language of plebeian prophets such as Southcott, Richard Brothers and John 'Zion' Ward found its way into the writings of figures like Thomas Spence, Robert Wedderburn, Thomas Evans and Allen Davenport. It is there in the previously mentioned ballad 'The Propagation of Spensonianism', in Spence's *The Restorer of Society to its Natural State* (1801), and in Wedderburn's *Axe laid to the Root* (1817). Spence was prosecuted for the publication of *The Restoration of Society to its Natural State* following the Committee for Secrecy's recommendation that the activities of prophets like Brothers be checked. Shelley tapped into the prophetic vein within radical politics when writing his dream-vision poem 'The Mask of Anarchy' (1819) in response to the Peterloo massacre. Dream visions also feature in Shelley's last major work 'The Triumph of Life' (1822), and in Keats's 'The Fall of Hyperion' (1819). Being from an early age immersed in London artisan culture, Bloomfield would have been at least as likely as Shelley and Keats to have been familiar with this tradition.

The shepherd's dream concerns a conflict between 'the fairies of the north' and 'the fairies of the south', and this also suggests possible literary antecedents. The behaviour of the fairies in battle might owe a debt to Swift's Lilliputians. In Chapter II, Part I of *Gulliver's Travels* (1726), Gulliver asks the Emperor 'to let a Troop of his best Horse, Twenty-four in number, come and exercise upon this Plain' (27). Gulliver goes on to describe their exercise as follows: 'As soon as they got into Order, they divided into two Parties, performed mock Skirmishes, discharged blunt Arrows, drew their Swords, fled and pursued, attacked and retired' (27). Notwithstanding the similarities between Bloomfield's fairies and the Lilliputians, the latter do differ in that they discover 'the best military Discipline ... [Gulliver] ever beheld' (27). Another possible source is Thomas Parnell's translation of the Homeric Parody entitled *Homer's Battle of the Frogs and the Mice* (1717). The tone of this is mock-heroic throughout, and it was often included with translations of Homer's *Iliad* and *Odyssey* during the eighteenth and nineteenth centuries. Bloomfield makes no reference to *Gulliver's Travels* or *Homer's Battle of the Frogs and the Mice* either in correspondence or elsewhere, but it is likely that he had read both. He could easily have regarded Swift as required reading, and the catalogue of effects compiled following his death includes an edition of Homer and an edition of Parnell.

The shepherd's descriptions of the conflict in 'The Shepherd's Dream' are marked by a similar mock-heroic tone and in many ways, like the Lilliputian's exercises or the clash between the frogs and mice, the battle does resemble a 'boundless frolic'. But both the narrator's description of John Armstrong, and the enigmatic tone established in the introductory passages of his poem, suggest that the reader should always consider alternative meanings. Significantly, the banners carried by both sides echo the carvings on the shepherd's staff. The fairies of the south carry 'silver birds upon poles' (15), and the fairies of the north 'Colour'd rags upon sticks' displaying 'a bird split in two' (38–40). These images could be said to imply that the fates are with the fairies of the north because the entrails of birds had traditionally been used for divining. But because they establish a direct link with the shepherd and the kind of and prophetic powers potentially possessed by him, they also indicate that the battle might not be just a 'boundless frolic'.

In dividing the combatants between north and south the shepherd might intend that his listeners make a connection with previous conflicts between England and Scotland. On the other hand the struggle between the two groups of fairies could just as easily represent the wars between England and France, because the appellations 'north' and 'south' apply equally well. Many aspects of the battle are evocative of the kind of behaviour that is often displayed in human conflict. Like human beings the fairies are concerned with all of the trumpery that usually accompanies soldiering, for example both sides carry banners of war. The fairies' wars are also marked by the same kind of blunders as any human conflict, and result in just as much collateral damage: ' I never could glean / Why the woodstack was burnt, or who set it on fire. / The flames seem'd to rise o'er a deluge of snow, / That buried its thousands,— the rest ran away; / For the hero had here overstrain'd his long bow, / Yet he honestly own'd the mishap of the day' (19–24). As in any human conflict the 'mishap' is followed by a desire for revenge on the part of the fairies of the north. The 'fays' of the north capture the 'hero' of the south 'And follow'd him down to the lake in a riot, / Where they found a large stone which they fix'd him upon, / And threaten'd, and coax'd him, and bade him be quiet' (26–8). The hero escapes, however, and the rapid displacement of his would-be usurper reveals the degree to which victory in war is transient: 'But the million beheld he could conquer alone; / After resting awhile, he leap'd boldly on shore, / When away ran a fay that had mounted his throne' (30–32). This passage could also refer to rapidity with which the seat of power had changed hands in France. The execution of Louis XVI in 1794 followed by the coronation of Napoleon as Emperor in 1804 and then the restoration of the Bourbon monarchy following Napoleon's defeat in 1814. Even the councils held by the combatants are chaotic and confused just like those in human conflicts: 'And the few that held council, were terribly hamper'd, / For some were vindictive, and some were afraid' (35–6).

The behaviour of the fairies throughout the battle is marked by pomposity and stupidity. Eventually the hero of the south falls during a desperate final encounter, but the narrator is keen to impress upon his audience that no one is really the victor in war: 'Death rattled his jawbones to see such a fray, / And glory personified laugh'd at them all' (43–4). The apparent victors are not united, and at no time are their actions preceded by moral or intellectual reflection:

> Meanwhile the north fairies stood round in a ring,
> Supporting his rival on guns and on spears,

> Who, though not a soldier, was robed like a king;
> Yet some were exulting, and some were in tears.
> A lily triumphantly floated above,
> The crowd press'd, and wrangling was heard through the whole;
> Some soldiers look'd surly, some citizens strove
> To hoist the old nightcap on liberty's pole. [49–56]

As had been the case during the temporary ascendancy of the south earlier in the conflict, there is no shortage of claimants for the vacant throne. The 'tears' of the crowd might be the regular product of 'glory personified', but their 'wrangling', and the 'surly' demeanour of some soldiers certainly suggests disapproval of the majority choice. The victorious army will also want its reward, which probably won't be forthcoming. On their return from conflict overseas British servicemen often experienced poverty and hunger. Moreover, civil unrest in the name of liberty threatens, as it did in England during the depression that followed the end of the Napoleonic wars.

The shepherd poet's account of the battle is both sophisticated and knowing. It combines entertainment with a considerable amount of 'serious lore'. 'The Shepherd's Dream' suggests that a poet who spends his life labouring, and learning from nature can produce poetry of the highest quality. Through the force of contrast, the poem that follows reiterates the message that only labouring-class poets of a particular kind have this potential. The fact that the principal narrator announces 'The Soldier's Home' in the context of 'The Shepherd's Dream' invites comparison. The soldier is introduced as a 'pension'd veteran, doom'd no more to roam' (5), thus foregrounding the fact that his experience is likely to be similar to that of the disbanded fairies. 'The Soldier's Home' is the work of a labouring-class figure very different from the shepherd. The shepherd is the product of 'honest labour' and serious reflection upon the 'language' of nature. But the soldier is a servant of the ruling class that is almost always responsible for human war. He is a product of the morality of war; the 'abrogation of language' that the keeper condemns in 'The Forester'. On many occasions individuals like Bloomfield's 'pension'd veteran' would not have been willing servants of the rich and powerful. In 'Walter and Jane' and 'The Miller's Maid', Bloomfield had explored the way in which through poverty the labouring poor were often forced to enlist. But the 'carnage, fire, and plunder' that all front-line soldiers experience in one way or another would still leave their mark (65). The soldier has not had the opportunity to develop the kind of skills that the shepherd possesses: 'My untried muse shall no high tone assume, / … / Brief be my verse, a task within my power' (1–3). His imagination has been crushed by the regimented horror of life as a soldier. This is reflected in his prosaic language, and the fact that his poem is not enriched by the kind of striking symbolic imagery and tonal variation that the shepherd introduces into 'The Shepherd's Dream'.

The soldier's is a voice that was heard all over the countryside during the period immediately preceding the publication of *May Day*. During the war years numerous poems about the soldier's return to his place of origin were published in the periodical press. 'The Soldier's Return', which appeared in *The*

Scots Magazine for April 1804, dwelt upon the apparent positive aspects of this event. Others like Robert Merry's 'The Wounded Soldier', which appeared in *The Spirit of the Public Journals* for 1799, focused upon the worst kinds of reunion: '... when he enter'd in such horrid guise, / His mother shriek'd, and dropp'd upon the floor: / His father look'd to heav'n with streaming eyes, / And Lucy sunk, alas! To rise no more' (Bennett, 245). Bloomfield's poem is a reworking of a piece entitled 'The Soldier's Return' published in the *General Advertiser* on 11 November 1786. It treats the same theme as the earlier poem, but in a quite different manner. 'The Soldier's Return' dwelt upon the soldier's homesickness and happy reunion with his lover. The much more subtle and confident later work explores the psychological trauma of homecoming which must have been faced by every surviving serviceman.

The 'The Soldier's Home' contrasts the physically and psychologically repressive life of a soldier with the kind of life that the speaker could have lived. He is reminded of the wasted years when he notices on his 'father's chair ... / ... / ... the rough initials of ... [his] name, / Cut forty years before' (20–23). The old almanacs that the wind disturbs, annals of the seasonal cycle of rural labour, represent all of the occupations that he could have taken up if he had not been a soldier: the wind 'caught the old dangling almanacks ... / ... / Then gently, singly, down, down, down, they went, / And told of twenty years that I had spent / Far from my native land' (27–31). He has been denied access to nature too, and the kind of nurturing power that, along with the rhythms of community life in the countryside, helped to produce the intellect of John Armstrong. Nature represented by a robin on the threshold of his cottage seems hesitant to welcome him back: 'At first he look'd distrustful, almost shy, / And cast on me his coal-black stedfast eye, / And seem'd to say (past friendship to renew) / "Ah ha! old worn out soldier, is it you?"' (33–6). The implication being that human wars take place on a moral plane that is neither part of nor sanctioned by nature. Despite the fact that he has lived as a soldier for twenty years, nature and his ancestral cottage have such strong associations for the speaker that they provoke a revelatory vision of the life he could have lived: 'The grasshopper, the partridge in the field, / And ticking clock, were all at once become / The substitutes for clarion, fife, and drum' (48–50). But eventually he is overcome by the sense of what he has lost, of a life not lived: 'I raved at war and all its horrid cost, / And glory's quagmire, where the brave are lost. / On carnage, fire, and plunder, long I mused / And cursed the murdering weapons I had used' (63–6).

The last poem to be recited is spoken by the kind of 'sturdy yeoman' that the soldier could have become. More importantly like the shepherd, the hero of the yeoman's poem is the possessor of special powers that link the production of poetry to an ability to understand nature and community life like the bards that Bloomfield had celebrated in 'Shooter's Hill' and *The Banks of Wye*. It represents a fitting conclusion to an event that Bloomfield hoped would become a monument that some future 'wandering bard might prize' because it represents a celebration of community labour and poetry. 'Alfred and Jennet' is not the work of a blind poet, but its theme is suggestive of the

Celtic tradition of blind bards and fiddlers. Significantly 'Alfred and Jennet' also makes a connection with great blind poets of the past such as Homer and Milton, toward whom Bloomfield was drawing closer because his own sight had been failing for many years when he began to write *May Day*.

At the beginning of the nineteenth century some believed that the blind possessed the ability to relate to their surroundings in a more profound manner than those who were sighted (Trumpener, 96). Although for the individual concerned this might not make up for the absence of sight, it is probably true that the blind are forced to rely upon other senses. In the context of the poetic tradition to which 'Alfred and Jennet' responds, the source and scope of Alfred's special power is significant. The blind Celtic bard, most influentially the figure of the bard in Gray's poem, was often endowed with the power of the seer, and generally had visions of death and destruction (Larissy, 46–53). Like David Wilkie in *The Blind Fiddler* (1807), Bloomfield counters the glamorization of the blind poet seer. Wilkie's fiddler is a moribund and pathetic figure surrounded by his wretched family. He is a man very much preoccupied by physical survival. Alfred does have special powers, but they are of a more gentle kind than those possessed by figures like Gray's bard; his senses of touch and smell are particularly refined. As a result he is able to respond to nature in a way that is not always available to the sighted: 'Each varying leaf that brush'd where'er he came, / Press'd to his rosy lip he call'd by name; / He grasp'd the saplings, measured every bough, / Inhaled the fragrance' (43–6).

His special powers give him greater access to the kind of virtue which for Bloomfield, as a disciple of Rousseau, emanates from and is located within nature. Despite being sighted his mother is unable to 'see' his love for Jennet: 'My boy / Dropped not a syllable of this to me! / What was I doing, that I could not see' (246–8). But Alfred is able to see that his mother's objection to Jennet is rooted in unnatural social distinctions and pride. His response to his mother's pride is ambiguous: 'Dear mother, share my fortune with the poor' (351). He is asking her to approve his courtship of Jennet, who is the daughter of a poor but 'sturdy' yeoman. But the phrase is a strange one to use in such circumstances because elsewhere he describes Jennet as 'my dearest love' and significantly 'my daylight' (357–8). In terms of Alfred's special power, however, the fact that he equates Jennet with 'the poor' in general does highlight the difference between his social vision and that of his mother. It suggests that he believes in the paternalistic system whereby the rich would support the poor through a network of customary rights and usages. But Alfred does not look for the deference that eighteenth-century paternalism demanded from the poor; he wants to 'share' his fortune with 'the poor [Jennet]'. In this respect the phrase could be said to express the kind of levelling sentiment that is appropriate in the context of the May-Day tradition in which the celebration on Oakly Manor is situated.

Alfred also communicates his understanding of nature and his concomitant sense of social justice in his dealings with humankind through the music and song that were central to the community life of the labouring poor. It is music that initially brings Alfred and Jennet together: 'When Alfred from his grand-piano drew / Those heavenly sounds that seem'd for ever new, / She sat as if to sing would be a crime, / And only gazed with joy, and nodded time' (107–10). The indefinable power of Jennet's song communicates with Alfred in a way that the spoken word had not: 'The soul of song: ... / ... / Her little tongue soon fill'd the room around / With such a voluble and magic sound, / ... / While Alfred trembled to his fingers' ends' (127–34). The union of Alfred and Jennet represents the power of song and indeed poetry to break down the barriers of social distinction, and in doing so it represents the 'triumph' of 'nature's music'. (144) It also suggests that inclusive celebrations of creative talent, like that which takes place on Oakly Manor, have the potential to transform social relations within human society.

All of the labouring-class poets that originate from Oakly Manor are implicated in this power of renewal in the pageant that takes place at the end of the poem. They are symbolically associated with the mythological source of poetry in the form of the classical muses represented significantly by nine 'ruddy' country 'lasses' (37). In that they are 'the very life and soul of Spring' (58), the muses are associated with the seasonal rhythm of agricultural labour. But they are also linked to the rural social calendar and the transformative potential of the labouring poor as exemplified by the kind of community event at which Bloomfield's poets have performed: 'Each in her beauty seem'd a May-day queen' (46). The roses carried by both Sir Ambrose's lady and the muses could have a variety of symbolic meanings, but historically the rose has been principally associated with fertility and renewal. When the Cybele, the mother of the Gods, passed in procession through the streets of Rome her image would be showered with roses. In Christian symbolism Mary's Immaculate Conception is held to have been brought about through the magic of a rose. The red rose is also associated with the shed blood of Christ or the bowl that caught his blood.

Sir Ambrose reveals that the creative and transformative potential which exists within the ranks of the labouring poor has not been exhausted: 'For untold tales must still remain behind, / ... / "The Soldier's Wife," her toils, his battles o'er, / "Love in a Shower," the riv'let's sudden roar; / Then, "Lines to Aggravation" form the close' (6–11). And he comes forward as a willing patron for the assortment of poets that have so far emerged from his estate: 'Your verses shall not die as heretofore; / Your local tales shall not be thrown away, / ... / I purpose then to send them forth to try / The public patience, or its apathy' (80–88). Like the frame narrative in general, his last remark appears to undercut the claim for freedom of access to the literary marketplace which emerges from the text elsewhere. But because the poem is mostly about progressive potential, and in view of Bloomfield's own struggle with Capel Lofft, it is reasonable to argue that on balance *May Day* is a celebration of artistic independence. It is certainly the case that through *May Day* Bloomfield symbolically passes on the mantle of poet of the countryside and community life to a new kind of labouring-class poet. The 'silence' that reassumes 'her reign' (114) at the end of the revels on Oakly Manor, also presages the silencing of Bloomfield's own voice as a poet of the countryside in general and the labouring poor in particular.

Reflections on Otaheite: Cooks second Voyage

(endnote to *The Farmer's Boy*, 1800, 101–102)

'Destroys life's intercourse; the social plan'

"Allowing for the imperfect state of sublunary happiness, which is comparative at best, there are not, perhaps, many Nations existing whose situation is so desirable; where the means of subsistence are so easy, and the wants of the People so few ... The evident distinction of ranks, which subsists at *Otaheite*, does not materially affect the felicity of the Nation as we might have supposed. The simplicity of their whole life contributes to soften the appearance of distinctions, and to reduce them to a level. Where the climate and the custom of the country do not absolutely require a perfect garment; where it is easy at every step to gather as many plants as form not only a decent, but likewise a customary covering; and where all the necessaries of life are within the reach of every individual, at the expense of a trifling labour ... ambition and envy in a great measure be unknown. It is true, the highest classes of people possess some dainty articles, such as pork, fish, fowl, and cloth, almost exclusively; but the desire of indulging the appetite in a few trifling luxuries can at most render individuals, and not whole Nations, unhappy. Absolute Want occasions miseries of the lower class in some civiliz'd states, and is the result of the unbounded voluptuousness of their superiors. At *Otaheite* there is not, in general, that disparity between the highest and the meanest man, that subsists in England between a reputable tradesman and a labourer. The affection of the Otaheitians for their chiefs, which they never fail'd to express on all occasions, gave us great reason to suppose that they consider themselves as one family, and respect their eldest born in the persons of their chiefs. The lowest man in the Nation speaks as freely with his King as with his equal, and has the pleasure of seeing him as often as he likes. The King, at times, amuses himself with the occupations of his subjects; and not yet deprave'd by false notions of empty state, he often paddles his own canoe, without considering such an employment derogatory to his dignity. How long such an happy equality may last is uncertain: and how much the introduction of foreign luxuries may hasten its dissolution cannot be too frequently repeated to Europeans. If the knowledge of a few individuals can only be acquired at such a price as the happiness of Nations, it were better for the discoverers and the discovered that the *South Sea* had still remain'd unknown to *Europe* and its restless inhabitants."

APPENDIX 2

A Chronology of Bloomfield's Publications and their Contents

1800

The Farmer's Boy: A Rural Poem

1802

Rural Tales, Ballads and Songs
'Richard and Kate: Ballad'
'Walter and Jane: a Tale'
'The Miller's Maid: a Tale'
'Market Night: Ballad'
'The Fakenham Ghost: Ballad'
'The French Mariner: Ballad'
'Dolly: Ballad'
'A Visit to Whittlebury Forest'
'A Highland Drover: Song'
'A Word to Two Young Ladies'
'On hearing of the Translation of the Farmer's Boy'
'Nancy: Song'
'Rosy Hannah: Song'
'The Shepherd and his Dog Rover: Song'
'Hunting Song'
'Lucy: Song'
'Winter Song'

1804

Good Tidings; or, News from the Farm

1806

Wild Flowers; or, Pastoral and Local Poetry
'Abner and the Widow Jones, a Familiar Ballad'
'To My Old Oak Table'
'The Horkey, a Provincial Ballad'
'The Broken Crutch, a Tale'

'Shooter's Hill'
'A Visit to Ranelagh'
'Love of the Country'
'The Woodland Halló'
'Barnham Water'
'Mary's Evening Sigh'
'Good Tidings; or, News From the Farm' (revised version)

1808

Nature's Music. Consisting of Extracts from Several Authors; with Practical Observations, and Poetical Testimonies in Honour of the Harp of Æolius

1809

The Poems of Robert Bloomfield. Revised versions of *The Farmer's Boy*; *Rural Tales, Ballads and Songs*; and *Wild Flowers: or; Pastoral and Local Poetry*

1811

The Banks of Wye; A Poem

1815

The History of Little Davy's New Hat

1822

May-Day with the Muses
'The Invitation'
'The Drunken Father'
'The Forester'
'The Shepherd's Dream: or; Fairies' Masquerade'
'The Soldier's Home'
'Rosamond's Song of Hope'
'Alfred and Jennet'

1823

Hazelwood-Hall: A Village Drama

Bibliography

Manuscript Sources

Bloomfield, Robert [The Farmer's Boy], Houghton Library, MS Eng. 776.
— [The Farmer's Boy], Houghton Library, MS Eng. 776.1.
— [Printed copy of the preface to *The Farmer's Boy* with corrections in the hand of Robert Bloomfield], British Library, Add. MS 29 896.
— [*The Farmer's Boy: A Rural Poem*, 7th edn, London: Printed for Vernor and Hood, 1803, incorporating loose leaf corrections in the hand of Bloomfield], British Library, Reference C.61.a.3.
— [A Tour Down the Wye 1807], British Library, Add. MS 28 267.
— [Correspondence], British Library, Add. MS 28,268.
— [Correspondence], Suffolk Record Office / B, MS 317/3.
Clare, John [Correspondence], British Library, MS Eg. 2245.
Lofft, Capel [Correspondence], Suffolk Record Office / B, MS E1/20/6.1.

Printed Primary and Secondary Sources

The following periodicals contain at least one review article cited in the body of the text: *Annual Review and History of Literature for 1806*; *British Critic*; *Critical Review*; *Eclectic Review*; *Edinburgh Review*; *The Guardian*; *Literary Journal, A Review of Domestic and Foreign Literature*; *Monthly Magazine*; *Monthly Mirror*; *Monthly Review*; *New London Magazine*: *Enlarged and Improved*; *New London Review*; *Poetical Register and Repository of Fugitive Poetry for 1802*; *Political Register*.

Abrams, M.H. (1965), 'Structure and Style in the Greater Romantic Lyric', in *From Sensibility to Romanticism: Essays Presented to Frederick A. Pottle*, eds Frederick W. Hilles and Harold Bloom, New York: Oxford University Press.
Allmand, Christopher (1992), *Henry V*, London: Methuen Publishing.
Altick, Richard D. (1957), *The English Common Reader: A Social History of the Mass Reading Public 1800–1900*, Chicago, IL, London and Toronto: University of Chicago Press.
Amarasinghe, Upali (1962), *Dryden and Pope in the Early Nineteenth Century: A Study of Changing Literary Taste*, Cambridge: Cambridge University Press.
Anon. (1827), *Observations on Some of the Popular Amusements of this Country, Addressed to the Higher Classes of Society*, London: Hatchard and Son.

— (1827), *The Voice of Humanity: Observations on A Few Instances of Cruelty to Animals*, London: Sherwood and Co.
— (1831), *Ordinance Survey Old Series Map 43*, London: Lt. Colonel Colby.
Bakhtin, Mikhail (1984), *Rabelais and His World*, trans. Hélèn Iswosky, Bloomington: Indiana University Press.
Barrell, John (1972), *The Idea of Landscape and the Sense of Place: An Approach to the Poetry of John Clare*, Cambridge: Cambridge University Press.
— (1980), *The Dark Side of the Landscape: The Rural Poor in English Painting 1730–1840*, Cambridge: Cambridge University Press.
— (1992), 'Sportive Labour: the farmworker in eighteenth–century poetry and painting', in *The English Rural Community: Image and Analysis*, ed. Brian Short, Cambridge: Cambridge University Press.
— and Bull, John (eds) (1974), *The Penguin Book of Pastoral Verse*, London: Allen Lane.
Bennett, Betty, T. (ed.) (1976), *British War Poetry in the Age of Romanticism: 1793–1915*, New York and London: Garland Publishing.
Blackstone, Henry (1788), 'Steel vs Houghton and Uxor, 1788', in *Reports of Cases Argued and Determined in the Court of Common Pleas in Easter and Trinity Terms, in the Twenty–eighth Year of George III*, London: Printed by His Majesty's Law Printers.
Bloom, Harold (1997), *The Anxiety of Influence*, Oxford and New York: Oxford University Press.
Bloomfield, B.C. (1993), 'The Publication of *The Farmer's Boy* by Robert Bloomfield', *The Library*, 15, 75–94.
Bloomfield, Nathaniel (1803), *An Essay on War, in Blank Verse; Honington Green, A Ballad; The Culprit, an Elegy; and Other Poems on Various Subjects*, London: Printed for Thos Hurst and Vernor and Hood.
Bloomfield, Robert (1800), *The Farmer's Boy: A Rural Poem*, London: Printed for Vernor and Hood.
— (1800a), *The Farmer's Boy: A Rural Poem*, 2nd edn, London: Printed for Vernor and Hood.
— (1800b), *The Farmer's Boy: A Rural Poem*, 3rd edn, London: Printed for Vernor and Hood.
— (1801), *The Farmer's Boy: A Rural Poem*, 5th edn, London: Printed for Vernor and Hood.
— (1802), *Rural Tales, Ballads and Songs*, London: Printed for Vernor and Hood.
— (1804), *Good Tidings; or, News From the Farm*, London: Printed for Vernor and Hood.
— (1806), *The Farmer's Boy: A Rural Poem*, 9th edn, London: Printed for Vernor and Hood.
— (1806), *Wild Flowers; or, Pastoral and Local Poetry*, London: Printed for Vernor, Hood and Sharpe.
— (1809), *The Poems of Robert Bloomfield*, 2 vols, London: Printed for the Author by Longman, Hurst, Rees, Orme and Co.

— (1813), *The Banks of Wye*, 2nd edn, London: Printed for B. and R. Crosby and Co.

— (1822), *May Day with the Muses*, London. Printed for the Author.

— (1823), *Hazelwood-Hall: A Village Drama*, London: Printed for Baldwin, Cradock and Joy.

— (1824), *The Remains of Robert Bloomfield*, 2 vols, ed. J. Weston, London: Baldwin, Cradock and Joy.

— (1968), *Selections from the Correspondence of Robert Bloomfield; The Suffolk Poet*, ed. W.H. Hart, FSA, London: Spottiswoode and Co., 1870; repr. Walton on Thames, Surrey: Robert Ashby, FLA.

— (1998), *Selected Poems*, eds John Goodridge and John Lucas, Nottingham: Trent Editions.

Blum, Carol (1986), *Rousseau and the Republic of Virtue: The Language of Politics in the French Revolution*, Ithaca, NY and London: Cornell University Press.

Borst, Arno (1993), *The Ordering of Time: From the Ancient Computers to the Modern Computer*, trans. Andrew Winnard, Cambridge: Polity Press.

Boswell, James (1934), *Boswell's Life of Johnson*, ed. George Birkbeck Hill, rev. L.F. Powell, Oxford: Clarendon Press.

Bowles, William Lisle (1855), *The Poetical Works of William Lisle Bowles*, 2 vols, ed. George Gilfillan, Edinburgh: James Nichol.

Brayley, E.W. (1806), *Views in Suffolk, Norfolk and Northamptonshire Illustrative of the Works of Robert Bloomfield Accompanied with descriptions to which is Annexed A Memoir of the Poet's Life*, London: Vernor, Hood and Sharpe.

Bromwich, David (1998), *Disowned by Memory: Wordsworth's Poetry of the 1790s*, Chicago, IL and London: University of Chicago Press.

Burke, Tim (2006), 'Colonial Spaces and National Identities in *The Banks of Wye*: Bloomfield and the Wye after Wordsworth', in *Robert Bloomfield: Lyric, Class and the Romantic Canon*, eds Simon White, John Goodridge and Bridget Keegan, Lewisburg, PA: Bucknell University Press.

Burnett, John (1966), *Plenty and Want: A Social History of Diet in England from 1815 to the Present Day*, London: Thomas Nelson and Sons Ltd.

Bushaway, Bob (1982), *By Rite: Custom, Ceremony and Community in England 1700–1880*, London: Junction Books.

— (1995), '"Tacit, Unsuspected, but still Implicit Faith": Alternative Belief in Nineteenth-Century Rural England', in *Popular Culture in England, c. 1500–1850*, ed. Tim Harris, Basingstoke: Macmillan.

Byron (1996), *Selected Poems*, eds Susan J. Wolfson and Peter J. Manning, London: Penguin.

Carafelli, Annette Wheeler (1995), 'The Romantic "Peasant" Poets and their Patrons', *Wordsworth Circle*, 26, 77–87.

Chadwick, Nora (1971), *The Celts*, London: Penguin Books.

Charlesworth, Michael (1994), 'The Ruined Abbey: Picturesque and Gothic Values', in *The Politics of the Picturesque: Literature, Landscape and*

Aesthetics Since 1770, eds Stephen Copley and Peter Garside, Cambridge: Cambridge University Press.

Charlotte, Princess (1949), *Letters of Princess Charlotte*, ed. A. Aspinall, London: Home and Van Thal.

Christmas, William J. (2001), *The Lab'ring Muses: Work, Writing, and the Social Order in English Plebeian Poetry, 1730–1830*. Newark, NJ and London: University of Delaware Press.

— (2006), '*The Farmer's Boy* and Contemporary Politics', in *Robert Bloomfield: Lyric, Class and the Romantic Canon*, eds Simon White, John Goodridge and Bridget Keegan, Lewisburg, PA: Bucknell University Press.

Clare, John (1820), *Poems Descriptive of Rural Life and Scenery*, 3rd edn, London: Printed for Taylor and Hessey.

— (1982), *The Rural Muse*, 2nd edn, ed. R.K.R. Thornton, Ashington and Manchester: Mid Northumberland Arts Group and Carcanet Press.

— (1984), *The Oxford Authors John Clare*, eds Eric Robinson and David Powell, Oxford and New York: Oxford University Press.

— (1985), *The Letters of John Clare*, ed. Mark Storey, Oxford: Oxford University Press.

Clark, Anna (1995), *The Struggle for the Breeches: Gender and the Making of the British Working Class*, Berkeley, Los Angeles and London: University of California Press.

Clark, Timothy (1997), *The Theory of Inspiration: Composition as a Crises of Subjectivity in Romantic and Post-Romantic Writing*, Manchester and New York: Manchester University Press.

Cobbett, William (1967), *Rural Rides*, ed. George Woodcock, London: Penguin Books.

Coleridge, Samuel Taylor (1956), *Collected Letters of Samuel Taylor Coleridge*, 2 vols, ed. Earl Leslie Griggs, Oxford: Oxford University Press.

— (1970), *The Collected Works of Samuel Taylor Coleridge*, 16 vols, ed. Kathleen Coburn, London: Routledge.

— [and Wordsworth, William] (1991), *Lyrical Ballads*, 2nd edn, eds R.L. Brett and A.R. Jones, London: Routledge.

Constable, John (1968), *John Constable's Correspondence*, 3 vols, ed. R.B. Beckett, Ipswich: Suffolk Records Society.

Cowper, William (1994), *The Task and Selected Other Poems*, ed. James Sambrook, London and New York: Longman.

Coxe, William (1985), *A historical tour in Monmouthshire*, London: L.T. Cadell Junior and W. Davies, 1801; repr. Cardiff: Merton Priory Press.

Crabbe, George (1991), *Selected Poems*, ed. Gavin Edwards, London: Penguin Books.

Crowe, William (1989), *Lewesdon Hill*, ed. Jonathan Wordsworth, Oxford: Woodstock Books.

Dart, Gregory (1999), *Rousseau, Robespierre and English Romanticism*, Cambridge: Cambridge University Press.

Davies, Damian Walford (2002), *Presences that Disturb: Models of Romantic Identity in the Literature and Culture of the 1790s*, Cardiff: University of Wales Press.

Davies, John (1994), *A History of Wales*, London: Penguin Books.

Davis, Leith (2004), 'At "sang about": Scottish song and the challenge to British culture', in *Scotland and the Borders of Romanticism*, eds Leith Davis, Ian Duncan and Janet Sornesen, Cambridge: Cambridge University Press.

Donald, Diana (1996), *The Age of Caricature: Satirical Prints in the Reign of George III*, New Haven, CT and London: Yale University Press.

Drummond, J.C. and Wilbraham, Anne (1939), *The Englishman's Food: A History of Five Centuries of English Diet*, London: Jonathan Cape.

Dryden, John (1821), *The Works of John Dryden*, 18 vols, 2nd edn, ed. Walter Scott, Edinburgh: Printed for Archibald Constable.

Duck, Stephen and Collier, Mary (1989), *The Thresher's Labour, The Woman's Labour*, eds E.P. Thompson and Marian Sugden, London: The Merlin Press.

Dyer, John (2000), *Selected Poetry and Prose*, ed. John Goodridge, Nottingham: Trent Editions.

Dyck, Ian (1996), 'The Town and Country Divide in English History', in *Living and Learning: Essays in Honour of J.F.C. Harrison*, eds Malcolm Chase and Ian Dyck, Aldershot: Scolar Press.

Elledge, Scott (ed.) (1961), *Eighteenth Century Critical Essays*, 2 vols, Ithaca, NY: Cornell University Press.

Ellis, Stanley (ed.) (1970), *Suffolk Words and Phrases*, London: R. Hunter, 1823; repr. Newton Abbot: David Charles.

Everitt, Alan (2000), 'Common Land', in *The English Landscape*, ed. Joan Thirsk, Oxford: Oxford University Press.

Ferguson, Moira (1993), 'The Unpublished Poems of Ann Yearsley', *Tulsa Studies in Women's Literature*, 12, 13–46.

Finley, M.I. (1987), *The Use and Abuse of History*, London: Penguin Books.

Foster, George (2000), *A Voyage Around the World*, 2 vols, eds Nicholas Thomas and Oliver Bergoff, assisted by Jenifer Newell, Honolulu: University of Hawaii Press.

Freud, Sigmund (1977), *The Penguin Freud Library: On Sexuality*, ed. Angela Richards, London: Penguin Books.

Genette, Gerard (1997), *Paratexts: Thresholds of Interpretation*, trans. Jane E. Lewin, Cambridge: Cambridge University Press.

Gill, Stephen (1989), *William Wordsworth: A Life*, Oxford and New York: Oxford University Press.

Gilpin, William (1994), *Observations on the River Wye, and Several Parts of South Wales, &c. relative chiefly to Picturesque Beauty; made in the Summer of the year 1770*, in *The Picturesque: Literary Sources and Documents*, vol. I, ed. Malcolm Andrews, Mountfield, East Sussex: Helm Information.

— (1994a), *Three Essays: on Picturesque Beauty; on Picturesque Travel; and on Sketching Landscape: to which is added a Poem, on Landscape Painting,*

2nd edn., in *The Picturesque: Literary Sources and Documents*, vol. II, ed. Malcolm Andrews, Mountfield, East Sussex: Helm Information.
Goldsmith, Oliver (1969), *The Poems of Thomas Gray, William Collins and Oliver Goldsmith*, ed. Roger Lonsdale, London and New York: Longman Group Ltd.
Goodridge, John (1995), *Rural Life in Eighteenth-Century Poetry*, Cambridge: Cambridge University Press.
— (2001), 'Editorial', in *The Robert Bloomfield Society News Letter*, 2, 1–2.
Graham, James (1790), *A Short Treatise on the All-cleansing, – all-healing, – and all-invigorating Qualities of the Simple Earth*, Newcastle Upon Tyne: Printed by Hall and Eliot.
Gravil, Richard (2003), *Wordsworth's Bardic Vocation, 1787–1842*, Basingstoke: Macmillan.
Gray, Thomas (1969), *The Poems of Thomas Gray, William Collins and Oliver Goldsmith*, ed. Roger Lonsdale, London and New York: Longman Group Ltd.
— (2001), *Thomas Gray's Journal of his Visit to the Lake District in October 1769*, ed. William Roberts, Liverpool: Liverpool University Press.
Greene, Richard (1993), *Mary Leapor: A Study in Eighteenth-Century Women's Poetry*, Oxford: Clarendon Press.
Griffin, Dustin (1996), *Literary Patronage in England, 1650–1800*, Cambridge: Cambridge University Press.
Griffin, Mary Theresa (1981), 'Dyer's Grongar Poems and "Picturesque" Sensibility', *Studies in English Literature, 1500–1900*, 21.3, 457–69.
Groom, Nick (1999), *The Making of Percy's Reliques*, Oxford: Oxford University Press.
Hartman, Geoffrey H. (1970), *Beyond Formalism: Literary Essays 1958–1970*, New Haven, CT and London: Yale University Press.
Hay, Douglas and Rogers, Nicholas (1997), *Eighteenth Century English Society: Shuttles and Swords*, Oxford and New York: Oxford University Press.
Hazlitt, William (1930), *The Complete Works of William Hazlitt*, 21 vols, ed. P.P. Howe, London and Toronto: J.M. Dent.
Henken, Elissa R. (1996), *National Redeemer: Owain Glyndŵr in Welsh Tradition*, Cardiff: University of Wales Press.
Hibbert, Christopher (1973), *George IV: Regent and King 1811–1830*, 2 vols, London: Allen Lane.
Howitt, William (1838), *The Rural Life of England*, 2 vols, London: Longman, Orme, Brown, Green, and Longmans.
Janowitz, Anne (1990), *England's Ruins: Poetic Purpose and the National Landscape*, Cambridge, MA and London: Basil Blackwell.
— (1998), *Lyric and Labour in the Romantic Tradition*, Cambridge: Cambridge University Press.
Johnson, Samuel (1905), *Lives of the English Poets*, 3 vols, ed. George Birkbeck Hill, Oxford: Clarendon Press.

— (1968), *The Yale Edition of the Works of Samuel Johnson*, 16 vols, ed. Arthur Sherbo. New Haven, CT and London: Yale University Press.

— (1976), *The History of Rasselas, Prince of Abissinia*, London: Penguin Books.

Keats, John (1970), *Letters of John Keats*, ed. Robert Gittings, Oxford: Oxford University Press.

Keegan, Bridget (2001), 'Cobbling Verse: Shoemaker Poets of the Long Eighteenth Century', *Eighteenth Century: Theory and Interpretation*, 42.3, 195–217.

Keen, Paul (1999), *The Crisis of Literature in the 1790s: Print Culture and the Public Sphere*, Cambridge: Cambridge University Press.

Kenyon-Jones, Christine (2001), *Kindred Brutes: Animals in Romantic-Period Writing*, Aldershot: Ashgate.

King, Peter (1991), 'Customary rights and women's earnings: the importance of gleaning to the rural labouring poor, 1750–1850', *Economic History Review*, 44, 461–76.

Kussmaul, Ann (1981), *Servants in Husbandry in Early Modern England*, Cambridge: Cambridge University Press.

Labbe, Jacqueline (1998), *Romantic Visualities: Landscape, Gender and Romanticism*, London: Macmillan.

Landry, Donna (1990), *The Muses of Resistance: Labouring-Class Women's Poetry in Britain, 1739–1796*, Cambridge, New York and Melbourne: Cambridge University Press.

— (2006), 'Georgic Ecology', in *Robert Bloomfield: Lyric, Class and the Romantic Canon*, eds Simon White, John Goodridge and Bridget Keegan, Lewisburg, PA: Bucknell University Press.

Larissy, Edward (1999), 'The Celtic Bard of Romanticism: Blindness and Second Sight', *Romanticism*, 5.1, 43–57.

Laslett, Peter (1988), *The World We Have Lost: further explored*, 3rd edn, London: Routledge.

Lawson, Jonathan (1980), *Robert Bloomfield*, Boston: Twayne Publishers.

Leapor, Mary (1748), *Poems on Several Occasions*, London: Printed by J. Roberts.

Lennox, Charlotte (1751), *The Life of Harriot Stuart*, London: Printed for J. Payne and J. Bouquet.

Levinson, Marjorie (1986), *Wordsworth's Great Period Poems: Four Essays*, Cambridge: Cambridge University Press.

Lofft, Capel (1788), 'On the Gleaning Question', in *Annals of Agriculture*, vol. X, ed. Arthur Young, Bury St. Edmunds: Printed for the Editor by J. Rackham.

— (1791), *Remarks on the Letter of Mr Burke to a Member of the National Assembly; with Several Papers in Addition to the Reflections of Mr Burke on the Revolution in France*, London: Printed for J. Johnson.

Lucas, John (1994), 'Bloomfield and Clare', in *The Independent Spirit: John Clare and the self-taught tradition*, ed. John Goodridge, Helpston: The John Clare Society and The Margaret Grainger Memorial Trust.

— (1998), 'John Clare: The Shepherd's Calander', in *A Companion to Romanticism*, ed. Duncan Wu, Oxford: Blackwell.
— (2006), 'Hospitality and the Rural Tradition: Bloomfield's *May-Day with the Muses*', in *Robert Bloomfield: Lyric, Class and the Romantic Canon*, eds Simon White, John Goodridge and Bridget Keegan, Lewisburg, PA: Bucknell University Press.
Luthi, Max (1982), *The European Folktale: Form and Nature*, trans. John D. Niles, Philadelphia, PA: Institute for the Study of Human Issues.
Lynch, Deirdre Shauna (1998), *The Economy of Character: Novels, Market Culture, and the Business of Inner Meaning*, Chicago, IL and London: University of Chicago Press.
Lynch, J.J., Hinch, G.N. and Adams, D.B. (1992), *The Behaviour of Sheep: Biological Principles and Implications for Production*, Wallingford, Oxfordshire: CAB International.
Malcolmson, Robert W. (1973), *Popular Recreations in English Society 1700–1850*, Cambridge: Cambridge University Press.
Mali, Joseph (2003), *Mythistory: The Making of Modern Historiography*, Chicago, IL and London: University of Chicago Press.
Marks, Arthur Sanders (1968), 'The Paintings of David Wilkie to 1825', unpublished PhD thesis, Courtauld Institute of Art.
Maxwell, Anne (1997), 'Fallen Queens and Phantom Diadems: Cook's Voyages and England's Social Order', *Eighteenth Century: Theory and Interpretation*, 38, 247–58.
McCalman, Iain (1988), *Radical Underworld: Prophets, Revolutionaries and Pornographers in London, 1795–1840*, Cambridge, New York and Melbourne: Cambridge University Press.
McEathron, Scott (1999), 'Wordsworth, *Lyrical Ballads*, and the Problem of Peasant Poetry', *Nineteenth-Century Literature*, 54, 1–26.
— (2006), 'An Infant Poem on War: Bloomfield's "On Seeing the Launch of the Boyne"', in *Robert Bloomfield: Lyric, Class and the Romantic Canon*, eds Simon White, John Goodridge and Bridget Keegan, Lewisburg, PA: Bucknell University Press.
Mee, Jon (2003), *Romanticism, Enthusiasm and Regulation: Poetics and the Policing of Culture in the Romantic Period*, Oxford: Oxford University Press.
Montagu, Elizabeth (1772), *An Essay on the Writings and Genius of Shakespeare*, 3rd edn, London: Printed for Edward and Charles Dilley.
More, Hannah (1799), *Cheap Repository Shorter Tracts. A New Edition*, London: Sold by F. and C. Rivington.
Morgan, Prys (1981), *The Eighteenth Century Renaissance*, Llandybie: Christopher Davies.
Morton, Timothy (1994), *Shelley and the Revolution in Taste: The Body and the Natural World*, Cambridge: Cambridge University Press.
Mulvey, Christopher (1983), *Anglo-American Landscapes: A Study of Nineteenth Century Anglo-American Travel Literature*, New York: Cambridge University Press.

Myers, A.R. (1971), *England in the Middle Ages*, 8th edn, London: Penguin Books.

Neeson, J.M. (1993), *Commoners: Common Right, Enclosure and Social Change in England, 1700–1820*, Cambridge: Cambridge University Press.

O'Flaherty, Wendy Doniger (1988), *Other Peoples Myths: The Cave of Echoes*, New York: Macmillan.

Ong, Walter J. (1982), *Orality and Literacy: The Technologizing of the Word*, London and New York: Routledge.

Paine, Thomas (1984), *The Rights of Man*, eds Eric Foner and Henry Collins, London: Penguin Books.

Palmer, Roy (ed.) (1986), *The English Country Songbook*, London: Omnibus Press.

Peacock, Thomas Love (1967), *The Works of Thomas Love Peacock*, 10 vols, eds H.F.B. Brett-Smith and C.E. Jones, New York: AMS Press.

Pedersen, Susan (1986), 'Hannah More Meets Simple Simon: Tracts, Chapbooks, and Popular Culture in Late Eighteenth Century England', *Journal of British Studies*, 25, 84–113.

Percy, Thomas (1858), *Reliques of Ancient English Poetry*, 3 vols, Edinburgh: James Nichol and James Nisbet and Co.

Perkins, Maureen (1996), *Visions of the Future: Almanacs, Time and Cultural Change*, Oxford: Oxford University Press.

Place, Francis (1972), *The Autobiography of Francis Place*, ed. Mary Thale, Cambridge: Cambridge University Press.

Pope, Alexander (1965), *The Poems of Alexander Pope*, ed. John Butt. London and New York: Routledge.

Porter, Enid (1969), *Cambridgeshire Customs and Folklore*, London: Routledge.

Postgate, M.R. (1962), 'The Field Systems of Breckland', *The Agricultural History Review*, 10, 80–101.

Pyne, W.H. (1971), *Microcosm*, London: M.A. Nattali, 1806; repr. New York: Benjamin Blom Inc.

Radcliffe, W. (1828), *Origin of the New System of Manufacture Commonly Called "Power-Loom Weaving"*, Stockport: Printed and Sold by James Lomax.

Ritson, Joseph (1884–86), *Ancient English Metrical Romances*, 3 vols, rev. E. Goldsmid, Edinburgh: E. and G. Goldsmid.

Rizzo, Betty (1991), 'The Patron as Poet Maker: The Politics of Benefaction', *Eighteenth Century Culture*, 20, 241–66.

Rochefoucauld, François de La (1988), *A Frenchman's Year in Suffolk*, trans. Norman Scarfe, Woodbridge, Suffolk: The Boydell Press.

Roper, Derek (1978), *Reviewing Before the Edinburgh: 1788–1802*, London: Methuen and Co. Ltd.

Rosenmeyer, Thomas G. (1969), *The Green Cabinet: Theocritus and the European Pastoral Lyric*, Berkeley and Los Angeles: University of California Press.

Rousseau, G.S. (1993), 'Medicine and the Muses: an approach to literature and medicine', in *Literature and Medicine During the Eighteenth Century*, eds Marie Mulvey Roberts and Roy Porter, London and New York: Routledge.

Rousseau, Jean-Jacques (1968), *The Social Contract*, trans. and ed. Maurice Cranston, London: Penguin.

— (1991), *Emile: or; On Education*, trans. Allan Bloom, London: Penguin Books.

Ruggles, Thomas (1788), 'On Gleaning', in *Annals of Agriculture*, vol. IX, ed. Arthur Young, Bury St. Edmunds: Printed for the Editor by J. Rackham.

Sales, Roger (1983), *English Literature in History 1780–1830: Pastoral and Politics*, London: Hutchinson and Co.

Sambrook. A.J. (1967), 'The Farmer's Boy: Robert Bloomfield, 1766–1823', *English*, 16, 167–73.

Scott, Walter (1932), *Minstrelsy of the Scottish Border*, 4 vols, ed. T.F. Henderson, Edinburgh and London: Oliver and Boyd.

Sharpe, Jim (2001), 'History from Below', in *New Perspectives on Historical Writing*, 2nd edn, ed. Peter Burke, Cambridge: Polity Press.

Shelley, Percy Bysshe (1964), *The Letters of Percy Bysshe Shelley*, ed. Frederick L. Jones, Oxford: Clarendon Press.

— (1993), *The Prose Works of Percy Bysshe Shelley*, ed. E.B. Murray, Oxford: Clarendon Press.

Siskin, Clifford (1998), *The Work of Writing: Literature and Social Change in Britain 1700–1830*, Baltimore, MD and London: Johns Hopkins University Press.

Smiles, Sam (1994), *The Image of Antiquity: Ancient Britain and the Romantic Imagination*, New Haven, CT and London: Yale University Press.

Smith, Bernard (1985), *European Vision and the South Pacific*, 2nd edn, New Haven, CT and London: Yale University Press.

Smith, Ginnie (1985), 'Prescribing the rules of health: Self-help and advice in the late eighteenth century', in *Patients and Practitioners: Lay perceptions of medicine in pre-industrial society*, ed. Roy Porter, Cambridge: Cambridge University Press.

Snell, K.D.M. (1985), *The Annals of the Labouring Poor: Social Change in Agrarian England, 1660–1900*, Cambridge: Cambridge University Press.

Southey, Robert (1925), *The Lives and Works of the Uneducated Poets*, London: Humphrey Milford.

— (2000), 'Wat Tyler' in *Five Romantic Plays, 1768–1821*, eds Paul Baines and Edward Burns, Oxford: Oxford University Press.

— (2004), *Poetical Works 1793–1810*, 5 vols, ed. Lynda Pratt, London: Pickering and Chatto.

Spence, Thomas (1807), *Spence's Songs*, London: Printed for the Author by Scale and Bates.

Stone, Lawrence (1979), *The Family, Sex and Marriage in England 1500–1800*, London: Penguin Books.

Storey, Mark (ed.) (1973), *Clare: The Critical Heritage*, London and Boston, MA: Routledge.

Sutherland, Kathryn (1994), '"Events Have Made Us A World of Readers": Reader Relations 1780–1830', in *The Penguin History of Literature: The Romantic Period*, ed. David B. Pirie, London: Penguin Books.

Swift, Jonathan (1986), *Gulliver's Travels*, ed. Paul Turner, Oxford and New York: Oxford University Press.

Sylvester, Dorothy (1969), *The Rural Landscape of the Welsh Borderland*, London: Macmillan.

Taylor, Anya (1999), *Bachus in Romantic England: Writers and Drink, 1780–1830*, London: Macmillan.

Taylor, Christopher (1975), *Fields in the English Landscape*, London: J.M. Dent.

Taylor, Jeffrys (1832), *The Farm: A New Account of Rural Toils and Produce*, London: John Harris.

Thelwall, John (2001), *The Peripatetic*, ed. Judith Thompson, Detroit, MI: Wayne State University Press.

Thomas, Claudia N. (1994), *Alexander Pope and His Eighteenth-Century Women Readers*, Carbondale: Southern Illinois University Press.

Thompson, E.P. (1963), *The Making of the English Working Class*, London: Penguin Books.

— (1993), *Customs in Common*, London: Penguin Books.

Thomson, David (1950), *England in the Nineteenth Century*, London: Penguin.

Thomson, James (1908), *Poetical Works*, ed. J. Logie Robertson, Oxford: Oxford University Press.

— (1972), *The Seasons and The Castle of Indolence*, ed. James Sambrook, Oxford: Clarendon Press.

Tonkin, Elizabeth (1992), *Narrating Our Pasts: The Social Construction of Oral History*, Cambridge: Cambridge University Press.

Trumpener, Katie (1997), *Bardic Nationalism: The Romantic Novel and the British Empire*, Princeton, NJ: Princeton University Press.

Turner, A.J. (1982), '"The Acomplishment of many Years": Three Notes Towards a History of the Sand-glass', *Annals of Science*, 39, 161–72.

— (1984), *The Time Museum: Time Measuring Instruments*, Rockford: The Time Museum.

Turner, John (1986), *Wordsworth, Play and Politics: A Study of Wordsworth's Poetry 1787–1800*, London: Macmillan.

Turner, Victor (1981), 'Social Dramas and Stories about Them', in *On Narrative*, ed. W.J.T. Mitchell, Chicago, IL and London: University of Chicago Press.

Unwin, Rayner (1954), *The Rural Muse: Studies in the Peasant Poetry of England*, London: George Allen and Unwin.

Vasina, Jan (1985), *Oral Tradition as History*, Madison: University of Wisconsin Press.

Vaughan, Henry (1986), *The Oxford Authors George Herbert and Henry Vaughan*, ed. Louis L. Martz, Oxford and New York: Oxford University Press.

Waldron, Mary (1996), *Lactilla, Milkwoman of Clifton: The Life and Writings of Ann Yearsley 1753–1806*, Athens and London: University of Georgia Press.

Warnock, Mary (1989), *Memory*, London: Faber and Faber Ltd.

Warton, Joseph (1762), *An Essay on the Genius and Writings of Pope*, 2nd edn, London: Printed for R. and J. Dodsley.

Wesling, Donald (1970), *Wordsworth and the Adequacy of Landscape*, London and New York: Routledge.

Wells, Roger (1988), *Wretched Faces: Famine in Wartime England 1763–1803*, Gloucester and New York: Alan Sutton and St. Martin's Press.

White, Simon (2003), 'Rural Medicine: Robert Bloomfield's *Good Tidings*', *Romanticism*, 9.2, 141–56.

Williams, Raymond (1993), *The Country and the City*, London: The Hogarth Press.

Winks, William Edward (1883), *Lives of Illustrious Shoemakers*, London: Sampson Low, Marston, Searle and Rivington.

Woodhouse, James (1764), *Poems on Sundry Occasions*, London: Printed for the Author.

Wordsworth, William (1967), *The Letters of William and Dorothy Wordsworth; The Early Years, 1787–1805*, ed. E. de Selincourt, rev. C.L. Shaver, Oxford: Oxford University Press.

— (1979), *The Prelude 1799, 1805, 1850*, eds Jonathan Wordsworth, M.H. Abrams and Stephen Gill, New York and London: W.W. Norton and Company.

— [and Coleridge, Samuel Taylor] (1991), *Lyrical Ballads*, 2nd edn, eds R.L. Brett, and A.R. Jones, London: Routledge.

Yearsley, Ann (1787), *Poems on Various Subjects*, London: Printed for T. Cadell.

— (2003), *Selected Poems*, ed. Tim Burke, Cheltenham: The Cyder Press.

Young, Arthur (1801), *Inquiry into the Propriety of Applying Wastes to the Better Management of The Poor*, Bury St Edmunds: Printed by J. Rackham.

— (1969), *General View of the Agriculture of the County of Suffolk*, London: Printed for Sherwood, Neely and Jones, 1813; repr. Newton Abbot: David and Charles.

— (1970), *General View of the Agriculture of the County of Lincolnshire*, London: Printed for Sherwood, Neely and Jones, 1813; repr. New York: Kelley.

— (1970), *General View of the Agriculture of the County of Sussex*, London: Printed for Sherwood, Neely and Jones, 1813; repr. New York: Kelley.

Young, Edward (1759), *Conjectures on Original Composition in a Letter to the Author of Sir Charles Grandison*, 2nd edn, London: Printed for A. Millar and R. and J. Dodsley.

Zimmerman, Sarah M. (1999), *Romanticism, Lyricism and History*, New York: State University of New York Press.

Zionkowski, Linda (1989), 'Strategies of Containment: Stephen Duck, Ann Yearsley, and the Problem of Polite Culture', *Eighteenth Century Life*, 13, 91–108.

— (2001), *Men's Work: Gender, Class, and the Professionalization of Poetry, 1660–1784*, Basingstoke and New York, Palgrave.

Index

Abrams M.H. 57, 63, 66, 79
abstraction 67, 70
Addison, Joseph 10
agricultural reform 51, 52, 53, 55, 61, 130, 136
allegory 134–5
anapestic metre 139
ancient Britons 110
animals 19, 27–8, 47–8
Annual Review 34, 48, 96
aristocracy 49, 82, 98
artisan culture 9, 10, 67
authorship 82, 99, 103, 127–8

Baker, Mrs Lloyd 101–3, 105
ballads 3, 72, 95, 96, 117, 133
  and Lofft's notes 97–8
  sentimental 35, 36, 46
  Suffolk 35, 37
  traditional 35, 46, 49, 64
  types of 35
  Wordsworth and 31, 35–6, 38, 39, 46–7, 49
  see also tales
bards 108–11, 118, 119, 143, 144
Barrell, John 13, 16, 115, 116
benevolence 40, 42, 62
Bennet, John 83
Bentley, Richard 108
birds 12, 13, 64, 138
Blake, Dr Nathan 97
blindness 144
Blomefield, William 74
Bloomfield, Charles 67–8, 102
Bloomfield, George 10, 68, 86, 87, 88, 89, 90
Bloomfield, Mary 67, 68
Bloomfield, Nathaniel 122
Bloomfield, Robert
  ancestry 74
  attitude to animals 19, 27–8, 47–8
  and community 2, 7
  complexity of 8, 16, 22, 30, 48, 49, 121, 131, 134, 139
  critical views of 2, 75
  decline 4, 5, 95
  dispute with Lofft 83–4, 90–93, 97, 99–100
  family problems 67–8, 76, 102, 127–8
  finances of 68, 92, 99, 127–8
  health problems 68, 69, 71, 76–8, 102, 105
  identity crisis 66, 67, 72, 76, 79
  and Johnson 32–4
  and labouring poor 2, 3, 5, 7–8, 12, 15, 16, 25, 26, 28, 45–6, 64, 65, 66, 79, 123, 126, 131, 133
  language of 2, 33–5, 46–7, 139
  'natural' qualities of 95, 96
  originality of 10, 95, 97
  and patrons 4, 11, 42–3, 64, 75–6, 81, 83–4, 86–9ff., 100–103
  poetic diction 17, 33–4, 96
  poetic inspiration 73
  poetics of 31–4, 54, 66, 79, 101, 124
  politics of 46, 51–2, 62, 87, 91, 115, 121, 136–7
  popularity of 4–5
  and Romanticism 2–3
  as shoemaker poet 9, 12, 14, 74, 76, 79, 127
  social status 11–12
  and war 44–5
  and Wordsworth 1–2, 7, 9, 10, 15, 20, 26, 30, 32, 35–6, 38, 46–7, 49, 54, 107–8, 119, 121
  Works
    'Anecdotes and Observations' 17
    Banks of Wye, The (1811) 4, 101–3, 105–119
      bards in 108–11
      compared to 'Tintern Abbey' 107–108
      and Dyer 106
      gleaners in 113–14
      and labouring poor 110, 115–16, 119
      landscape in 105, 106, 107, 109
      monuments in 119
      originality of 105
      preface 105–6
      reviews of 105, 122

ruins in 111–17
songs in 111, 118, 119
structure 122
'Gleaner's Song' 111, 112
'Maid of Llandogo', The 111
'Morris of Persfield' 111, 118, 119
Farmer's Boy, The (1800) 1, 2, 4, 5, 7–30, 70, 78, 88
appendix 22, 23
authenticity of 99
biographical elements 12, 29
community in 19–21
complexity of 3, 7, 8, 22, 25, 30
composition of 8–9, 30
editing of 11, 29, 75, 86–7, 91–2, 97, 98, 99, 100
invocation 8, 9
and labouring poor 7, 12, 25, 45–6
and politics 21–4
preface 11, 21, 86, 89, 91, 100
and *The Prelude* 3, 7, 9, 10, 15, 20, 26, 28ff.
reviews of 7, 8, 31–2, 75, 89, 96, 97
royalties from 128
structure and modes 7, 8, 11, 12
subject matter 7, 9–10, 11, 18, 21, 22–3, 25, 31–2
Good Tidings; or, News from the Farm (1804) 100
Hazelwood- Hall: A Village Drama (1823) 49
May-Day with the Muses (1822) 5, 35, 81, 121–46
community in 125, 126
complexity of 121, 131, 134, 139
labouring poor in 123–4ff., 133, 138, 142, 145
originality of 125
preface 122–3, 124
structure and frame 122, 131
subject matter 124
tone 121, 122, 123, 124, 131
'Alfred and Jennet' 143–5
'Drunken Father, The' 129, 131
'Forester, The' 132–8
'Shepherd's Dream, The' 138–42
'Soldier's Home, The' 142–3
'On Revisiting the Place of my Nativity' 86
Poems of Robert Bloomfield, The (1809) 8, 23, 63, 87, 88, 99, 105, 126
Remains of Robert Bloomfield, The 1, 15, 46
Rural Tales, Ballads and Songs (1802) 1, 3, 4, 31, 32, 33, 42, 43, 46, 81, 93–4, 95, 100
preface 32, 34, 42
'Dolly' 43, 44–5
'Fakenham Ghost, The' 46, 47
'French Mariner, The' 43, 44, 45–6
'Hunting Song' 133
'Market Night' 1, 46–7, 95
'Miller's Maid, The' 39, 40–42, 43, 96, 98, 142
'Richard and Kate' 35–9, 75, 95
'Visit to Whittlebury Forest, A' 63–7, 68, 71, 79
'Walter and Jane' 39–40, 41, 42, 43, 96, 142
'Widow to her Hour-Glass, The' 57–63, 79, 93, 95
Selected Poems (1998) 2
Wild Flowers; or, Pastoral and Local Poetry (1806) 3, 31, 32, 33, 34, 46, 47, 93, 94, 101, 122
preface 32–5, 101
'Abner and the Widow Jones' 28, 47–9, 54
'Broken Crutch, The' 3, 17, 49–54, 62
'Horkey, The. A Provincial Ballad' 34, 132
'Shooter's Hill' 57, 67–72, 79, 105, 106, 124, 126
'To My Old Oak Table' 57, 124, 73–80
Boswell, James 84, 121
Bowles, William Lisle 57, 59
Brayley, E.W. 74
Breckland 12
Brimble, William 83
British Critic 21, 87
Brunless Castle 115, 116
Bryant, John Frederick 83
Brydges, Sir Samuel Egerton 128
Buchan, Earl of 101, 109

Burke, Tim 110, 111, 113
Burney, Frances 83
Burns, Robert 5, 109, 111, 131
Byron, Lord 5, 121, 124, 133, 139
    English Bards and Scotch Reviewers 121–2, 126

Cambridge Intelligencer 44
capitalism 2, 20, 21, 27, 39, 40, 61, 62, 130, 133
carnival 128
Celtic cultures 71, 108–10, 144
Charlotte Augusta, Princess 136–7
children 40
Christianity 145
Christmas, William 16, 17, 19, 22, 83
Clare, John 17, 35, 51, 67, 68, 75, 97, 103, 126, 127, 128
Clark, Timothy 2
classical literature 97
Clifford, Rosamond 117–18
Clifford Castle 117
Cobbett, William 15, 20, 21, 27, 70, 91, 136
Coleridge, Samuel Taylor 1, 3, 4, 30, 31, 45, 46, 57, 63, 64, 65–6, 67, 73, 75, 77, 96, 128
    'Dejection: an Ode' 57, 73
    'Frost at Midnight' 57, 63, 66, 67
    'This Lime Tree Bower My Prison' 57, 63, 64, 66
common land 51, 52, 67
community 2, 7, 12, 19–21, 26, 28, 29, 38, 39, 41–2, 54, 61, 65, 66, 125, 143
    decline of 21, 26–7
    and history 116
    ideal 23, 24, 53, 126
    and poetry 126
    see also rural communities
consciousness *see* mind
conversation poem 3, 57, 63, 65
'Cook's Voyage' 23–4
copyright 90, 128
Corbould, Richard 108
Corn Laws 135–6
Cowper, William 82, 89, 123
    'Diverting History of John Gilpin, The' 47
    Task, The 25
Coxe, William 110, 112, 115, 118
Crabbe, George 37, 38, 82, 89
Critical Review 4, 41, 122
Crowe, William
    Lewesdon Hill 63–4
Cumberland 20, 21
customs 20, 22, 24, 25, 34, 38, 52, 60, 61–2, 114

debating societies 10, 19, 21, 91
deference 81, 126, 144
Denham, Sir John 63
dialect 33–4, 35
diet 19
Drake, Dr Nathan 89, 101
dream-vision poems 139, 140
drunkenness 129–30, 131–2
Dryden, John 33, 82, 96, 97, 118, 123
Duck, Stephen 94, 95
    Thresher's Labour, The 16
Duff, William 95
Dyer, John 10
    Fleece, The 7, 107, 111
    Grongar Hill 69–70, 106–107, 113

Eclectic Review 75, 105
Edinburgh Review 1
Eleanor, Queen 117–18
enclosure 12, 17, 51, 52, 61, 122, 136
endnotes 93–4, 95, 96, 98, 100
England 66, 67, 113, 134–5, 141, 142
episodic structure 7, 12

'Fair Rosamond' 117–18
fairies 140, 141
farm service system 26–7
farmers 19, 21, 23, 26, 28
Fawcett, Joseph 21
folktale 39, 40, 50
    and helpers 39–41
Forster, George 23
France 43, 45–6, 85, 129, 141
freedom 9, 18, 19–20, 25, 26, 38, 132
Freemantle, Bridget 42

Garrick, David 45
gender 82–3
General Advertiser 143
Genette, Gerard 32, 34
genius, natural 70, 75, 86, 88, 95, 109, 121, 126, 127, 138
georgic 10, 12, 16, 111
Gilpin, William 106, 111, 112, 113
gleaning 59–62, 113–14
Goldsmith, Oliver 37
Goodrich Castle 112–13
Goodridge, John 2, 7, 69
Gothic literature 95, 124
Grafton, 3rd Duke of 64, 67, 68, 79, 81, 85, 89, 127, 134, 138

Grafton, 4th Duke of 134
Graham, James 68, 69
Gravil, Richard 108
Gray, Thomas 16, 70, 108, 109, 118, 144
Greene, Richard 77
Griffin, Dustin 82, 90, 103
Groom, Nick 72

Hartman, Geoffrey H. 67
harvest 19–25, 115–16
  harvest-home 119–25
Hazlitt, William 75
health 67–9, 71, 76–7, 100, 101
Henry IV 113, 116
Henry V 113
Hesiod 12
history 4, 110, 111–117, 134
Homer 95, 140, 144
Hood, Thomas 4, 75, 89–90, 92, 93, 94, 127
hour-glass 57–9, 62–3, 79
Howitt, William 130
humour 47, 49, 50, 54, 121, 122, 123, 124, 131, 132
Hunt, Henry 91, 136
hunting 133

imagery 13, 14, 16, 18, 26, 46, 134
imagination 107, 124
inspiration *see* poetic inspiration
intellect *see* mind
irony 48, 123
isolation 26, 29, 30, 37, 38

Jago, Richard 63
Janowitz, Anne 24, 111
Jeffrey, Francis 1
Jenner, Edward 81, 100–101
Johnson, Samuel 32–4, 41, 82, 84, 96, 97, 121, 122
Jones, Thomas 108

Keats, John 31, 107, 121, 140
Keegan, Bridget 2

labour 12, 13, 14, 37, 38, 58, 121, 125, 133, 142, 143, 145
  in art and poetry 15–16
labourers 21, 23, 26, 28, 37
labouring-class poets 1, 2, 9, 10, 11, 31, 74, 127, 142, 145
  economic position 72–3
  narrative of decline 2, 4, 5, 95
  and patrons 42, 83, 87
  prejudice against 75, 87, 94, 95, 96, 121–2, 133–4
  readership of 3
  see also poetics
labouring poor 19, 42, 47, 79, 144
  abilities of 123, 126, 145
  behaviour of 129–32
  Bloomfield's response to 2, 3, 7–8, 12, 15, 16, 25, 26, 28, 64, 65, 66, 110, 115–16, 119
  communal tradition 12, 26–7, 38, 114
  and history 115–16
  impact of war on 43–5
  and landscape 70, 71, 115–16
  popular culture of 111, 114, 116–17, 129–30
  representation in art 15–16, 33, 115
  resistance of 50, 51–2, 136, 137
  and time-pieces 58–9, 62
  Wordsworth's response to 2, 3, 38
  see also labouring-class poets; poverty
Landry, Donna 83, 89, 133
landscape 12, 67, 105, 106, 107, 109
  changes in 16–18, 53
  labouring poor and 115–16
  open-field 12
  poems 69–70
  and the sublime 107, 108, 109, 113, 119
Langland, John 139
law 60, 61, 62
Lawson, Jonathan 2, 7, 8, 13, 22, 105
Leapor, Mary 42–3, 77, 87
leisure 9, 18, 28, 67, 79
Lennox, Charlotte 42, 83
Levinson, Marjorie 112
Literary Journal 47
literary marketplace 4, 5, 75, 82–3, 92, 99, 103, 128, 131
literary reviews 75, 94, 122
Lloyd, Sarah 85, 88
loco-descriptive poem 63–4
Lofft, Capel 4, 10, 21, 42, 43, 60, 61–2, 75, 81, 114, 122
  as author 85
  biography of 84
  dispute with Bloomfield 83–4, 90–93, 97, 99–100
  editorial changes 11, 29, 90–92, 97
  as patron 89–91
  prefaces 11, 86, 89
  presentation of Bloomfield 86–91, 96–9

and readers 98–9
radical politics of 84, 85, 86, 88, 91
London 8, 10, 14, 19, 20, 21, 24, 29, 49
lost-child-found plot 40, 42
Loughborough, Lord 61
Lucas, John 2, 5, 7, 8, 21, 124, 125
luxury 23, 24
Lynch, Deirdre 95, 96
lyric 3–4, 51, 53, 57, 63, 66, 67, 71
meditative 57–8, 63, 66, 67
Romantic 57, 63, 66, 79

McEathron, Scott 2, 10, 31, 37, 45
marriage 49
Martin, John 108
May-Day 128–9, 131, 135, 144
meat 19
memory 12, 13, 14, 15, 18, 57, 66, 116, 117, 118
mental health 25–6, 68
merit 74, 75
middle class 18, 21, 98
millenarianism 140
millers 40, 41, 42
Milton, John 5, 9, 139, 144
mind 13, 14, 15, 107, 126
minstrels 71–2, 109, 118, 119
mock-heroic mode 47, 48, 50, 140
Monmouthshire 106, 110-11, 112, 113, 118
Montagu, Elizabeth 83, 86–7, 89
Monthly Magazine 4
Monthly Mirror 86, 89, 99
Monthly Review 31–2, 94
morality 66, 72, 110, 129–30, 131, 132
More, Hannah 83, 84, 89, 94, 127, 129–30
Morganwg, Iolo *see* Williams, Edward
Mosaic Law 60, 61
muses 145
music 114, 144–5
see also songs
mutuality 39–40, 41, 42, 125, 132
myth 66, 116, 145

nature 13–14, 30, 54, 62, 64, 70, 109, 112, 119, 132, 133, 138, 139, 143, 144
'general' 32–3
and health 68–9
New London Magazine 36
New London Review 1
nostalgia 2, 24, 124, 126, 136
'Nut-Brown Maid, The' 64–5, 66

old age 37–8
oral culture 68
Otaheite society 23–4
Owain Glyn Dwr 113, 115, 116

Paine, Thomas 44, 84, 135
painting 15, 16, 108, 132
Park, Thomas 102, 123
pastoral mode 14, 22, 32, 37, 69
paternalist system 39, 55, 125, 126, 127, 129, 144
patronage 41–3, 64, 71, 127, 128
authority and 99
Bloomfield and 81, 83–4ff., 100, 101
changes in 82–4, 90, 92, 103
patrons 4, 35, 75, 94
see also patronage
Peacock, Thomas Love 109, 119
Pearl 139
Pentridge rising 136, 137
Percy, Thomas 71–2, 95, 97
Phillips, Sir Richard 4
ploughing 12, 16
poetic inspiration 7, 13, 14, 73, 95
Poetical Register 93
poetics 7, 57
labouring-class 31–4, 54, 66, 121, 122, 123, 124, 126, 128ff., 133, 138, 142, 145
polite audience 2, 3, 4, 7, 10, 16, 61, 87, 95
politics 21–5, 27, 46, 52, 61, 87–8, 113ff., 121, 134–8
Pope, Alexander 5, 82, 118–19
popular culture 111, 112, 114, 116–17, 129, 130, 132
Porter, Enid 77
Portland, Duke of 85, 86
poverty 9, 15, 45, 60, 70, 79, 142
property 3, 20, 27, 38, 61
prophecy 110, 139–40
prospect poem 106
providence 21
publishers 4, 75–6, 83, 92, 99, 103

Radcliffe, W. 58
radical politics 21, 24, 46, 51, 52, 62, 84, 85, 86, 87–8, 91, 108, 110, 135, 136, 140
Radstock, Lord 127, 138
Raglan Castle 114–15, 116–17
rationalism 24
readers 2, 3, 7, 10, 11, 16, 34, 36, 50, 54, 61, 87, 98, 103

Reform movement 136
religion 21–2, 78, 139–40
Richardson, Samuel 42–3, 49
Ritson, Joseph 72
Rizzo, Betty 42
Rogers, Samuel 102
romance mode 48
Romanticism 2–3, 7, 14, 31, 57, 63, 66, 70, 121
Rosenmeyer, Thomas G. 12
Rousseau, G.S. 77
Rousseau, J-J 132–3, 144
Ruggles, Thomas 60, 61
ruins 111–17
rural communities 2, 20, 21, 24, 26–7, 28, 43, 66, 115, 123, 125
  complexity of 25
  decline of 38, 53
  impact of city on 25
  positive aspects of 28, 29, 30, 37
rural poetry 1–2, 7–8, 123, 124

Sales, Roger 9, 22
satire 47
Savage, Richard 82
science 138
Scots Magazine 143
Scott, Walter 96, 97, 98, 118, 123
sentimentality 25
Shakespeare 95
sheep 17–18, 28, 124
Shefford, Bedfordshire 124
Shelley, P.B. 31, 73, 121, 137, 140
  'Epipsychidion' 73
shepherds 28–9, 124, 138, 140
shoemaker poets 8, 14
Siskin, Clifford 73
Smiles, Samuel 108, 110
Smith, Ginnie 68–9
Snell, K.D.M. 27
social class 74, 75, 76, 88, 126, 145
social relations 3, 23, 24, 26, 30, 38, 42, 43, 54, 126, 145
social status 9, 11, 37, 126, 134
social unrest 44, 121, 135, 136, 137
soldiers 142–3
songs 16, 66, 72, 111, 114, 118, 119, 124, 145
Southey, Robert 4, 35, 94, 123
  Wat Tyler 135
Spence, Thomas 135, 140
Suffolk 8, 9, 11, 12, 18, 19, 26, 32, 60, 78, 136
  ballads 35, 37
  enclosures 51, 52
  vernacular 33, 34, 35
Suffolk Garland, The (1818) 51
Swift, Jonathan 140

tales 3, 11, 31, 39, 66, 72, 95, 96, 116–17
taxes 43–4
Taylor, Jefferys 60
Thelwall, John 21
Thompson, E.P. 39, 52, 114
Thomson, James 10, 16
  Seasons, The 7, 9, 15, 17, 31, 69
time 58–9, 62, 110, 117
tracts 129–30
tradition 12, 114, 116, 117
Turner, Victor 117

Unwin, Rayner 95

vernacular 31, 33–4, 35
Vernor, Thomas 4, 89–90, 92
versification 8–9

Waldron, Mary 83
Wales 71, 108, 110, 111–17
war 43–6, 141, 142
Warnock, Mary 12, 13
Warton, Joseph 86
wealth 20, 51
Wedderburn, Robert 140
White, Simon J. 2
Wilkie, David 132, 144
Williams, Edward 108, 111, 115, 119
Winks, W.E. 8
women 70, 82–3
Woodhouse, James 83, 86, 87, 94, 121, 128
Wordsworth, William 27, 73, 75, 77, 96, 119
  attitude to labouring-class poets 1, 9, 10
  attitude to rural poor 2, 3, 16, 20, 35, 38, 54, 112, 119, 130–31, 133–4
  ballads 31, 35–6, 38, 39, 46–7, 49
  individualism of 3, 9, 20, 29, 30, 38, 40, 130
  and landscape 16, 17, 18, 107
  and mutuality 39–40
  poetics of 32, 35, 36, 126
  readership 10, 36
  self-image as poet 1, 9, 30
  subject matter 10
  and war 44, 45

works
'Female Vagrant, The' 39, 44
'Idiot Boy, The' 1, 46, 47
Lyrical Ballads 1, 2, 3, 10, 17, 25, 31, 32, 35, 36–7, 40, 46–7, 49
'Michael' 16, 130
Prelude, The 1, 2, 3, 7, 9, 10, 15, 16, 18, 20, 26, 28, 29, 30, 45, 73, 107, 110, 130, 134
'Ruined Cottage, The' 41, 44
'Simon Lee, the Old Huntsman' 36–7, 42
'Tintern Abbey' 4, 57, 66, 67, 107–108, 111, 112, 119

Yearsley, Ann 25, 83, 84, 86, 88, 89, 92, 94, 99, 127
Young, Arthur 52, 60, 70
Young, Edward 86

Zionkowski, Linda 82, 103

www.ingramcontent.com/pod-product-compliance
Ingram Content Group UK Ltd.
Pitfield, Milton Keynes, MK11 3LW, UK
UKHW020350010325
455677UK00021B/390